S0-BFD-503

INFORMATION RESOURCES MANAGEMENT:
CONCEPT AND CASES

Library of Congress Catalog No. 79-53322

Horton
  Information Resource Management
  Ohio Association for Systems Management
  250 pg.

ISBN 934356-01-7

Printed in the United States of America

INFORMATION RESOURCES MANAGEMENT: CONCEPT AND CASES

FOREST WOODY HORTON, JR.

ASSOCIATION FOR SYSTEMS MANAGEMENT
24587 Bagley Road, Cleveland, OH 44138

CONTENTS

ACKNOWLEDGEMENTS

My principal debt is to my colleagues at the Commission on Federal Paperwork who argued, debated, criticized, and, in general, suffered my incessant questions throughout 1976 and 1977 when this manuscript was being prepared. To Commission Chairman, Cong. Frank Horton from the State of New York, and to Commission Director Warren Buhler must go a special note of thanks for providing me with the opportunity for juxtaposing my own research objectives closely with the work program of this important Congressional Commission. Commission staff members Steve Baratz, Jerry Calderone, Dick Bullock, and Murray Haber were a constant source of ideas and inspiration.

Additionally, I want to thank Donald Marchand, John Stucker, Dick Nolan, Dave Robinson, Aaron Hochman, Dick Brown, Chet Guthrie, Bob Kelley, Wally Haase, Fred Lilly, Bill Flury, Dave Snyder and Bill Kenworthey for suggesting useful avenues to explore and for giving me critical feedback.

Also to A. James Andrews, ASM's Director of Publications, who has pursued me almost around the world encouraging me to write on the burgeoning future of information technology. A rare publisher, it was his foresight of trends in information systems that has brought this book to print.

Last, but most important, a very large dose of appreciation must go to Bill Price for his continuous flow of ideas and extraordinary grasp of the technical details of the entire field of information technology. And to Hazel Higginbotham and Cynthia Karels for the drudgery of putting it all together, a chore which they handled with characteristic sparkling good humor, but careful attentiveness to details. Ted Schuchat then made sure all the commas and colons were in place, a chore he approaches with zest and experience.

DEDICATION

To Tina and Ingrid

PREFACE

Information is fast becoming man's critical resource. The planet's natural resources—air, water, land, minerals, and so on—are man's oldest assets. Then man produced artifacts, combining available raw materials to create and manufacture physical and material goods. Eventually, financial resources were needed to facilitate marketplace transactions because man was producing and trading too many goods in too many places, too frequently, to rely on barter alone. In the Twentieth Century, man's very own role in the scheme of enterprise he had invented demanded more explicit recognition and management of human resources.

In each case, the role of the fledgling resource category evolved gradually, over a long period of time. With awareness, recognition, and acceptance of each new resource category came a body of doctrine—a formal collection of principles, standards, rules and practices—to guide, in an orderly fashion, the efficient and effective utilization of the resource.

By now we have well established bodies of doctrine that deal with natural, physical, material, financial, and human resources. But only recently, with the advent of the information and data explosion, has man's attention turned to a serious discourse on how to manage and control the data and information resource. Many disciplines and professions are hard at work testing hypotheses—information scientists, computer specialists, systems experts, library scientists, statisticians, mathematicians, linguists, semanticists, philosophers, and a broad array of social scientists. In each instance both pure and applied research, and the technologies flowing from them, are moving forward on a broad front of theorizing and experimentation. It is much too early to predict where information science, for example, will eventually come to rest in a taxonomy of knowledge, nor is there any good reason to try to push, prematurely, for epistemological immutability at this point.

What is important, it seems to me, is that in both private and public enterprise we must learn to harness our enormous capital investments in information handling resources. These capital investments, as well as their associated operating expenses, are becoming much too large to treat as "overhead expenses." Conventional approaches to managing the printing plant, the information center, the library, the computer room, microfilming operations, and other central information service activities no longer adequately illuminate risks, trends, and deficiencies in information resource utilization. Too high a proportion of overhead is tied up in information-related activities. Moreover, every organization is experiencing rising overhead and administrative expenses at a time when the fires of inflation, budget deficits, unemployment, and geopolitical crisis are burning everbrighter. Why is this happening?

We needn't search far for the reasons. Ours is perhaps above all else a technological society. The proliferation of knowledge and the need to communicate and exchange that knowledge rapidly among large numbers of specialists, working in compartmentalized institutional and organizational environments and in many geographically dispersed locations, is placing a heavy burden on data resources. Computers, satellites, telecommunications networks, electronic miniaturization and other technologies which affect information handling make inescapable the data resource's crucial role in our post-industrial society.

The second reason has to do with the convergence of information handling technologies and information functions and fields of specialization (see Figures i-1 and i-2). Whereas these different technologies and fields developed more or less independently, the newer, more powerful information technologies are permitting—nay, *forcing*—the

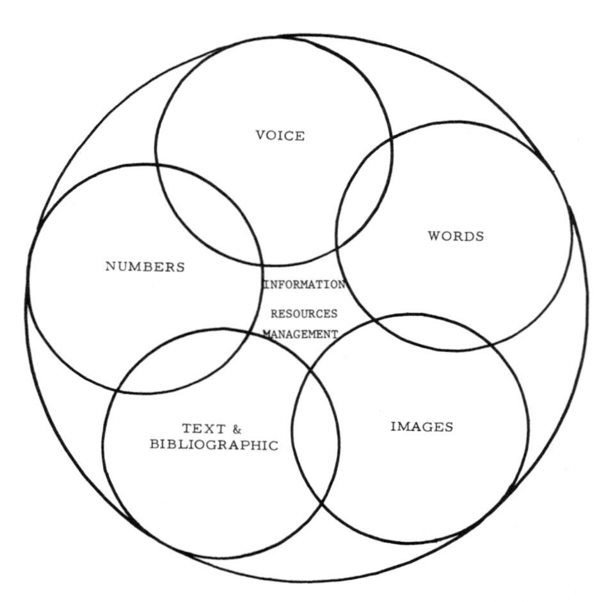

Figure i-1. **The convergence of information handling technologies**

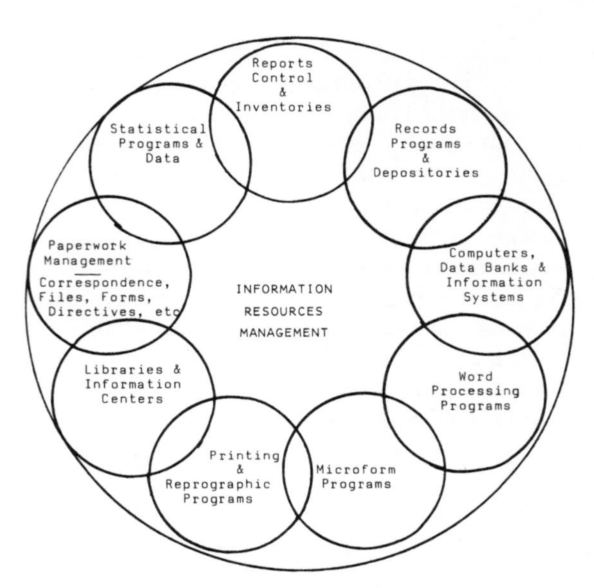

Figure i-2 **The convergence of information functions and fields of specialization**

integration of hithertofore independent technologies into coordinated hardware, software and procedural frameworks. Thus text, voice, visual and graphic technologies, when interconnected, offer a far more effective and efficient array of information capabilities than each of the separate ones did taken individually. Scientists, engineers, financial analysts, librarians, and researchers can now move back and forth swiftly between digital and analog modes, between data and word processing modes, between full text/bibliographic and abstract modes, and so forth. Their manipulative powers, in short, are multiplied enormously using the newer, ultra-modern information handling technologies.

Moreover, in the context of the Office of the Future concept, these information technologies can be harnessed in more productive settings than our more traditional office environment, cluttered with piles and reams of paper files and records and reports, offers. Indeed, the Office of the Future offers the bright promise of finally enabling us to move from a rapidly disintegrating post-industrial society to the dawning of the Information Age where data, information and knowledge are the driving force.

The public sector, particularly government at all levels, has relied heavily on the data resource. Of course the other resources—human, physical, financial, and natural—all play their roles too, but data and information are the key, the common denominator; data links all other resources together. Information is a unique resource in that it can be viewed either abstractly (ideas) or physically (as a commodity): physically, when it takes the form, for example, of a statistic, a document, a report; abstractly, when it takes the form of literature, an invention, an artistic creation, or an entire body of knowledge.

This uniqueness, this pervasiveness, this amorphous and intangible quality of information, has created extraordinary problems for us, however, in trying to harness data to advance mankind's goals. Except perhaps for the librarian, the archivist, or the historian, data has not traditionally been thought of as a "resource" in any formal sense—a resource to be organized and managed in the same way that we look, say, upon people, typewriters, missile systems, dollars or an endangered species of wildlife.

Quite the contrary. Until relatively recently, many businessmen and government officials tended to regard information as virtually a free good. To be sure, the most obvious, tangible, and concrete physical forms and expressions of data—the report, file, record or book, for example—have often been costed out and a price tag assigned at some point. Usually, however, only the most direct and obvious elements went into the cost calculation. Most information has escaped rigorous cost accountability, for a number of reasons.

First, separating the physical expressions, representations and uses of data from the abstract ones is an enormously difficult task. Second, both the value and the cost for information have traditionally been poorly defined and measured on scientific, political, and humanistic grounds. The archivist, for example, resists measuring the value of data because he views almost all information, potentially at least, as historically significant. He supports his position with the thesis that the relevance of "current facts" can only be ascertained in some kind of ultimate historical context. The scientist resists measuring the intrinsic value of data (not its functional value) because he views all information as knowledge and admonishes that those who would control, manage or destroy data risk the destruction of potential knowledge if not mankind's heritage. The political scientist's resistance to measuring the value of data is grounded in the democratic rights of citizens in our free, pluralistic society—rights to access, retrieve and use public information "for the public good," when and in whatever form desired. He points out that the obligation of government is to store and furnish data upon demand, subject only to limiting constitutional safeguards such as those protecting state secrets, business and trade and financial secrets and personal privacy.

The lack of a body of doctrine for organizing and managing information resources costs us dearly. For example, can a Congressional or State legislator, or an executive agency official in government, hire, transfer, promote or fire employees in any manner he chooses? Hardly. There is a long and well-established and detailed set of rules, guidelines, sanctions and procedures which tells the official exactly how those actions should be accomplished. Moreover, come budget time, officials are told precisely how to define, measure and count "on-board" personnel; they are directed to tally both positions authorized and present for duty, as well as man-years, by a host of yardsticks—organizational unit, category of expense, permanent vs. temporary positions, and on and on. The Office of Personnel Management at the Federal level has a whole body of management doctrine (the Federal Personnel Manual) that pulls together all of these rules. At each successive level of government, State and local, there are counterparts to this Federal doctrine.

Would a company's property officer allow a company official to requisition as many fancy chairs, tables, desks or typewriters as he wanted? Of course not. We have in this area, too, tables of allowances, authorization schedules, and other standards, criteria and formulas which set forth exactly the deployment of each one of these commodities. In short, most large corporations and public agencies have promulgated, over a long period of time, a detailed body of doctrine to manage and account for the organization's real and personal property assets.

The analogy can be extended to financial and natural resources as well. Certainly when it comes to financial resources the "rules of the game" are even less flexible. The penalties and other sanctions for misuse of company or public financial assets are perhaps even more severe than they are for the other assets, probably for good reason.

When we come to the data and information resource, not only is there no central, cohesive body of management doctrine in organizations, but we don't always do a very good job in giving managers informal guidance on a fragmented basis—a little bit for computers, a little bit for designing information systems, some for microform, some for reprography and so on. In few cases do we have comprehensive policies, much less procedures, to guide officials when they are, for example, selecting data-handling media on a cost effective basis or weighing the expected benefits of a new or upgraded information system against the total capital and operating investments.

I contend here that top corporate and government officials are more and more often trapped into making incremental decisions to "buy and build bigger and better data and information capabilities." Then, when things begin to go wrong, the investments are already too big to write off as sunk costs and the problems are too intractable to back away from. Managers have, in a real sense, become a captive of these powerful and inexorable new information handling technologies of ours. It is small solace to say that top officials should have become more closely involved at an earlier stage and participated more intimately in the investment decision-making processes.

To deal effectively with this situation, managers must first understand the risks and opportunities of data resources. Then they must learn to deal with information as a valuable organizational resource, the use of which must be planned, budgeted and managed.

Now this may seem to some to be too efficiency-oriented. That is, do we risk over-controlling this uniquely valuable resource—information—by using words like "management" and "control" in this way? To be sure, "information manipulation"—or, even worse, the stifling of creativity and the free flow of ideas—are inherent possibilities and to warn against them is useful. Fair enough, and legitimate criticism. In rejoinder, if we are ever to realize the full potential of our new computer, communication and other information-handling technologies, we must make sure, particularly in this era of inflation and the tight budget dollar, that our monies are well spent. I contend that, to unleash the full power of modern information handling technologies, we must plan the collection, use and reuse of our data resources more judiciously and cost-effectively. A doctrine of accountability, Information Resources Management, would, in my view, go a long way to help us meet that challenge. That is what this work is all about.

To deal comprehensively with the subject, I've organized the material into twelve chapters, beginning with broader conceptual considerations and moving by progressively narrower and more technical stages into the detailed treatment. At the end of each chapter are some questions which can serve several purposes. At the end of the book are several short cases designed to reinforce and further illuminate the theoretical material. Because the subject of Information Resources Management is still in its infancy, there is a shortage of well-formulated, tested and evaluated case material.

Much of the work was drawn from the author's experience with the Commission on Federal Paperwork, which found that the paperwork burden on the American public was far more than a matter of physical pieces of paper, but, instead, had its roots in ineffective data and information policies of the Federal Government. Of necessity, then, examples and illustrations were drawn from government, but they have direct applicability to business, and more broadly, to the private sector.

In a sense, this book is a primer. Therefore, I hope it will be useful to practicing information professionals, students of information science, businessmen concerned with rising information handling costs, and government officials concerned with mounting paperwork and information costs on the American taxpayer.

1 BACKGROUND AND FRAMEWORK

By now the term "information explosion" has surely become a cliche. In an earlier work, I said, "some cynics call the information explosion 'information pollution.' Whichever view you choose, clearly the production, handling and dissemination of information has come of age as a respectable industry. And yet those primary disciplines concerned with improving the management of information—including Computer Science, Automation, Library Science, Telecommunications, and Information Science—have not yet fully intermeshed theory and practice to harness information resources in very efficient and effective ways to support and service users."[1]

Since writing those words, I have seen many researchers pursuing the same general theme in two closely related fields. First, computer scientists are speaking of the data explosion. They refer to the proliferation of computerized data files, data bases and information systems. In a related vein, authors in the fields of public administration and political science are writing of a knowledge explosion. Caldwell, for example, says: "Perhaps the single most important factor in the present transition (from what he calls modern society to the post-modern society) is the availability of information, organized and distilled into knowledge, regarding the physiology and psychology of the human animal. It may be argued that every major historical transition involves a change in man's self image and that the manner in which information is evaluated has been a significant factor in these changes. It seems probable that more factual information regarding the human animal has become available in the past generation than in all previous history. One might expect that the accelerating growth of information would by its sheer magnitude, diversity, and utility affect the state of knowledge and man's evaluation of the significance of knowledge and his own position on the earth."[2]

Another authority, Nanus, said: "In fact, information is the very stuff from which human society is made and, thus, any major change in the way information is collected, stored or distributed will, of necessity, have the most profound implications for the way in which society functions and is structured. Increasing access to the vast evolving store of human knowledge may very well provide the most fundamental and dramatic resolution of all, for it can lead to the transformation and expansion of human awareness and sociel intelligence itself."[3]

It will be useful for our purposes to conceive of all three of these "explosions"—of knowledge, information, and data—in a kind of nested hierarchy and then to continue the search for the solution to our "information dilemma" by looking at resource management theory and into other considerations.

There seems to be fairly general agreement that data can be defined as unevaluated raw facts, while information may be thought of as evaluated data, that is, facts which have been interpreted in some manner so as to give them more value than they had in the natural state. Knowledge, at the top of the pyramid, may be thought of as representing a still higher order of intelligence. It is useful in this regard to keep in mind Daniel Bell's reminder that the post-industrial society is a "knowledge society" in a double sense:

> . . . first, the source of innovation are increasingly derivative from research and development (and more directly, there is a new relation between science and technology because of the centrality of theoretical knowledge);
>
> second, the weight of the society—measured by a larger proportion of Gross National Product and a larger share of employment—is increasingly in the knowledge field.

Relatively few now assert that the "information problem" is exclusively one of a lack of information. Rather, more of those who have thought about the problem seem to have come to the conclusion that there are two factors at work. First, there is a lack of useful or relevant information. At the same time there is a glut, or at least an overabundance, of irrelevant or marginally useful information. One might go further and say that the two conditions are inter-dependent; that is, the glut of marginally relevant information is clogging our communications channels and thereby preventing useful information from reaching our decision-makers.

PROLIFERATION OF INFORMATION NEEDS

Let us take up these two conditions separately. First, the need for facts and data in government, for example, certainly has increased enormously at all levels, in part because government programs are increasing in number. We now have, for example, in the Federal Government's *Catalog of Federal Domestic Assistance*, over 1,100 programs. This does not count the large number of international programs or the large number of programs which regulate commerce rather than serve individual citizens. Also, government programs have become increasingly difficult to manage and implement as they have become larger. This is in part because larger programs require more civil servants to administer them and they are administered, more and more, at the local geographical level. They also require a larger number of specialists, each of whom tends to operate in his own compartmentalized environment with his own independent data and information needs. The problems of attempting to coordinate the relatively larger numbers of organizational units associated with each one of these programs is much greater than it was a decade ago. Both government organizational structure and numbers of government employees have grown enormously in absolute terms. Both, of course, "feed," in a manner of speaking, on data and information.

Moreover, each level of government, beginning with the Federal level and moving down to State, regional, subregional and finally to the local level, develops and promulgates its own unique information requirements. Sometimes information can be shared between and among these levels of government, but more often than not each level collects its own information in its own way for its own purposes. Figure 1-1 depicts the dramatic growth of several of these key information markets, programs, products and services at the Federal Government level in the six year period 1971–1976.

The consequences of this enormous growth of bureaucracy in both the public sector and large organizations in private enterprise, have become almost too well known to require recapituation. Let us briefly review them, nevertheless. First, there is inevitable duplication and overlap because requirements for data are not fully coordinated, and organizational units typically do not share their data. Second, similar facts collected by so many organizational units and at different levels are often inconsistent and incompatible. Next, communication channels are clogged by much irrelevant, marginally useful data. What is the result of all this? Bad decisions are made; program effectiveness and efficiency suffer; and program goals and objectives are not achieved.

Fiscal Year	1971	1972	1973	1974	1975	1976
Federal Information Index						
Fed. Register Pages	21,864	26,053	33.284	42,372	44,847	59,605
Index	100	119.2	152.2	193.8	223.4	272.6
NTIS Publications	45,000	53,200	55,600	59,000	63,000	60,000
Index	100	116.4	121.7	129.1	137.9	131.3
Number of Computers	5,934	6,731	7.149	7,830	8.649	9,600
Index	100	113.4	120.5	132.0	145.8	161.8
GPO Spending (mil$)	224	262	292	366	418	500
Index	100	109.7	118.9	140.0	147.7	173.4
Congressional Printing (mil$)	41	48	54	62	74	85
Index	100	109.8	117.3	127.8	141.6	157.5
Spending on Statistical Prgms. (mil$)	204.8	237.6	280.8	371.9	428.1	498.4
Index	100	108.8	122.7	158.2	170.1	193.6
Spending on R & D (mil$)	15.1	16.4	17.8	18.3	19.5	21.3
Index	100	101.3	103.5	97.8	90.2	91.3

Fed. Info. Index	100	111.4	122.4	139.8	151.0	168.8
Federal Press Release Index						
Dept. of Labor	100	116.7	128.2	117.5	106.4	144.5
Dept. of State	100	93.3	109.2	139.3	161.6	170.0
Housing & Urban Development	100	95.9	72.8	49.0	52.4	55.2
Dept. of Transport.	100	100.3	92.3	97.5	87.1	70.2
Civil Aeronautics Board	100	115.8	133.2	137.5	133.7	156.0
Small Business Administration	100	90.1	61.4	77.2	50.5	76.3
Dept. of Defense	100	91.9	65.7	52.7	60.7	52.5
Veterans Admin.	100	128.0	120.0	121.6	120.8	100.0
Dept. of Commerce	100	115.2	106.1	114.8	85.9	103.0
Federal Press Release Index	100	105.6	98.9	100.1	95.6	103.3

For computing an index all dollar figures were converted into 1971 dollars by using the Federal Purchases Deflator.
by permission: Washington Researchers, Washington, D.C.

***Figure 1-1.* Federal information index**

The ultimate consequence is that organization officials, the Congress (or the board) and the public (or stockholders) are all frustrated, dissatisfied, and confused.

With the passage of the Freedom of Information Act, the Congress believed it had taken a giant stride in "opening up government to the people." The legislation, passed auspiciously on July 4, 1967, spelled out the intent of Congress to disclose all government records, except for certain privileged types of data which agencies deem exempted (for example, personal data on individuals, trade secrets, or classified defense information). From the very beginning, compliance with the law was less than adequate, not necessarily because agencies were unwilling to disclose their records, but because their information—files, records, forms, directives, technical reports, library holdings, data holdings in computer data banks, and so forth—were disorganized, diffused, dispersed and fragmented. In short, agencies simply didn't know what information they had, where it was, or how they themselves (much less the public) could lay their hands on it! To the citizen, this sounded incredible. How could the situation have reached this point? To the bureaucrat, on the other hand, this state of affairs is perfectly understandable because government's controls on its own data and information flows, both inward and outward, are seriously deficient. We do not have, for example, a single, authoritative, and comprehensive Federal information locator directory, nor do we have indices and catalogs that lead us to where data is hidden: in records, in files, in libraries and in computer data banks. In summary, there is very little information resources management in the Federal Government.

The aphorism "out-of-sight, out-of-mind" seems particularly appropriate when we consider the fact that our preoccupation with physical records, their filing and storage, instead of with the data content of those records, has left us with the situation shown in Figure 1-2.

Although much data and information is collected in government by ad hoc methods using simple correspondence and the telephone, the structured collection of data and information is accomplished conventionally by use of the information system. All kinds of people use information systems, and there is an almost infinite variety of systems. But in government, far and away the most expensive capital investments in information resources are in automated or computerized information and communication systems. Later it will be instructive for us to review briefly how disorders in communication and information systems have, in no small measure, been responsible for the proliferation of marginally useful information, that is, the "glut of irrelevant information," mentioned earlier, which is clogging our

Figure 1-2. **This isn't the answer**

information channels. For the moment, let us continue the search for the roots of the information dilemma elsewhere.

INACCURACY, IRRELEVANCY, DISTORTION

The difference between reality and representations of reality is one source of the dilemma. Information systems demonstrate the illusory nature of reality as presented by recorded information and the need to monitor these realities continually so as to take into account the multiple images of those realities as they are represented by dynamic and not by static systems. From a communication point of view, meanings are continually changing. Language, seen from the coign of everyday life and not from the static view of a dictionary definition, is continually in flux. Further, experience, a dynamic concept, continually seeks to break the bounds of defined and accepted meanings to include in language descriptors of those experiences which are not contained in words. Poetry, for example, is the clear locale of expanded experiential terminology; yet the process, as incorporated in poetry, is very much evident in everyday life, no less governmentese.

The disjunctions between governmentally imposed standards and the day-to-day realities of business, as well as those of individuals, may be a function of the loss of contact between the "real world" of the private sector and the actions and decisions taken by public officials.

Information systems, then, reflect a frozen cut of reality. Hence they are vulnerable to complaints about the adequacy of the match or the fit between the information content thereof and the reality they are supposed to mirror. Moreover, their influencing the way decision-makers view a situation—influencing their perception of reality—determines the way external realities are perceived by receivers. That is, information affects the very realities it is supposed to reflect. Therefore, in a real sense, information contains the seeds of its inadequacies.

These disjunctions are often discussed by authors in these terms; for example, "what starts out as a management information system too often ends up as a management mis-information system." One can translate that complaint in the context of the preceeding discussion to mean that information of use for a particular reality becomes "frozen" because the technical processes by which it is stored, disseminated and handled do not take into account its changing substance.

What is not so clear, following the above, is whether one must say that information, in the end, is utterly context-dependent and that removing data from its original milieu constitutes such radical surgery as to distort substantially its intended meaning. Must one conclude, instead, that we live in such an age of changing external realities—future shock—that information, as a tool of language in communication, is hopelessly doomed to a state of flux? Which of the two interpretations is "correct"? Or, are both explanations at work? Or others?[4]

INFORMATION IS POWER

Another root of our dilemma is the question of who should establish and oversee information policies. To be sure, knowledge producers have themselves entered into the political system. This means that the management of information is to be shared with those who produce the information. The policies which guide the management of that information should be similar to those which guided its production in the first place. Interestingly, those policies are similar in spirit to the policies laid out in the Bill of Rights and very similar to the issues dealt with in many cases involving freedom of the press. Certainly, therefore, any exploration of knowledge management policies, or information management policies, must include policies relevant to the "management" of scientific information.

One of the problems of information science is that it often talks about information without considering substance, much as a schizophrenic person talks about his experiences as if they have no meaningful context. Surely policies surrounding the use of information must be separated from policies surrounding its objectives. The reader would probably not want an automobile mechanic to tell him where he could drive, to illustrate the difference between a technical and a substantial problem. Information management, as practiced by the recent Administration of Richard Nixon, was considered by some to have been a case of the mechanic telling you where you can drive. Consequently, abuses of the information function now constitute criteria against which public officials are evaluated in part.

The abuses of the Nixon Presidency centered on the manipulation of information, not the management of information. Still there is a thin line between manipulation and management. Because the abuses of the past are still fresh in the public mind, and manipulation depends upon sophistication in the management function, we must clearly distinguish between management and manipulation.

Finally, much of the preoccupation with information manipulation by recent U.S. Congresses seems subsummable under a complex of issues centering on problems associated with the potential abuses and misuses of government-held data collected from the public. The Freedom of Information Act and the Privacy Act, for example, are two of the clearest expressions of this concern. As Elliott Richardson has written: "But if the wrongs of Watergate were sins against the sactity of information, the events leading to redress of those wrongs were acts of redemption for the sanctity of information—investigating it, extracting it, leaking it, confessing it, revealing it, and publishing it." And ". . . in a sense, all the abuses of Watergate have been abuses of information: its theft, distortion, fabrication, misuse, misrepresentation, concealment, and suppression. Once you see it, the thread is plain. It runs from one Watergate abuse to the next and binds them all."[5]

IS INFORMATION PROPERTY?

We must review still other causes of the information dilemma. Another important avenue has to do with the advent of modern reprographic technologies such as the Xerox machine. Jovanovich, in quoting William Saroyan, says: "Yes, xerography will confound human life still more along with other things, help to cancel it out."[6] Jovanovich later asks, "What is writing worth as a human act, and what is it worth as a form of property? We have presumed for more than two centuries that writing is a kind of property that is concentrated and transacted in such a way that unauthorized copying or transmission has been declared illegal. Writing as property is the basis of copyright law in most western countries, even though some otherwise conservative manufacturers and educators put forth the criticism that copyright is a monopolistic practice that deprives 'the people.' Communist countries tend to ignore copyright, or they waffle; and the 'emerging nations' ask special dispensation in order to catch up with the West, that is, to copy the works of the West. As for the first part of the question—writing is a human act—it is related to the second. Is the artifact resulting from writing—the book, the article, the journal, the script—as important as the discrete, individual act of writing?"

Certainly reprography is indeed an easy way by which one can, if one wishes, break the law since we can all reproduce a work without compensating its author. But how far can we go in the attribution of rights and obligations and privileges to information? In short, how far can we go with the analogy that information can and should be compared legally with property? Snyder reminds us that today we have come to accept the notion that our "good name" is a property right, despite the fact that it is intangible and an abstract concept.[7] He seems to support the idea that we can extend that general notion further to a general rule that states "any and all data pertaining to our describing an individual is the property of that individual." In buttressing his point, he mentions that the meaning of the word *property* in its legal sense is "that which belongs exclusively to one." The new Swedish Data Act (1974) identifies the misuse of personal information as "data trespass," a new form of crime. So it would appear that personal information, like clean air and clean water, may be becoming a very precious commodity indeed.

Snyder urges that we openly acknowledge the economic implications of information as property, "in other words, to uniformly treat information as an economic commodity." Under information economics, data would be paid for as would any other resource, individual persons or corporations receiving some remuneration for the use of their individual data. In a direct challenge to the government, he says that such a treatment, providing "direct, economic incentives for increased efficiency in data handling," would be far more effective in curtailing burdensome public reporting requirements "than a dozen Hoover Commissions."

The Commission on Federal Paperwork seemed to agree, for the notion of treating information as an economic commodity instead of a "free good" was a centerpiece of its final recommendations to the Congress in 1977.

ECONOMICS OF INFORMATION

More than ten years earlier, Adrian McDonough, in testimony before the Nix Subcommittee on Census and Statistics of the House of Representatives, made a plea for the use of what he called Information Economics in government instead of traditional measures of paperwork.[8] He reminded us that "paperwork is a term which originated more than fifty years ago when the composition of the labor force was very different." He mentioned that our production methods, even as recently as fifty years ago, were primitive. It took a very large percent of the labor force on the farm and in the factory, doing hard, physical work, to produce the bare necessities of life. Therefore, only those workers involved in contributing to the stock of food, shelter, and clothing were considered productive. All other workers, especially the white-collar employees, were, logically enough at the time, labeled negatively as overhead, burden, or nonproductive labor.

McDonough emphasized that we can no longer justify the reasoning that the white-collar worker, by economic and accounting definitions is non-productive. If we continue to treat the white-collar worker as non-productive, we are greatly inhibiting the progress that can be made in our society. In the past we have said that "paperwork" should be kept to a bare minimum because it was non-productive. Therefore, the white-collar worker who did the paperwork was also non-productive and thus a primary target for all sorts of cost-reduction measures. At what point were we eliminating a document that was not only a cost but also a paper which carried valuable information? This is the situation on which McDonough's Information Economics concentrates.

Information Economics he defines as "the study of the allocation of certain scarce resources of an organization to achieve the best decisions for that organization."[9] In particular, Information Economics concentrates on the storage of knowledge, on obtaining information through data processing, and on the effective utilization of both stored knowledge and processed information. The word "economics" is attached to the word "information" to emphasize the need to understand the demand for information as well as the supply of information. The demand for information determines the value of information, whereas the supply of information determines its cost.

Perhaps we can carry the notion of information as a resource as far as our scholars and lawyers have carried the notion of property resources, and even natural resources, so long as we recognize that:

- people with knowledge are resources;
- people, not machines, organize knowledge; and
- since there are many different ways to organize knowledge in a democratic system, management of information must be pluralistic.

It is principally the *location* of property that determines its value. Similarly, it is the *context* of information that transforms data into information and eventually information into knowledge. *Context*, therefore, is what produces value, and information in context produces meaning. This process is poorly understood. It has not been studied often. There are still too many misleading treasure maps lying around.

The organization of information for consumption by a computer, in anticipation of later analysis and utilization, does not, by itself, produce meaningful information, nor does the filing system of a secretary give meaning to the contents of her files. Along the same lines, neither the card catalog of a library nor the filing system for its books produces the value of the contents of the library. The enhancement of value for information context can only occur when the information is organized in such a fashion that the process of organization is compatible with the individual who is to use it; value is decreased when the organization of the information does not meet the organized framework of the user. Traditionally, we've approached the information organization task by looking at the "container," the physical file or record. But Figure 1-3 tries to make the point that silent, dusty archives are not the solution.

Results cannot always lead to the conclusion that information does or does not have value. Where there are no results from an action, or where the results are negative, information used in the decision-making and problem-solving processes can be considered to be "value neutral," or even counterproductive or "counter value." Where the results are positive, we may say we have achieved meaningful solution, but in the last two cases, we must say the results are not meaningful.

Figure 1-3. **This isn't the answer**

Information may be of value since the outcome for which it is used can be influenced by a variety of factors both intrinsic to the decision-making process itself and extrinsic to it. Of the intrinsic factors, the human factor is by far the most important. Here, elements include the existing knowledge structure of the decision-makers, their ability to understand and assess information, the limits of their abilities to integrate new information to create new knowledge, and their capability of applying the new knowledge.

Thus, information that is relevant may reside in a situation where human decisions and actions cause negative or neutral outcomes, despite the potential value of the information. Results, in short, cannot be used fully to infer information value. The final outcome, moreover, comes at too late a stage to make this assessment. Some benchmarks must be established much earlier to make the assessment. We will come back to this algorithm several times in later chapters.

DATA, DOCUMENTS, AND LITERATURE

Computers, telecommunications, and their associated technologies, have now become the most important and the most expensive information-handling tools in modern society. Paperwork may still be the most visible and perhaps even the most pervasive medium for handling information, but paperwork can no longer claim to be either the most important or the most expensive one. The computer has taken over! Eventually, some contend, we shall evolve into a paperless society. Already the electronic collection, transfer and storage of data are commonplace in banking, brokering, retailing and other important business sectors. To be sure, significant data standardization, data ownership and data confidentiality problems remain to be resolved, and these problems have important philosophical, legal and even Constitutional consequences. But the technological breakthroughs are already at hand or in sight. The remaining technical barriers will most certainly be surmounted within the decade. Now, what are the consequences of the ascendancy of the computer?[10]

First, because the unit cost of storing and processing data is cheaper, using automated capabilities, than using paper media, particularly in the light of the extraordinary speeds of the machines, there are increasingly stronger economic incentives to switch from paper to electrons. Second, as the knowledge explosion is generating more and more information, there is no shortage of "raw material" to feed the machines. Quite the contrary. Third, there is strong evidence that the switch to electronics and computers is creating more, newer and different kinds of red tape problems than the conventional ones experienced with paper systems because:

- one cannot footnote or annotate a machine record; entire special "routines," as they are called, must be developed;
- people discontinue their old, informal "cuff" records slowly and painfully when new computer systems are installed. As a consequence, two sets of records, often incompatible, exist side by side and compound the transition from the old manual system to the new computerized one;
- Capital investments in hardware, software, and human resource support staffs are substantially greater for most large computerized systems than those corresponding costs supporting equivalent conventional paperwork systems, even though unit costs may be substantially lower in automated systems;

Fourth, the computer offers very substantial technical information-handling capabilities indeed, capabilities vastly superior to manual approaches or conventional machine-assisted approaches such as tabulating machines. These capabilities include computational powers; "logical" powers to edit, reorder and correlate data; graphic display powers; search and retrieval powers; modeling and simulation powers; and extraordinary speeds that enable some operations (e.g., airline reservations) to be processed in "real time" (that is, as transactions occur). On the positive side, these exceptional capabilities provide the scientist and administrator with the means, at least in theory, of solving increasingly complex technical, scientific and managerial problems. On the "negative" side, these very same capabilities are creating even more enormous problems for organizations trying to manage their data resources judiciously. These problems may take the form, for example, of imperatives to: buy more capacity than may actually be needed "just in case;" buy larger numbers of machines for use at lower and lower organizational levels with some loss of centralized control; and buy smaller modules of capabilities and fragment them into larger numbers of organizational units, with a similar loss, not only of control, but of the ability to integrate, correlate and summarize comparable data. Before looking at these problems in further depth, however, let us first look more closely at the three major classes of information holdings—data, documents, and literature.

Figure 1-4 identifies some nine variables which help us discriminate between these three major classes of information holdings, that is, ways in which information is stored and processed in the broadest

Discriminating Variable	DATA	DOCUMENTS	LITERATURE
1. Method of representation; unit of measure	Fact, number, symbol	Report, record, message, memorandum	Monograph, serial periodical
2. Storage / *Machines* and handling media	*Documents* Magnetic tape, punched card, microform, paper	*Literature* Microform, paper	*Libraries, archives* Bound volumes, recordings, films
3. Structural combinations	Data banks, data bases, tables, charts, graphs	Files, dossiers, dockets, correspondence	A body of writings, histories, biographies
4. Half-life measured (transience) (value decay function)	Fractions of seconds, seconds, minutes, hours	Days, weeks, months, a few years	Years, decades, centuries, millenia

5. Changeability	Very permutable	Moderately permutable	Infrequently permuted
6. Uses	Research, analysis, experimentation, validation	Recordkeeping, legal evidence financial accounting	Recording man's heritage, achievements, discoveries, conflicts
7. Method of generation	Observation, experimentation	Writing, typewriting, printing, photograph	Dissertation, composition, inspiration
8. Arrangement	By acquisition source and method, location, condition	By subject, classification category	By author, title, subject
9. Methods of replication and transmission	Automation, telecommunication	Reprography, facsimile	Father-to-son, Mother-to-daughter, institutions

***Figure 1-4.* Three major forms of information holdings**

sense. The computer and telecommunications and electronics revolutions brought with them extraordinary capabilities to deal with information unhampered by physical paperwork. Whereas the conventional method of storing and processing information prior to the advent of those technologies had been the document, with their introduction came the means to "free" information from the shackles of rigid forms and formats and the inherent constraints imposed by the handling of paperwork. It is the center column in Figure 1-4, then, that is being transformed most radically in our post-industrial society. In the view of this author, it is the center column that is causing us most of the difficulty at the moment, during this transition between the document era and the electronics era. Just look at your desk! Or into your mailbox! Have you tried to get anything out of your files lately?

It is in the rightmost column, literature, that knowledge management will have its greatest impact, that is, in the efficiencies with which data and information are assimilated into the body of literature. By contrast, information resources management seeks to deal with the interplay between the left and middle columns. We will come back to this in Chapters 4 and 5.

THE SYSTEM INSTEAD OF THE INFORMATION

These sophisticated information handling tools are mixed blessings. Their ability to process massive volumes of information cheaply and efficiently has sandtrapped organizations into concentrating on data *processing* and data *systems* at the expense of *data management*. The equipment's speed, capacity, and economies of scale have more glamor and excitement than ways of organizing and manipulating data and information so that it is more *useful and relevant* to users. Oversimplifying and generalizing, it has been only since the advent of the decade of the 1970's that managers and computer users have begun to focus seriously on considerations of effectiveness. One could argue that this has come about primarily because of tighter budgets and the inflationary situation, not because the problems were unforeseen, overlooked or ignored. Clearly, data resources and data capabilities must be used more judiciously and circumspectly if the *information dollar* is to be a dollar well spent.

Next, source data automation techniques, such as the use of mark-sensed tabulating cards, or optical character recognition, do avoid, or at least minimize, costs and errors associated with the transposition of data from hard-copy source forms to key-punched cards or typewritten form. However, research seems to indicate that the lion's share of costs is not in such transposition steps, but rather in the earlier stages of data capture and recordkeeping. The high costs begin much before input to the machines.

Continuing, the temptations to collect all possible data "just in case" it might be needed have simply been too great for many organizations to resist. Because organizations have not planned their data needs carefully, or even defined their problems carefully, the computer administrator has been subjected to this kind of pressure: "We don't have the time to define our problem carefully, but it really doesn't matter because the computer is such a powerful tool that we can collect and store all the information we could possibly need. Surely, even on a hit or miss basis, enough of it will be useful. What isn't useful we don't care about, because it is so cheap to store; anyway, who cares?"

The result? Data banks are not getting any smaller; more and more irrelevant, obsolete and inaccurate data is clogging our storage and processing channels. This situation is not just a matter of expense. We cannot quickly locate the data that is relevant, timely and valid because there is so much of the irrelevant, untimely and invalid to screen out to get to what we do need. The irony of the situation is that, in many cases, we do have the system capability to identify and "track" user identity, frequency, patterns of use, and so on, but we don't feed this intelligence back to data managers. Figure 1-5, then, doesn't depict a very sanguine situation. The answer must lie elsewhere.

WHAT LESSONS HAVE WE LEARNED?

Now the mini- and micro-computer equipment and software revolution is upon us. Again we are being treated to a bewildering array of bright, brand-new bells and whistles that dazzle the jaded computernik and novice alike. It is no exaggeration to say that everyone now wants his or her personal computer, or at least a computer terminal. Isn't that what technology is all about? Shouldn't every scientist, technician, analyst and decision-maker have a data set at their fingertips, able to call forth computational and manipulation routines for the quick and efficient resolution of problems as they come up? Such is the inevitability and inexorable consequence of this development that the endemic management problems attendant to fragmentation, specialization, and compartmentalization will most assuredly increase

***Figure 1-5.* This isn't the answer either**

once again, and perhaps geometrically.

Have we learned any lessons from the third generation of equipment now passing from the scene that we might apply as we now move into the era of the fourth generation? Let us hope so. One general lesson might be that moving information-handling technologies closer to their ultimate users does indeed heighten and sharpen the responsiveness of the technology to the user, but at the same time it creates new problems not present when such capabilities were centralized and managed on a service concept basis.

PROBLEMS OF INFORMATION TECHNOLOGY

There are many problems here. For one, the collection, storage, transfer and disssemination of duplicative and potentially conflicting and incompatible data is compounded in proportion to the number of new units using the new capabilities. For another, top management is confronted with the problem of how to deal with conflicting and incompatible information. This problem has been dramatically manifest in very large public organizations such as the Department of Defense where the Secretary, until recently (since the creation of the new Information Directorate), was faced with the military services giving testimony to Congress and releasing information to the media that used different sets of data (e.g., troop strength, missile numbers, budget figures, etc.) which were often inconsistent or, in some cases, downright contradictory. Now, with minicomputer decentralization, the problem of tracking, auditing and reconciling differences in data sets is certainly going to be considerably more difficult, absent suitable controls. In some cases it may turn out to be merely data disparity due to dysynchronous cut-off or input dates or the lack of data element standardization.

More is involved than the ire or embarrassment of a Cabinet officer. The scientist in charge of the laboratory will now have his assistants collecting and storing data used in vital experiments on, for example, health, safety and security programs which potentially is inconsistent, incompatible and conflicting. Without adequate controls and policies, simply reconciling differences would be a time-consuming and expensive job quite aside from the potential dangers that such irreconcilable information may pose. The reader is familiar with the various "horror stories" which every large Federal agency already has in its files: cases where key officials didn't have access to the right information at the right time in the right form because it was buried in inaccessible places, and there was no "system" to retrieve it when needed.

Communication, even on simple matters and in routine fashion, is made inordinately difficult by the use of terms and phrases which are not standardized and uniformly designed in all parts of the organization's operations and activities. If the Personnel Department defines on-board strength as excluding temporary part-time employees as of the end of the reporting period, but the Payroll Department includes them in its definition, clearly time and money will be wasted.

Another problem is miniaturization. The micrography technologies and the newer holographic technologies make storage of data in textual form cheaper and more accessible to use. In many cases these technologies complement and supplement computer technologies which may deal with data in digital or analog form. It is tempting, therefore, to collect, store, process and disseminate data in *both* forms simply because "the technology is there," without careful consideration of the *needs and uses* for handling data in multiple media forms. Certainly exercising both options will make sense in some data settings; but in other cases the use of both media will result in unnecessary redundancy that, again, is expensive and time-consuming.

The telecommunication and satellite technologies must also come under our scrutiny. Without them we would be unable to move masses of data quickly and efficiently. It is difficult to quantify the value of ringing the earth with communication satellites that bring people and nations closer together and capture events of international scope as they occur. Multinational corporations and governments can communicate rapidly with their plants, ambassadors and emissaries and give them instructions on-the-spot. "Instant" problem-solving and decision-making is not always efficacious, however. The results may be disastrous because actions taken were ill-considered, premature or untimely. Again, the *mere existence and availability of cheap technology* has lead to improdent and irreversible action, in many cases, in the political, social, economic and commercial arenas.

INFORMATION: A MANAGEABLE RESOURCE

In the end, it seems to me that one is left with the inescapable notion that information must be viewed as both a resource—or a "commodity"—and also as an abstraction, an idea. One must be extremely careful in the development of information theories, concepts, policies, and programs to make clear which of the two primary connotations is being addressed. It is a thesis of this work that the time has come for society in general, and the public and private enterprise sectors in particular, to explore seriously and systematically the notion that information be viewed as a resource. One consequence that flows from that hypothesis is that it is necessary to maximize the effectiveness and efficiency dealing with the use of the information resource, for several reasons. First of all, the demand for data, like the demand for dollars, or people, or supplies or office space, tends to exceed the supply. Economists tell us that when this happens we usually assign a price tag to bring buyers and sellers together in the market place. Second, we tried to argue earlier that, while indeed there may be a "glut" of irrelevant and/or marginally useful information, we still have a shortage of facts. Senators, Congressmen, bureaucrats, scientists, technicians and others allege, with boring uniformity, that they are not getting all the facts they need to formulate public policy, undertake experiments and research, or manage and administer public programs.[11]

Searching for greater efficiencies and managing data and information as a resource—or as a commodity—inevitably will lead us to consider carefully its implications from the standpoint of both scientific methodology and our democratic, pluralistic free-enterprise traditions. Both demand that nothing be done to stifle the unbridled and rapid interchange of information as knowledge and as a check or balance on the system—as Watergate demonstrated. Therefore, it would appear that one maxim which the information manager should adopt is to assure that whatever steps he takes in the name of managing information resources more efficiently should be pursued only to the extent that such a course would simultaneously enhance and strengthen the free creation and dissemination of ideas and knowledge. At the very least, one should say that such a path should make certain that recommendations to enhance the efficiency and the utilization of information not impinge upon the free flow of knowledge and take into account the need to balance such efficiencies with the need to assure that the communication of knowledge is not unnecessarily constrained.

The American Civil Liberties Union Foundation has been less than bashful in criticizing the potential abuses of government through misuse of confidential data. In a recent report which excerpted a speech by John H. F. Shattuck, ACLU national staff counsel specializing in government secrecy and privacy, at a conference of social services professionals in Athens, Georgia, the Foundation said:

> The principal commodity of power in our society is information. Power may come out of the barrel of a gun, but far more power comes out of a computer or a databank, particularly if the information in it relates to people who do not know that it has been collected or cannot challenge its accuracy or use. It is no accident that many of the great governmental power abuses that have come to light in the last few years—wiretapping, enemies lists, political surveillance, counter-intelligence, secrecy and deception—have revolved around information practices.[12]

At the annual conference of the American Society for Information Science in Washington, D.C., held in 1976, Mrs. Hazel Henderson

Figure 1-6. **Will the answer lie in more machines and technologies?**

said that the Nation was passing from a phase of "maximum thruput of non-renewable resources" to a phase of "minimum thruput of renewable resources which can be recycled." She strongly implied that we should look for tradeoffs between our diminishing natural resources, such as coal and gas, with resources which, while not necessarily infinite, nevertheless offered the promise of giving the plant a respite while we decide whether, if, and how we could and should deal with the natural resource problem.[13] Two years before, in the keynote address to this same distinguished Society, then-Governor of Georgia Jimmy Carter had this to say on the same subject:

> How can we even measure the character of knowledge? What is knowledge? What is important about it? How can we assess the monetary value of it, so that when we exchange information with Russia, or with England, France, Germany, or Japan, we will know how much monetary value

> we can attach to the gift of one of our great natural resources? Knowledge is a resource which is not consummable. It is not wasted when it is used. In fact, it enhances itself. Perhaps this nonconsummable resource can be substituted for some of the consumable resources, like energy, in the enhancement of the quality of the lives of our people.[14]

Surely the Governor, now President, expressed one of the greatest challenges to mankind itself, and a worthy goal for Information Resources Management. Will the answer lie in new machines and technologies as Figure 1-6 would imply? Perhaps—but, then again, perhaps not. Many believe the machines have already far outstripped our abilities to use them effectively. Whether the new ones not yet designed widen the gap, or help close it, is a challenge that lies at least partially under our control: Shall we manage the machines, or they us? Electronics engineers continue to snicker at the posing of the question. Social scientists continue to anguish over it. Perhaps the emerging information manager will help move the dialogue from confrontation to collaboration.

QUESTIONS FOR DISCUSSION

1. "Managing information as a resource" is a notion that has some very obvious parallels to other areas—such as human resources, financial resources, physical resources, and so on—but there are important differences. Compare and contrast the hypothesis that data and information can be treated as an economic resource with the corresponding treatment of the other "resource categories" such as labor, capital and property. What are the similarities? Differences?

2. Information systems can be said to *represent reality*. Unlike man's direct interaction with other human beings and with the environment, information systems must rely on *symbols*, and their manipulation. What do people mean, then, when they claim that "inadequate symbolization and inadequate processing of symbols lie at the root of our most serious information processing problems?"

3. Some persons are more comfortable with the phrase "information *resources* management" than they are with "information management." They allege the latter raises the spectre of information manipulation: knowledge is power. Is there a "legitimate" difference between the two concepts? How do they interrelate to one another?

4. Who "owns" information? Is there a property right in information that corresponds to real property and personal property? Give examples

of ownership, and indicate who the claimants are to information property rights. Are other legal property precepts applicable to the notion of information as a property? For example, what about the transfer of information; the ceding of information; the using of information owned by one party, by another party; and the expropriation of individually owned property by the State.

5. We are sometimes said to have become an "Information Economy." How might we go about measuring what share of our national wealth originates with the production, processing and distribution of information goods and services?

6. A recent report of the National Commission on Electronic Fund Transfers talked about the coming "Paperless Society" and the need to preserve competition among the financial institutions and other business enterprises using an electronic fund transfer system. How will the electronic deposit of bill payments to bank accounts, without the use of checks or cash, affect the rights and obligations of consumers, merchants and financial institutions? What differences might there be from existing practices where there is a "hardcopy" back-up document of some kind?

7. In government at all levels, Federal, State and local, the debate continues about where to draw the line between a citizen's right to privacy, and the Public's right to know. That is to say, when should the government deny access to confidential information which it holds on the grounds that the purposes for which an agency plans to use it, or another citizen or "third party" wants it, do not outweigh the obligation to safeguard the information. Conversely, when might the public interest seem to outweigh the personal privacy considerations?

FOOTNOTES

[1]Horton, Forest W. Jr., "*How to Harness Information Resources: A Systems Approach*," (Association for Systems Management, 1974) pp i-ii.

[2]Caldwell, Lynton K., "*Managing the Transition to Post-Modern Society*," (Symposium on Knowledge Management, Public Administration Review, Nov/Dec 1975). This issue of the Review also contains some other excellent material, giving a fairly broad range of viewpoints.

[3]Nanus, Burt, "*Information Science and the Future*," (Bulletin of the American Society for Information Science, Vol. 2, No. 8, March 1976) pp. 57–58. This Special Bicentennial of the Bulletin also contains some other excellent material. In the words of its editor, Lois Lunin "The history of any field of science or technology is a tale of the strivings, the searchers, the successes of many individuals in many lands. Information science is no exception. We build on the past. We act on the present. We anticipate and plan for the future. We have before us the greatest challenge any field has been

offered—to analyze, to organize, to manage, and to use information for the good of all people. How we deal with the challenge may well affect the course of this nation in its next 200 years."

[4]The author is indebted to Stephen Baratz, who, during 1976 served with me on the Commission on Federal Paperwork. The ideas put forward here were in large measure the result of a dialogue during this time, when the Commission staff was considering objectives, assumptions and strategies for various key information-related studies. This dialogue, in the form of an exchange of memoranda, is available from the author, subject to Dr. Baratz's release approval.

[5]Richardson, Elliott, "*The Creative Balance*," Holt, Rinehart and Winston, 1976. While there have been many books on Watergate that have addressed the broad issue "information is power," Richardson's perspectives make him almost uniquely qualified to deal with the issue in the eyes of a bureaucrat-administrator, who must deal with the balance between the public's "right to know" and the individual's right to privacy. From that standpoint, this work offers useful insights.

[6]Jovanovich, William, "*The Universal Xerox Life Compiler Machine*," (The American Scholar, Vo. 40, No. 2, Spring 1975) pp. 249–250. This short article is as amusing as it is intellectually provocative. Highly recommended.

[7]Snyder, David P., "*Computers, Personal Privacy, and the Treatment of Information as an Economic Commodity," pp. 302–303, and "Privacy, the Right to What*?" Editorial, pp. 221–225, The Bureaucrat, Vol. 5, No. 2, July 1976.

[8]McDonough, Adrian M., Professor of Industry, Wharton School of Finance and Commerce, University of Pennsylvania, in testimony prepared at the request of Robert N. C. Nix, Chairman, Subcommittee on Census and Statistics of the Committee on Post Office and Civil Service, House of Representatives, May 25, 1966.

[9]Ibid. Op. cit.

[10]Horton, Forest W., Jr., "*Computers and Paperwork*," The Bureaucrat, Volume 6, No. 3, Fall, 1977, pp. 91–100. This brief paper reviews the evolution of the "paperless society;" and indicates how hard copy paper media is being increasingly replaced by electronic and holographic media for collecting, storing and disseminating data and information.

[11]See for example "Information for Government: Needs and Priorities," by Senator Hubert H. Humphrey, Bulletin of the American Society for Information Science, Volume 1, No. 1, June-July 1974. Senator Humphrey was for years in the forefront of the battle to develop more effective information systems to support public policymakers and the policymaking process. In his words: "To find solutions to these problems, we must do a much better job of establishing goals and setting priorities for our nation, backed up by effective systems of information collection, analysis and dissemination."

[12]"*The Privacy Report*," Volume III, No. 8, March 1976, issued by Project On Privacy and Data Collection, American Civil Liberties Union Foundation, New York, New York.

[13]Remarks by Hazel Henderson, Annual (Bicentennial) Conference, American Society for Information Science, "America in the Information Age," April 12–14, 1976, Washington, D.C.

[14]Remarks by former Governor, now President Jimmy Carter at 1974 Annual A.S.I.S. Conference, Atlanta, Georgia

2 RESOURCE MANAGEMENT: Principles and Practices

If we are to use the term "resource" we must be aware of the definitional problems associated with its multiple meanings. First of all, resources are traditionally thought of as "owned." Ownership of information, particularly where that ownership is not explicitly mandated by law, creates problems for society. For another, the appropriate allocation of publicly-owned information assets, particularly when those assets are considered close to personal or corporate interests is, in the end, a political question. It is here that the issues of overall societal benefits versus costs must be considered. For example, the public's right to know must be weighed against the personal right of privacy. It is also here that one must understand the differences between traditional notions of resource utilization and utilization and management of the kind of resource described here as data and information.

As has been pointed out, one useful way to begin this discussion is to compare the idea of unlimited resources, such as air, with the idea of a limited resource, such as coal or water. There are finite limits to even our "unlimited" resources, and the exact limits of such "unlimited" resources are different, particularly where the item in question—in this instance, information—has previously been considered to be a thing of no value, but now is declared to be a resource. What changes is the perception of "value" with concommitant changes in the perception of costs and burdens. For example, air pollution and the contamination of the environment have changed our perception of these apparently unlimited resources (air and water) to resources of limited availability. Much the same occurs with energy when changes in availability increase its price.

Thus we can say knowledge or information becomes a valued resource when demand increases to the point where the supply takes on a price. In the information area, for example, the supply of information may be to the detriment of the supplier. If so, legal questions arise which may place the issue in a legislative frame. The Privacy Act and the Freedom of Information Act are examples of national values placed upon ownership issues. Personal information, some say, may be the most valued asset we have. Since the term "resource" has been traditionally used to describe material objectives, the use of the term to apply to knowledge or information, in short, changes the types of definitional problems encountered. This is particularly true where the variables in the definition become social or psychological in character. Let us look now at some specific issues.

FUNCTIONAL MANAGEMENT PROGRAMS VS. RESOURCE MANAGEMENT PROGRAMS

It is sometimes said that the "management function" itself can be subdivided into two primary sets of responsibilities, functional responsibilities and resource responsibilities. The former set goes to the management of the production and distribution processes while the latter goes to the management of resource acquisition, allocation and utilization processes.[1] For example, functional programs in the automobile manufacturing business address the processes of design, fabrication, manufacture, assembly and shipment of automobiles. For each of these processes, a variety of financial, physical, material, human and information resources are required. The automobile manufacturer's functional programs would include all of these activities necessary to acquire, allocate and distribute those resources, in an "optimal mix," to support the various functional programs.

For both sets of responsibilities, questions of efficiency and effectiveness are important, and it is sometimes difficult to distinguish between the two. The classic distinction is that efficiency considerations involve questions of productivity, that is, input-output relationships. The more units of output produced per unit of input, the more "efficient" the process. The simple term used for this relationship is productivity. On the other hand, as we all know, an organization (or an individual for that matter) can sometimes use a resource "efficiently" but goals or results are still not achieved. In such an instance, the process or program is said to be "ineffective." To be sure, when we come to the information asset, both factors are at work. Nevertheless we will contend here that, while technological capabilities have increased productivity as a general rule, (and therefore efficiency in data and information acquisition, storage and dissemination has been good-to-excellent) still the information is not achieving sought-for results. Figure 2-1 shows this function: resource management dichotomy in a schematic "operating environment."

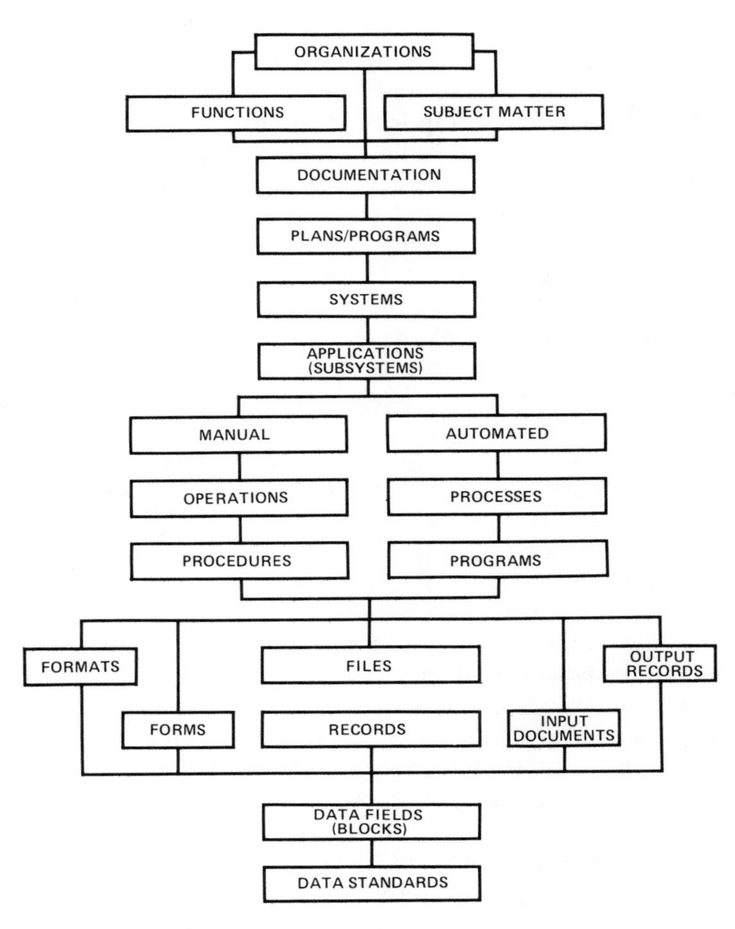

BY PERMISSION AARON HOCHMAN

Figure 2-1. **Resources operating environment**

WHAT IS A "RESOURCE?"

But first what are *resources?* Figure 2-2 depicts resources as that concept has been espoused by several well known economists and management theorists. There are close parallels between the two viewpoints, as Figure 2-2 shows. Taking each in turn, first, the money/capital resource: Doctrines relating to the definition, measurement, application, and use of this class of resource were developed in the 1920's, in response to heightened investment accuracy. Figure 2-3 summarizes this doctrine development in government. This is not to say that neither money nor capital were controlled prior to the 1920's; rather, it is to say that, until the 1920's and in particular until the stock market crash culminated that decade, doctrine relating to the money resource was fragmented and the trade-offs between various alternatives for the application and use of this valuable resource were not carefully defined, made explicit and followed.

Concomitant with the evolution of the resource management doctrine dealing with money and capital was the evolution of a new resource manager—the financial manager. It was to become his responsibility to manage this valuable resource. In some companies, he became known as the vice-president for finance, in others, the comptroller. Within government the term controller caught on, and there are other terms as well. Though names and titles are different in the public and private sectors, and within the same sector, the function is essentially the same.

Next, the people resource. The doctrine associated with the management of human resources did not evolve formally until around the end of World War II and it proceeded into the early fifties. It evolved in response to advances in the behavioral sciences and in response to compelling social forces. Among those forces were the emerging role of unions in industry and significant changes in work conditions. As in the case of the money resource, a parallel management function and a resource manager emerged to match the evolution of the doctrine of human resource management. That management function became known as manpower management, after passing through a phase when it was known as personnel management. In some organizations it still bears the latter name, and, again, other labels and terms are sometimes used.

Next, in the 1940's, primarily to assure the prudent and efficient use of increasingly expensive office and plant space, a third resource class emerged—land and building resources. In government, this new management function became known as space and property management. At about the same time, there emerged a fourth class of

FACTOR OF PRODUCTION TYPE	ECONOMISTS	MANAGEMENT THEORISTS		CARVED-OUT MANAGEMENT FUNCTION
	SAMUELSON	BAKKE*	FORRESTER**	
PRIMARY	NATURAL RESOURCES	MATERIALS	MATERIALS	PRODUCTION
	HUMAN RESOURCES	PEOPLE	PERSONNEL	PERSONNEL
INTERMEDIATE	CAPITAL GOODS	MONEY	MONEY CAPITAL EQUIPMENT	FINANCE
		MARKET	ORDERS	MARKETING
		IDEAS		RESEARCH AND DEVELOPMENT
			INFORMATION	EDP (ELECTRONIC DATA PROCESSING)

*E. Wight Bakke, The Human Resources Function, Yale Labor and Management Center, New Haven, 1958.
**Jay W. Forrester, Industrial Dynamics (Cambridge, Mass.: The M.I.T. Press) 1961.
Source: Richard L. Nolan, *Managing the Data Resource Function* (St. Paul, Minn.: West Publishing Company, 1974).

Figure 2-2. **Basic resources**

RESOURCE	MANAGEMENT FUNCTION	EVOLUTION BEGAN	CAUSES
Money/Capital	Financial Management	1920's	Heightened investment awareness, capital shortages, and depression
People	Manpower Management	1930's	Advances in behavioral sciences and to social forces (unions, working conditions)
Raw Materials	Materials Management	1940's	Critical shortage forecasts for key strategic stockpiles
Land & Buildings	Space & Property Management	1940's	Assure prudent use of office/plant/laboratory space
Information	(Information Management)	1960's	Information explosion, and the need to control the paperwork burden placed on the taxpayer

Figure 2-3. **Historical parallels in government**

resource—material and equipment. Supply and inventory management were the corresponding management functions.

Then, in the 1950's, as we moved from an industrial society to an increasingly technological, post-industrial one, ideas themselves became recognized as a valuable national asset. Developing countries were thirsting for knowledge. Certainly pure research could not easily be transferred, but applied research and technology were increasingly important avenues to achieve both the political and economic aims of the United States, domestically and abroad. On the organizational charts, we soon saw the research-and-development management function emerge.

And now, in response to the information and paperwork explosion, and the need for more facts and better organization of and accesibility to those data, statistics and facts, we are seeing the emergence of a new function: Information Resources Management. The corresponding resource? Data and facts.

RESOURCE ALLOCATION

Now where does resources management come in? The role of top management is, in effect, to integrate the mix of all resources to produce the most cost-effective set of resource alternatives for the production and distribution of the company's goods and services (or in the case of a government agency, the achievement of a program's goals). Taken both singly and collectively, the company's individual products and its total product line requires the meshing together of money, market, employees, materials, ideas, and information. See Figure 2-1 again. In short, for any basic resource to be effectively managed, it must be:

- understood—that is to say, its role in the organization's stable of resources, its uses, its limitations, and its opportunities;
- acquired wisely, since it is not a free good;
- conserved to avoid waste, abuse, and misuse; and
- exploited fully to maximize its uses and applications.

We might usefully summarize the basic objectives of resource management as:

- maximizing the value and benefits from the use of the resource in achieving the organization's goals and objectives;
- minimizing the cost of acquiring, processing, using, and disposing of the resources; and
- fixing accountability for the efficient and effective use of the resources on named officers and specific departments.

Under this concept, then, the "value" of the information resource should be defined as the benefits (results) obtained from its use. Like all resources, the value from utilization must then be weighed against the costs involved.

The central question in resource allocation is choice, that is to say, the choice among alternatives. In the case of government, for example, actions generate public benefits and incur taxpayer costs. The U.S. General Accounting Office has said, "These benefits and costs should be broadly defined to include both social and private aspects."[2] The key elements of the problem of choice in selection from among national goals in the public sector are:

- Government objectives are achieved by developing, adopt-

ing, and implementing policies and by creating and operating programs, *all of which consume or transfer resources*—tangible and intangible.
- There are many public needs. These needs are large and constantly changing. Demands for resources are much greater than the resources available.
- Decision-makers must choose among competing objectives and among the alternative programs and policies capable of meeting the choices of the chosen objectives at desired and affordable levels of achievement.

In the business sector, multiple products and services are manufactured and sold. Each of these incurs costs. Again, the choice confronting the general manager is to select which products and services he should market.

Each functional manager, in turn performs the task of determining and providing an optimal mix of resources to meet his particular responsibilities. For example, a production manager must mix together the optimal combination of inventories, space, equipment, and people to assemble and manufacture products. The financial manager must put together the company's financial portfolio. The marketing manager must come up with an optimal mix of resources for advertising, promotion, and marketing the company's products. The Personnel officer must decide what kinds of people to hire, with what sorts of skills, and for how long a period, and at what salary. The R & D manager must decide how much money should go into pure research versus how much should go into applied research to develop new products and services. In government the issues are analogous. Most government programs are interdependent and affect more than one national goal. This interdependency leads to a requirement for the use of evaluation and analytical techniques in two important resource allocation tasks: First, to effect choices within a major government program area; and second, to effect choices among major government program areas. In short, there is a *value framework* for resource management that embraces four key activities: acquisition, enhancement, retention and delivery. See Figure 2-4.

THE VALUE MANAGEMENT FRAMEWORK

To make choices within each of these four areas, there are several important and unique considerations. For example, for acquisition, is there an appropriate "level" specified for a given objective, and

Resource	Specialized Management Function	COST INCURRED—TYPES OF ACTIVITIES				Benefit Obtained
		Acquisition	Enhancement	Retention	Delivery	
Materials	Production	Purchasing	Manufacturing	Inventory Management	Distribution Logistics	Sale at a Profit
Money/ Capital	Finance	Attraction of Investment or Borrowing	N/A	Payment of Use Charges	Liquidity Management	Conversion Into Other Resources When Needed
Market/ Goodwill	Marketing	Advertising, Promotion, Distribution, Pricing				Enhanced Product Value
Employees	Personnel	Recruiting Hiring	Training	Management Of Rewards	Staffing Control	Improved Efficiency & Effectiveness
Ideas	R & D	Provide a Conducive Environment		Patient Protection Security	Liaison with Product Development	Development of Salable Products
(Data/ Facts)	Information	Collection	Synthesis and Analysis	Organized Maintenance	Accessability Responsiveness Packaging	Improved Human Effectiveness & Contribution

Figure 2-4. **The value framework for resource management**

are there preferred alternatives for achieving that level? For enhancement, are there barriers to adopting a preferred enhancement course of action, and what are the costs of breaking through those barriers? The U.S. General Accounting Office says: "Resolution of resource allocation issues should result in any of a number of actions:

1. Continue, modify, or abandon existing policies;
2. Adopt new policies; *or*
1. Continue, modify, expand, reduce or phase out current programs; and
2. Create new programs."[3]

Available resources will be viewed differently, depending upon the freedom of choice or degree of decision-making automony that is inherent in the manager's position in the organizational hierarchy. Entrepreneurs may bring into the enterprise resources it did not previously possess. Only a few top positions in an enterprise normally have discretionary access to sources of outside funds or the right to acquire major physical resources. Normally, managers work with resources already available within the enterprise or with resources that are regularly generated internally. At his own organizational level, each manager has a negotiating opportunity to secure for his unit some share of the total discretionary resources of the enterprise. But the amount of resources potentially available to each unit decreases sharply at each successively lower level of the organization. It is the general manager, therefore, at the top level of the enterprise, who has ultimate responsibility for acquiring, enhancing, conserving, and deploying resources among conflicting demands for the organization as a whole.

TECHNIQUES, TOOLS AND APPLICATIONS

The need to allocate available human, physical, material, financial, and information resources is a pervasive task that faces most managers at one time or another. Although the examples above relate primarily to the tasks for the organization's top level executive, other examples of tools and techniques used in resource allocation at other levels are:

- Capital investment
- Construction scheduling
- Programming financial resources

- Budgeting financial resources
- Transportation scheduling
- Location of plants
- The analysis of traffic patterns
- The design of research experiments
- Computer simulation
- Warehouse conveyor belt location
- Production scheduling
- Sales territory assignments
- Machine shop scheduling

Figure 2-5 lists additional tools and techniques. Indeed, an entire "new" management science, operations research, has evolved to help managers execute their resource allocation task. Allocation problems are one important major class of operations research problems. Allocation problems arise when given sets of resources can be combined in different ways to achieve desired ends or when there are not enough resources to perform all the necessary activities in the most efficient manner. Operations research is most effective in those instances where available resources are scarce. In that situation, one must optimize

RESOURCE/FUNCTION	TECHNIQUES
FINANCE (Money)	—Discount and Break-Even Analysis in Capital Investment Decisions —Return on Investment Decisions
PRODUCTION (Materials)	—Economic Order Quantity Formulas Which Balance Costs to Procure v.s. Costs to Carry Inventory —Make v.s. Buy Determinations
MANPOWER (People)	—Projected Losses in Production Due to Strikes, Absenteeism and Turnover, Balanced Against Benefit and Wage Packages
INFORMATION (Data)	—Paperwork v.s. Alternatives to Paperwork —Manual v.s. Automated Systems —Microfilm v.s. Hardcopy —Sampling v.s. "Total Coverage" —Produce In-House, Buy Outside

Figure 2-5. Other tools for managing resources

the resource mix in the best possible way. One might, for example, want to minimize resource inputs and maximize resource outputs.

Another tool in resource allocation is the programming system. A programming system is a management device designed to support the information and other decision-making needs of managers who are involved in resource allocation. Without programming, ideas and plans lie dormant or sterile, and budgets become perfunctory administrative mechanisms. A programming system serves both as an information system and as a management control system. As an information system it provides for the collection, manipulation, and presentation of management information to decision-makers. As a management control system, it provides a mechanism for controlling the use of resources to accomplish the organization's goals and objectives.

In the 1960's, formal programming systems had widespread application in both government and industry. During that period, budgeting systems and programming systems were increasingly integrated, at least in theory although seldom in practice. Early programming concepts were labeled performance budgets; later, program budgets came on the scene. Both terms are still used. Major emphasis toward the integration of programming and budgeting came in 1965 when President Lyndon Johnson directed the introduction of an integrated programming-planning-budgeting system (PPB System) in the Executive Branch of the Federal Government.

In Bulletin No. 66-3, issued by the Bureau of the Budget (now the Office of Management and Budget) on October 12, 1965, the need for the PPB system was justified in part on the ground that "to help remedy these shortcomings, the planning and budgeting system in each agency should be made to provide more effective information and analysis to assist line managers, the agency head, and the president in judging needs and deciding on the use of resources and their allocation among competing claims."

So much for the general theories and principles of resource management. While the many and varied approaches, doctrines, "axioms" and hypotheses developed in the traditional resource areas are not fully applicable to the information resource, nevertheless I believe the analogies are compelling and demand further research, testing and experimentation to determine their extent and usefulness in the information area. I believe, moreover, that there are four steps that must be taken to extend general resources management principles to the information resource. First, a full understanding of the similarities and differences between the information resource and the other resources. Second, establishing a discrete management function at the highest organizational level and vesting a senior official with overall responsibility for managing the organization's information resources efficiently and effectively. Thirdly, assigning specific authorities and responsibilities. And lastly, developing and installing the necessary policies, procedures and management systems to "operationalize" the information resources management function. Let us examine each of these.

STEP 1: UNDERSTANDING THE NATURE OF INFORMATION

When we come to the data and information resource area, not only is there no central, authoritative, and cohesive body of doctrine, but only in rare cases do we have clear, detailed, and explicit information policies, much less operating procedures, to guide officials in, for example, selecting from among possible data handling media alternatives on a cost-effective basis or weighing expected benefits of a new or upgraded information system against the total capital and operating investment costs.

In short, the data resource is poorly understood. There is no well-developed body of knowledge for understanding and managing the data resource. Observe that managers have not had a basic orientation toward data as a resource, to be "planned and managed." Computer hardware vendors have been a major source of useful technical knowledge, but understandably they have fostered a hardware orientation among their clients. The first step to be taken by those who would move in the direction this book suggests is to begin thinking of data, not just as abstractions—ideas—but as something tangible, physical, and concrete. To be sure, as we pointed out earlier, information must be thought of both ways—as abstractions (ideas) and as a physical commodity—and in the end, we must consider both ways of looking at information if we are to manage it effectively. But taking the very first step is, as usual, the most difficult one because it requires fundamental rethinking of traditional ways of looking at information.

Let's illustrate the utility of viewing information as a resource by using an analogy of a mineral resource like coal. Coal:

- has an acquisition cost;
- comes in several different grades, some harder and more expensive to mine than others;
- comes in various degrees of purity;
- must be refined and processed to enhance its value;

- passes through many hands from point of acquisition to point of use;
- has many synthetics to compete with—some cheaper, some more expensive;
- can be bought and processed in its raw material form and thus integrated vertically, or can be bought in more refined and processed forms; and
- is subject to the value-added principle at each stage in its life cycle; and transfer pricing principles and techniques can be applied as it moves along its path from acquisition to use.

Of course, like all analogies, there are some important differences between a mineral resource like coal and information. For example, minerals are "consumed" when they are used; information often is not—although information does often become obsolete. Notwithstanding these differences, I believe the similarities are compelling.

STEP 2: ESTABLISH A MANAGEMENT FUNCTION

Now let us try to build a case for managing information as a resource. First, the element of management control. To repeat, can anyone imagine that a corporate executive or top government agency official would be allowed to hire, transfer, promote, or fire his human resources in any manner he chose? Unlikely. Or can anyone imagine that the accountable property officer would allow us to requisition as many fancy chairs, tables, desks, or typewriters as we want and use them for whatever purpose we wanted? Of course not. The analogy, as has been pointed out, can be extended to financial resources too. We have allowances, allotments, and authorizations which tell us exactly how many dollars we may obligate and spend. In the Federal Government, the General Services Administration has promulgated, over a long period of time, a detailed body of doctrine in the area of managing and accounting for the use of real and personal property resources "loaned" agencies. Title is rarely transferred.

Drewry reminds us, for example, that traditionally we have thought of data and information's value as a resource in government in terms of physical paperwork—files, records, reports, evidentiary materials, and so forth. She says, for example, "a file's administrative value is its value in carrying on the activities of the agency or of the government as a whole."[4] All records have some administrative value for a period of time or they would not be created, she says. Those files and records pertaining to uncompleted actions are of administrative value to the agency, since their loss would impede the carrying on of its activities, while those of completed actions may quickly lose their administrative value to the agency. Records may have legal value to the Federal Government or to individual citizens, corporations, or even State and other governments. As in the case of administrative value, the duration of the period during which this legal value exists varies with the kind of right or legal question that is involved. There is enduring legal value to the government in laws and regulations and interpretations of them and in treaties and other international agreements.

Drewry mentions this research value of records must take into account the fact that papers should not be saved merely for the casual interest they may hold "for the curious," or because someone in the future may conceivably take a private interest in the information they contain. There must be more practical reasons for determining that records have research usefulness."[5]

Historically, then, we've seen that when resources get out of control, one obvious course of action is to establish a management function to deal with the problem. It then becomes a first order of business of the officer in charge of that management function to define, measure, package, manage, utilize, and dispose of that resource according to prescribed principles and practices. For our purposes, that set of principles and practices can be referred to as a body of doctrine.

But we see that, in the case of information, a management function has only infrequently been established to deal with the problems. The traditional and conventional treatment of data and information in the organization is to deal with it (or bury it) as an overhead cost. It is thus hidden and kept from evaluation and analysis by budget officers, accountants, middle and top management. An important consequence of this conventional treatment has been to obscure the skyrocketing costs of information activities. Another important consequence has been to mask effective and efficient consideration of alternatives open to management in making trade-off decisions between information resources and other resources.

STEP 3: ASSIGN AUTHORITIES AND RESPONSIBILITIES

In Step 1 we raised the consciousness level of managers and others by asking them to begin thinking of information as a manageable, physical commodity. In Step 2 we established a management function to deal with the problem. In some organizations, this may mean the creation of a completely new function on the organizational charts; in others, it may mean simply a regrouping of existing functions; and in still others, those which perhaps are farthest out on the leading edge of applying information resources management principles, we may need only to relabel or retitle an existing unit.

A few organizations already have a grasp of the function well in hand and are moving on to cement and reinforce organizational, technical, and human links in the chain. But most organizations will require a step-by-step, structured approach. We would then, here in Step 3, assign specific authorities and responsibilities to named individuals, and named units, to carry out the function. Later chapters discuss in more detail alternative organizational locations, pros and cons of each, and the kinds of individuals who will manage the new function.

STEP 4: DEVELOP NECESSARY POLICIES, PROCEDURES AND SYSTEMS

In some cases we will be able to build on existing doctrinal bases. Perhaps a certain amount of guidance already exists, for example, for the management of computers, the operation of libraries, microform program policies, and so forth, but in other cases there may be little or none. In most cases we shall need to articulate organization-wide guidance where before it may have been fragmented by type of organizational unit, function to be carried out, or whatever. Indeed, the integration of fragmented policies, rules, regulations, and guidelines relating to pieces, or facets, of the information resource is one of the most critical objectives of this step-wise process of applying the principles of information resources management.

In each of the chapters that follow, we will take up these major policy, procedural, and systems areas one at a time, beginning first with a more detailed discussion of the "commodity" itself—information. In the next chapter, for example, we will differentiate between knowledge, information, and data. This discrimination is crucial to further evolution of guidance. Then in the following chapter we will review ways of classifying information: typologies. Following that, we will begin a discourse on each of the processes in the management cycle, planning, budgeting, accounting, and so forth, related of course to information resources.

A very useful clue to the development of these policies and procedures is to look at the subject matter headings for the other resources being managed—financial, physical, human, and so forth. Often a study of these subdivisions will offer analogues for the data resource. For example, instead of "recruitment and selection," terms which apply to the human resource, we may have "collection" or "evaluation of sources" in the information resources area. Instead of "warehousing, storage and stockpiling," we may have "storage and retrieval."

The author does not intend that this step-wise process be followed in some cookbook, recipe fashion. It is only a guide. Clearly the exigencies of each organizational context will dictate the form, tempo, priorities, and level of resources which can be brought to bear on the problem, and it is almost axiomatic that we should plan the effort very carefully. After all, creating a new management function isn't something that happens everyday! My guess is that even in the most favorable organizational climates where top management supports the notion actively, where middle and lower management understand it and are committed to its precepts, and where employees and the rank and file are also willing to effect the necessary changes in their activities, the process will take years. Indeed, five to ten years is a likely estimate, and in those organizational contexts where there will, inevitably, be false starts, add additional years. Where the idea is actively resisted and necessary changes are frustrated, the likelihood is that major organizational development and change programs may have to be initiated as a pre-condition.

WHAT HAPPENS IF WE DON'T MANAGE INFORMATION RESOURCES?

What are the penalties of not moving in this direction? For one, as we approach the leading edge of the mini-computer revolution, employees on the lowest rungs of the organizational ladder are demanding bigger and more expensive hardware and software on the grounds that their information needs are more critical, and the unit cost of processing information is continually dropping. This is true whether we're talking about hard copy records and filing equipment, microform technology, digital equipment, optical scanning approaches, or the more exotic advanced holographic and other technologies. Therefore, we already have the capacity to proliferate, miniaturize and splinter data all the way down to the level of individual, personal control over data, held in the palm of the hand.

For example, how can information managers/users keep the lid on the information resource in the face of the following kinds of pressures:

- the head of the printing and reproduction plant tells us that his performance should be judged on the basis of the total number of units of printing; the longer the run, the lower the unit cost;
- the administrative records officer tells us that in storing the company's records, he should be judged on how small a space and how cheaply he can store records; so long as the unit cost of storing is lower than the unit cost of backing a document out of the system, it should be retained;
- the files chief tells us that his evaluation criterion should be how often a document in the files is referred to: if less than once a month per drawer, it should be transferred to a records depository, if more than once, retained;
- the small jobs duplication department manager tells us that overhead is generally more expensive than direct labor costs; therefore, by increasing volume, the unit cost is reduced by distributing overhead across the total number of units replicated;
- and so on, into the computer room, the library, the mail room, and elsewhere.

The "information explosion" can be illustrated in many different ways. Another of my favorites, in addition to the specious use of the economy-of-scale argument above, is to consider the following chain of events. A report comes into the company's mailroom. If only one copy arrives, it is automatically replicated. One of the copies automatically goes to the library. The librarian decides extra copies are needed (not knowing how many came in in the first place or who got them), so the librarian orders them for the bookshelves. Another copy of the report goes to a company official. The official decides several chapters are of interest to the immediate office, so it is sent to the printing plant where master plates are made and additional copies reproduced. An analyst sees the report somewhere along the line and decides that some of the data may be of general purpose interest to various groups, so some of it is key-punched and digitalized and put into the computer data banks. At the same time, the micrographics department notices that the report is big and bulky, so someone decides it should be filmed and entered into the micrographic holdings.

Then an addendum to the report comes in, and the cycle repeats itself. By this time, however, some of the same people who read and processed the original report have left or been reassigned. New people read the addendum; their decisions are different. Inevitably the data is splintered, fragmented, compartmentalized and dispersed to the point that problems of incompatibility, overlap, duplication and inconsistency are unavoidable because nobody can locate, identify, correlate and organize the original data. Bits and pieces of it are strewn across the organizational landscape. Some of this redundancy may be necessary, but is all of it?

It is apparent that the traditional approaches to the control and management of data and information do not suffice. Such approaches may offer temporary savings and relief, but they rarely result in lasting and permanent control. Why not? I contend the reason is that traditional and conventional approaches to managing data and information fail to develop the tools to control information within a formal resource management framework. In short, we now need to treat information as a manageable and budgetable resource—an approach which will help us to identify and measure the "full and true" costs of data and information.

What, in short, then are the consequences of the failure of an organization to treat data and information formally as a manageable resource? Here are some of them in the business world:

- lower echelons within the company are burdened with excessive demands for information from higher echelons;
- top management, the board, and stockholders are frustrated, dissatisfied and confused because information and paperwork handling costs appear to be consuming an ever-increasing portion of the overhead budget;
- duplication and overlap result because requirements for data are not fully coordinated between company divisions and departments—they don't share their data willingly;
- similar facts are collected by different departments and divisions, at different levels within the company, so as to create a real problem with the company's overall credibility to its stockholders and customers; different groups within the company issue similar information which is often inconsistent;
- company communication channels—both the formal ones and the informal ones—are clogged by much irrelevant data; the relevant data can't be separated; and
- bad decisions are made; the company assumes unnecessary risks and loses opportunity; sales drop and profits are lost.

Typically, top officers in the company react to this situation with what I call the "knee jerk" reaction by dealing with the form and shape of the problem instead of its cause. They launch attempts to control their ballooning overhead budgets by imposing arbitrary limits on the number of records, reports or forms which departments can promulgate and use. Such attempts admittedly offer temporary relief, but they hardly ever result in organic and enduring relief. Why? Because records and reports—like weeds—continue to grow back if they are not kept closely cropped—or better yet, pulled out by the roots!

I propose, instead, that we treat information as a critical resource, crucial to organizational health, which both deserves and needs the same kind of management disciplines as those applied to the management and control of other resources.

INFORMATION MANAGEMENT IS NOT INFORMATION MANIPULATION

It is a central contention of this work that we must now pay as much concern to questions of how to manage information as we have paid to questions of how to manipulate information. In short, is information in fact helping to achieve established and approved goals and objectives of the organization—and getting results?

Elliott Richardson put the question of juxtaposing information manipulation with information management rather neatly, in the context of Watergate, when he traced the thread from one Watergate abuse to the next, binding them together:[6]

- "Theft of information: the bugging of Democratic National Headquarters; the break-in of Dr. Lewis Fielding's office to get Ellsburg's psychiatric records; the hiring of spies to steal information from the camps of political opponents.
- "Distortion of information: this, for the electorate, was the net effect of illegal corporate campaign contributions; it also appears in the slanted editing of Presidential tape recordings.
- "Fabrication of information: this, included the forgery during the New Hampshire primary of a letter purporting to be from Senator Muskie in which the word "Canuck" was used; the forged cable implicating the late President Kennedy in the murder of Diem; the plan to use a national security "cover" for the Fielding break-in.
- "Misuse of information: under this heading came attempts to get the IRS to use income tax returns as the basis for investigating political enemies; efforts to exploit FBI files for "dirty tricks"; overtures to the CIA aimed at subverting

its intelligence-gathering function.

- "Misrepresentation of information: a polite word for lies like President Nixon's bold assertion, "Far from trying to hide the facts, my effort throughout has been to discover the facts;" schemes to make the public believe that the Watergate break-in was being thoroughly investigated; the perjury that stretched from one case to another in a rancid sequence relieved only by the unintentional humor of the Presidential Press Secretary's announcement that all previous statements on Watergate were "inoperative."
- "Concealment of information: the payment of hush money; the omission of damaging portions of tapes; the shredding and destruction of documents; the attempts to exploit executive privilege as a means of shutting off the flow of information.
- "Supression of information: the all-out effort to keep the lid on the investigation; the attempt to use "national security" as an excuse for covering up; the entire conspiracy to obstruct justice."

As a postscript, I believe I share the very real concern that "managing information" may be viewed by some under certain conditions as a threat to personal freedoms, a constraint to creative work, or a barrier to the free flow of ideas in our democratic society. Information is indeed power, and the line between "managing information" and "manipulating information" easily becomes blurred. To some, managing information may seem suspiciously like a return to the Orwellian "big brain" idea—a number for everybody and everyone a number—or the gigantic centralized data bank subject to so much debate and criticism in the late 1960's. To these people, or at least to many among them, no amount of explanation will suffice. Duplication, overlap, and redundancy, they say, are a small price to pay for checks and balances in our pluralistic society.

As pointed out in the Preface, however, we have yet to realize the full power of modern information handling technologies. The question is, are they leading us into a deeper quagmire of information overload? Or are we going to harness their power, direction, and application to the plow of national goals and priorities? I believe treating information as a resource, using the doctrines already developed in the other resource areas, is a necessary prerequisite to harnessing the data resource to decision-making and problem-solving plows.

QUESTIONS FOR DISCUSSION

1. Under what circumstances does information become "valuable?" What factors could be taken into account in establishing a price for information? Might information be valued on the basis of what an insurance company was willing to insure it for?

2. Under one scheme, the resource management *function* can be said to generally embrace five components: identification, classification, and description; inventory; acquisition; allocation and distribution; and support for organizational goals and objectives. Compare and contrast how raw materials* can be dealt with in such a framework, with how information might be viewed. Where are the similarities? Differences? * (For example, a mineral like coal).

3. A buzz word sometimes used in resource allocation methodology is "trade-off." We hear, for example, that dollars can be "traded" for people in carrying out some project; or labor for capital; or time for quality. How might "information resources" be traded with "manpower resources" in undertaking a marketing survey of consumer buying habits?

4. How would you value the usefulness of a particular record or set of records you company is contemplating holding for perhaps twenty or thirty years? On the basis of storage space costs? How many times the documents might be accessed? How the information might be used in some particular context? Some combination of these, or other factors?

5. How would you value the usefulness of a particular information system your agency is planning to develop? If you were in charge of the feasibility study that was to identify and cost out all of the "variables" on both the benefit/use side and the cost side of the equation, what considerations would you address?

6. What do the economist and financial analyst mean when they say a particular information cost should be *capitalized?* What is an example? How about the "corresponding" term *expensed?* When might we want to expense an information purchase? Give some examples.

FOOTNOTES

[1]For a good discussion of the basic concepts involved here, see the two volume report "Guidelines For The Management of Data Resources" prepared by Task Group 17 of the Federal Information Processing Standards program of the Institute for Computer Science and Technology, National Bureau of Standards (preliminary draft dated Sept. 20, 1977). The authors list five basic functions, regardless of the resource being managed: identification, classification, and description of the resource; inventory of the resource; acquisition of the resource; allocation and distribution of the resource; and support for management policies and goals. A companion volume is also available, entitled "Executive Guide to the Management of Data Resources."

[2]General Accounting Office, U.S. Government, "Evaluation and Analysis to Support Decisionmaking," September 1, 1976, pp. 4–5. In its preface, the GAO says "For a number of years, GAO has been expanding the scope of its work and capability of its staff to review the results and effectiveness of Government programs." This important publication deals with the resource allocation problem in the context of public policy decisionmaking; and talks of the "evaluation and analysis continuum." Both the theoretical and practical aspects of planning an evaluation study, conducting it, appraising results, and communicating results, are dealt with.

[3]Ibid. Op. cit.

[4]Drewry, Elizabeth B., "*Records Disposition in the Federal Government,*" Public Administration Review, Vol. 15, 1955, pp. 220–221.

[5]Ibid. Op. cit.

[6]Richardson, Elliott, "*The Creative Balance, Government, Politics, and the Individual in America's Third Century,*" Holt, Rinehart and Winston, New York, 1974, pp. 105–106.

3 KNOWLEDGE, INFORMATION AND DATA

Essential for information resources management is a clear understanding of the relationships between knowledge, information, and data. A simple schematic, as shown in Figure 3-1, can perhaps most easily be understood as depicting the "life cycle of a fact." Thus, in the first stage of its life cycle, a fact is "born" or emerges. At this stage, it is a raw fact—unevaluated. It has almost no significance standing alone, out of context. What is a number, for example, unless we have a context or referant within which or against which to ask a question?

As the fact "grows," it enters the second stage of its life cycle. Someone has chosen to evaluate the significance of the fact, to place some interpretation and meaning on it. Hence we often speak of information as evaluated data. Finally, in the third stage, the maturation stage, various bits and pieces of information are put together in an even broader context. Knowledge then helps us move from mere opinion or half-truth to "truth." It helps us point to principles, and it helps add to a body of doctrine. Finally, the fact "dies" as its identity and relevance are completed subsumed and submerged in the knowledge base.

A number of theorists have juxtaposed these four stages of the fact's life cycle into an integrated theory of one kind or another. Let us review some of the more important ones. First, Claude E. Shannon of Bell Telephone Labs developed his theory in an effort to define and measure information within the context of communication.[1] His theory goes something like this:

- Information is news. If someone tells you your own name,

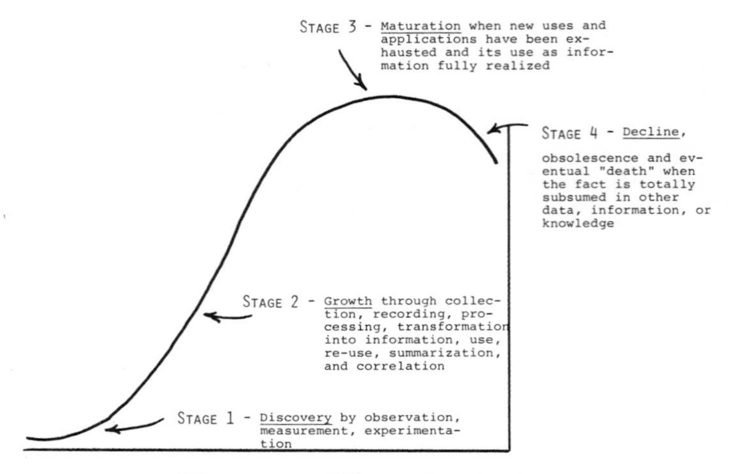

Figure 3-1. **Life cycle of a fact**

he transmits no information; you already know it, unless you are an idiot (or perhaps an imbecile).

- Such an informer hasn't "resolved any uncertainty" for you. Data or facts, to become information, must help to resolve uncertainty.
- Information is more than facts or data, because of the first two points made above.
- Data and facts fill *memory;* information, on the other hand, *feeds the intellect.*
- Mere facts and data can answer four of the six interrogatives: what happens; involving who; when; and where. But only information can answer the other two—how and why.

Herbert Simon also evolved a theory of the relationship between knowledge, information and fact.[2] Although Simon may not have formally considered the closeness of some of his ideas to those of Claude Shannon, it does appear his notions reinforce and build on Shannon's. Here are the essential elements of Simon's theory:

- Facts and information vie for attention. Either may "win" because the intellect may not be able to discriminate between the two.
- The trained intellect can discriminate more efficiently between the two than can the untrained intellect.

Now, when one adds hypotheses of additional theorists, one might go still astep further and construct the following:

- All acquired facts were at one time information, beginning with the early prenatal and postnatal processes of sentience, cognition, recognition, and perception.
- Knowledge is an organized body of information, or the comprehension and understanding consequent to the acquisition thereof. Information is therefore the narrower term of the two.
- Two or more facts may be correlated by the intellect to produce information. Both facts may already be in memory, or one may be in memory and the other in the process of being brought into memory.
- Semantically and epistemologically, the second "fact" in the above example is information, insofar as this hypothesis is concerned, because of some dialectic such as induction or deduction.
- The value of information is the extent to which it helps to resolve uncertainty. The value of information is zero if uncertainty is not resolved to any degree; "complete" if uncertainty is completely resolved.
- In this theoretical framework, the burden imposed on those persons who furnish information might be defined, measured, or weighed against the value of the information furnished in psychological value/burden terms only, not in economic terms.
- One man's data may be another man's information and vice versa.
- Typically, as we go up the organizational/authority ladder, information at the lower level becomes data at the upper level. Part of the reason is summarization and aggregation of data to correspond to broader responsibilities. Part of the reason goes to interpretation differences, because significance and relevance are, in part, circumstantial and contextually-dependent, not rooted in absolute or immutable conditions or situations.

The problem with the "resolve uncertainty hypothesis" is that it almost appears too "slick." Indeed, most authors would use a much longer list of criteria for measurement of the value of information. Surely the purposes of information are much broader than merely the resolution of uncertainty. For example, what of the broad "for your information—FYI" class? Moreover, we read some books, not because they help us to resolve some sort of uncertainty, but rather for sheer pleasure. See Figure 3-2 for a list of some ways to think of information.

WAYS TO THINK OF INFORMATION

1. Information is data understandable to someone, somewhere.
2. Information is a valuable resource.
3. Information is the "organized, intelligible, and meaningful result once data is processed."
4. Information is mental in character.
5. Information is "all sensory stimuli."
6. Information is the stuff we fill in our heads when we think and act.
7. Information is facts and knowledge that are believed to be true.
8. Information is the content of communicative messages.
9. Information can only be understood as a part of the communication process.
10. Information is utterly context-dependent, and has no meaning outside of context.
11. Information theory is an abstraction of a very human process.
12. Information is a representation of reality.
13. People are the ultimate and only users of information.
14. People produce information.
15. Machines produce data.
16. Information is physical in character.
17. Information is abstract in character.
18. Information is books, articles, technical papers, audio tapes, memos, computer printouts, all stored data.
19. Information is a commodity.
20. Information is a resource.
21. Information is an asset.
22. Information isn't consumed when it is used.
23. Information is a national treasure.
24. Information is an economic resource; it can be bought and sold in the marketplace.
25. Information is an organizational resource.
26. Information is a personal resource.
27. Information is power.
28. Information is money.
29. Information is the same as knowledge.
30. Information isn't the same as knowledge.

Figure 3-2.

SOCIAL SCIENCE DEFINITIONS

Baratz reminds us that a great deal of work on the definition of these terms according to the context of their use has already been done in the Social Sciences, particularly Psychology.[3] An informed discussion of these varied uses should, according to social scientists, recognize that the definition of the term *information* is context-specific. That is, information is a convenient abstraction for the stuff which fills our heads whenever we think and act. We never really think of the "stuff" in abstract terms, except when we are thinking about it out of context of real-time, real-life situations. Psychologists have done a great deal of thinking about information both in and out of context. Attempts have been made to conceptualize the role of stimuli as they lead to action and behavior. Psychologists are not univocal in the way in which they conceptualize the problem, yet they recognize the limits of their conceptions; that is, they recognize that the abstractions, when they are put into use in a particular context, may miss some very critical aspects of the process they purport to describe. Even the simplest of these conceptions, Stimulus-Response theory, recognizes the character of different types of stimuli (read data).

When we define information exclusively in terms of its attributes, we may miss the variety of characteristics recognized by even the most simple theory of human behavior/action, because a particular theory of the communication or reception of knowledge or intelligence has been substituted for the abstract problem itself, without recognizing that the theory is itself an abstraction and that the abstraction may limit our conceptualization of the information process itself, since it is, in reality, an abstraction of a very human process, engaged in by most without much thought as they go about their daily business in the world.

Such an abstraction of the conception of information is contained in an economic definition of information as a commodity. The use of the economic definition with its own set of meanings, is itself an abstraction, with its own encumbrances. Describing the term *information* in terms of the processes of collection, recording, processing, storage, and dissemination, while adequate for the computer, does not adequately define *information.* Use of these processes to define information predisposes us to the limits, not only of the computer, but also to the search for alternative processes by which information in context can be understood. *Commodity* is an adequate way of describing an object, such as a *bit,* but it says very little about the way in which value is ascribed to that bit of information. The market, as well as other mechanisms, ascribe value to a commodity. To the extent that we deal with the market for information in commodity terms, we are constrained to think of the seller—not the buyer.

On the demand side, particularly when the buyer is the Federal Government, appear all of the concerns about datamation as an abstraction. This is of particular moment when the buyer is also what has been called a "decision-maker." He or she may have different values placed on information, and when he or she leaves the scene so may the values. So it goes with the information that appears of "value." Since we have introduced the term *context* we may therefore talk about the term *value-context,* convenient but abstract for the term *person.* When that person needs information, a value is automatically placed on it—defined by the statement of need. One might, in the best of all possible worlds, turn to one's information specialists for help. In the best of all possible worlds, that specialist presses a few buttons and gets it. More often than not, alas, such is not the case, so the specialist seeks to collect it. Given this process, a great deal of information is collected which might be of value at one time but is worthless at another. "Need to know" turns into "nice to know," which turns into known or worthless.

Discussion of the problem of using an economic or commodity definition for information illustrates two points: 1) The difficulty of compounding meanings as presented by terms forced to meet usages for which they were not originally intended; and (2) that the term *commodity* conceals a defect in the conceptualization of the term *information* which it is intended to modify.

This latter element is worth exploring further. Use of the term *commodity* to modify a particular point of view (read theory of information) piles onto one level of abstraction (information is "facts and data which are collected, recorded, processed, stored, and disseminated") another level of abstraction which totally obscures the original problem—"information as the communication or reception of knowledge or intelligence."

The linear trend evident in the commodity formulation piles excess meaning on excess meaning, leading to confusion. This is a very ordinary mistake often made by theoreticians: the original formulation of the problem is never questioned.

IS INFORMATION AN INTRINSIC PROPERTY OF SYMBOLIC DATA?

Dunn and other authors have emphasized that information is not merely an object or a thing but an act or a process.[4] Information processing, then, is a process of giving meaning or imparting form ("informing"). Under this conception, information is not an intrinsic property of symbolic data; that is, it cannot be assumed that "the more symbolism, the more information." Any element of symbolic data only represents a meaning or set of meanings. Information, then, is both a process which incorporates the objectives, values, logic and perceptions of the individual and a series of objects in the form of data elements, records, reports, files, and messages which are an integral part of the process by which the individual collects, stores, transmits, and communicates symbolic data that has meaning or value to the person.

An important characteristic, then, of the individual's information processing is that it involves the use of symbols. An individual understands, describes, and interprets the real world through the use of symbols. In a sense, therefore, important root causes of information problems lie in the use of symbols. The ways we organize, conceptualize, ascribe significance to, and give meaning to the symbols have important bearing on our effectiveness as decision-makers and problem-solvers.

A CONCEPT USE ANALYSIS

Diener develops a "concept use analysis" perspective for stratifying information in a generic sense into our three categories—data, information, and knowledge.[5] He contends that data are sensory and perceptual phenomena, while information and knowledge are conceptual phenomena and are therefore at the cognitive level of perception. Under this approach, data which would be perceptually entered into the human process via the sensory stimuli routes—visual, auditory, tactual, taste, and olfactory—are "encoded neurochemically." Then the data either may be retrieved in raw form or used as "raw material for the cognitive processes (thinking). The interpretations of these perceptions, their conceptualizations, are socio-culturally defined phenomena, shared by the group experiencing the data." In distinguishing between information and knowledge, this author, too, suggests equating the four interrogatives *what, when, where* and *who* as falling within the realm of information, whereas only knowledge would answer the other two interrogatives, *how* and *why.*

Diener also seems to reject any objective criterion for the assessment of the value of information. He contends that information is, indeed, "in the eyes of the beholder." The problem with this notion is that, set in an organizational context, it might lead the investigator to conclude that every user, in the end, should be the final arbiter of whether the information he needs is useful. That thesis runs partially counter to other arguments put forward in this work that information must be treated as a manageable resource and that, if every user is allowed unilaterally to dictate the value of the information he uses, we might very well end with a kind of data resource anarchy or chaos. Why, for example, should we allow the individual organizational user such latitude in the information resource area, when we don't in the other resource areas (money, chairs, people, and so on)?

CURRENT TRENDS IN KNOWLEDGE MANAGEMENT

A number of leading theorists in the fields of public administration and information science developing the resource management theme are using the terms *knowledge management* or *knowledge administration.* Caldwell, for example, has said that: "The effective organization and wide sharing of knowledge should enable the public agency to more readily achieve public goals with reduced probability of error, yet also enabling an informed public to challenge administrative action where the use of public authority appears to be improper or unwise. Knowledge may be power when effectively organized, and the organization and management of knowledge is essential to moving society through its present transition. Under the organization and management of knowledge may be the most critical aspect of managing this transition toward a world hopefully more stable and enduring than the one we now know."[6]

Perhaps one of the most carefully articulated theories of the relationship of knowledge, information, and data is that developed by Berry and Cook.[7] In 1976 and 1977, they began to develop a theory of knowledge "as a foundation for many of the concepts involved with establishing a knowledge resource for a department (in government)." They begin much of their background discussion with the computer, the general problem of the data explosion, and the clogging of management decision-making channels. It soon becomes clear that their primary focus is not so much in raising knowledge to a "peer level" with other economic resources available to government departments (human, physical, financial, and so on) but rather in elevating the knowledge resource to a unique position somewhat above the level of the other resources. These authors are not content to deal with data and information alone. "In this paper," they say, "we suggest that the *real* resource which a department should be seeking to understand and extend is not just its data, but is knowledge. Extending the data-as-a-resource philosophy to the concept of knowledge-as-a-resource can be a complicated process, but one which we feel can yield real benefits to a department." See Figure 3-3 for a schematic diagram of the Berry-Cook hypothesis.

I quibble with the contention in one important respect. I believe that all three levels—data, information and knowledge—are each important in their own right. It is not a case, I would submit, of knowledge being "more important" than data, or of slightly higher importance than information. All three have their special and unique contribution to make to organizational problem-solving and decision-making. There will be direct trade-offs between them when, for example, organizations cannot afford, or take all the time in the world, to "develop knowledge." Usually time runs out, or money runs out, or both run out, and we then are forced to settle for less than we would like to have. Typically, information or sometimes data is simply presented, and staff units find themselves being forced to suggest that a problem be "studied further." See Figure 3-4, for example, for a list of trade-offs.

In short, I would say we have three levels, knowledge resources, information resources, and data resources, each with its special niche. But the Berry/Cook research is extremely helpful to us here, and we should look at it further. They divide knowledge into three main classes: factual, procedural, and judgmental. Factual knowledge is

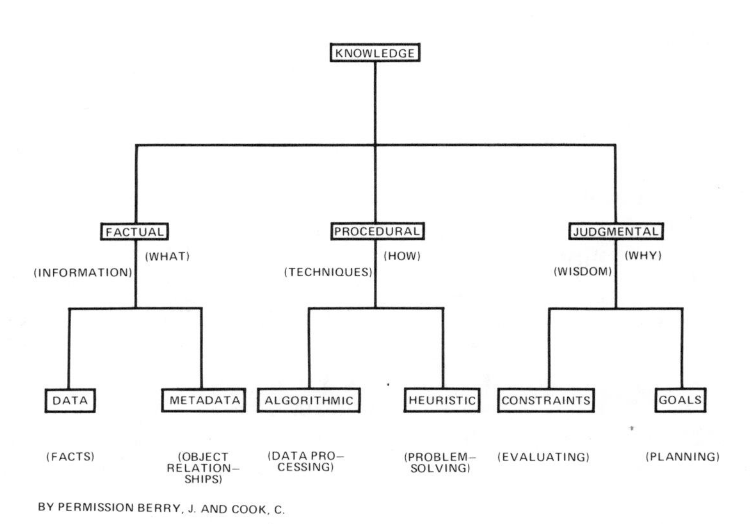

Figure 3-3. **A knowledge taxonomy**

Data and Information Trade-Offs

FORM AND MEDIA	
Alphabetic	Numeric, statistical
Verbal	Written
Hard copy	Microform
Microform	Digital
Hard copy	Digital
Telephone	Letter
Night letter	Telegram
Black and white	Color
Abbreviated	Spelled out
People-to-people	Paper-to-paper
362636 (data)	36″26″36″ (information)
Rare	Common
Sample	Universe
Geographically related	Non-geographically related

PACKAGING, COLLECTING AND DISSEMINATING	
Text "in clear"	Text codified, symbolized
Book	Book review
Full text	Abstract, synopsis, precis
Primary journal	Secondary journal
Hard cover	Paperback
Bound	Looseleaf
Captured at source	Transcription
Narrative	Codified, symbolized
Qualitative	Quantitative
Tabular	Textual
Graphic	Narrative
Full dissemination	Selective dissemination
Search purposefully	Browse
Annual subscription	Monthly subscription

PROCESSING, STORING, RETRIEVING AND MANAGING	
Off-line	On-line
Batch	Real time
Sequential	Random access
Time-shared	Dedicated
Integrated data bases	Fragmented data bases

Centralized holding	Decentralized holding
Standard data definitions	Unstandardized data definitions
Dialogue	Monologue
QUALITY AND MEANING	
Source pinpointed	Source unidentified
Edited	Unedited
Verified	Unverified
Current	Obsolete
Relevant	Irrelevant

Figure 3-4. **Data and information trade-offs**

defined, in turn, as being of two types, data and metadata. Data are raw, unevaluated facts; metadata is data on data or data about the relationships between other data. See Figure 3-3 again.

Procedural knowledge relates to the "how," as they put it, or the techniques, methods, and approaches by which an organization does its business. Again they subdivide this second class into two categories, algorithmic and heuristic. Algorithmic procedural knowledge deals with techniques which follow specific, prescribed decision rules which are applicable to a wide variety of situations; that is, the applications of the algorithms are to routine, repetitive kinds of activities and operations. On the other hand, the second category, heuristic procedural knowledge, is more discovery-oriented; that is, decision-rules are impossible to articulate, or they are so difficult or uneconomical to use as to be impractical. *Learn by doing* is the term one often sees in the context of heuristics. Over the long run, some heuristic methodology gets transformed to algorithmic methodology as experience, testing, verification, and scientific validation proceeds.

INFORMATION AND KNOWLEDGE AS HISTORY

We must not overlook the definition of data, information, and knowledge as the archivist and historian would view them. The archivist and the historian have long conceived of information "as a resource," but their definition is really to be taken in the context of the third major class of information holdings we discussed in an earlier chapter, namely, literature. In that sense, then, they see information as the primary tool for recording man's heritage in written form for all posterity. They are not particularly concerned with the technical distinction between data, information, and knowledge; indeed, they would be content to preserve all three in limitless quantity if they could be persuaded that the utility of the material would be of value to some yet-to-be-born historian. They delight in pointing out that some long forgotten, obscure facts in the history books may elucidate meanings in today's world.

The problems of the archivist have been compounded by the modern information-handling technologies. Whereas prior to their arrival the archivist could be content with the dusty manuscript, the computer posed new and unforeseen problems. Should a computer printout be preserved? "It all depends" has been an unsatisfactory answer.

Finally, their third main class, judgmental, is also subdivided into two categories, constraints and goals. Those two terms are ascribed their conventional meanings in organizational and linguistic theory. Constraints are laws, rules, regulations, policies and the like; the authors cite codes of ethics and the Ten Commandments as examples. Goals refer to the direction in which the organization is moving and its raison d'etre. In the private sector, making a profit is the common objective; in government, serving the people is an objective. Nonprofit organizations may have philanthropic or altruistic goals, and religious organizations theological ones.

One minor flaw in the Berry/Cook presentation (as opposed to the theoretical underpinnings) is that the authors show a computer-bias. Their "outside world" is the computer *application;* some may allege an insensitivity to politics and the problem of information viewed as power. With the profound understatement so characteristic of the computer fraternity, they say at one point that their notions must be "sold" to top management, and the presentation cannot be the "usual hour-long briefing." But my criticism here is a friendly one. They have, in my view, made an outstanding contribution to this field.

In a recent report, "Toward a National Program for Library and Information Services: Goals for Action," the National Commission on Libraries and Information Science said:

> Information, whether in the raw form of empirical data, or in a highly processed form we call 'knowledge,' has come to be regarded as a national resource as critical to the Nation's well-being and security as any natural resource, such as water or coal. The wealth of popular, intellectual, scholarly, and research resources in the libraries and information facilities of the United States is one of the great strengths of the Nation. But like many natural resources, knowledge resources, uncoordinated in growth and usage, are in danger of being wasted and inefficiently utilized.

> In advanced societies, a substantial part of the culture is handed down to successive generations in the form of recorded knowledge. This resource consists of books, journals, and other texts; of audio and visual material; and of smaller units of information or data which can be separately manipulated, as by a computer. In recent years, these records have become increasingly varied—through technological extention of written words, pictures, and sounds. For example, a significant part of the country's information resource is now on film, on video tapes, and in computer files. As the Nation's knowledge grows and the number of records increases, our dependence on them increases, and the need to gain access then becomes crucial.[8]

The problem has been that too much of the Nation's information heritage is stored and administered by custodians in places which are too remote and in systems too difficult to access. The reason, in short, is that the archivist tends to view all information as historically significant, supporting his position with a thesis that the true relevance of "current facts" can only be ascertained in some kind of historical context. But surely not all information can be considered history or knowledge! Certainly much of it must be peripheral in value, and much of it is soon obsolete.

The difficulty in reconciling the views of the archivist with those of the modern information technologist can perhaps best be illustrated, albeit in some oversimplified fashion, by the observation: The archivist wants to preserve everything; the modern information technologist wants to preserve very little. Tefko Saracevic points out that the problem is as much a qualitative one as a quantitative one. He mentions that:

> Documentation at one time defined the problem as one of organization of knowledge and at another time information retrieval defined it as one of retrieval and dissemination. One definition does not exclude the other; they supplement each other. However, both definitions resulted in approaches that essentially concentrated on controlling the *quantitative* flood of information perceived in terms of the information explosion.
>
> There were attempts to define the problem from still another point of view, one of quality. From this third viewpoint, difficulties in communication arise not so much because we do not have adequate organization, retrieval, or dissemination, but because practically we are quite unable to get to the qualitative information (data, articles, documents) which is buried under all that quantity. We have difficulties in separating wheat from chaff, although we mastered the processing of both together.
>
> The qualitative definition of the problem, where accepted, resulted in creation of information analysis centers as suggested by information scientists from Battelle Memorial Institute in the late 1950's and early 1960's. However, since the view was not widely accepted we have very

few such centers. This view also resulted in proposals for creation of encyclopedic systems by H. G. Wells in the 1930's and more recently in Manfred Kochen. None have been created as yet.

Documentation and information retrieval provided several relatively successful solutions to the problem of controlling the quantity of information being published today. The time is overripe for the third problem—that of quality—to be attacked. Perhaps information science will tackle this problem. However, it is entirely possible that a new discipline will be developed around the qualitative definition of communication problems in science and technology in particular and in society in general. Will what has previously happened to librarianship, and then to documentation, also happen to information science? Somebody else took the ball and ran.[9]

A MULTI-DISCIPLINARY APPROACH

I believe Saracevic is on the right path when he hints that a new discipline may need to be developed. I believe we must move from a traditional, single-discipline approach to defining, conceptualizing and managing information toward a modern, multi-discipline approach.

The development of disparate theories, hypotheses, and notions about how to deal with information is not unique to that resource, as the history of the evolution of doctrines relating to other resources reveals. For example, in the development of theories concerning the management of human resources, we've seen and are still seeing contributions made by psychology, industrial engineering, business administration, public administration, political science, management science, and many other specialists within social science. In the evolution of computers, the contributions of semantics, philosophy, physics, chemistry, engineering and many fields are well known. Statistics have seen major innovations developed by biometricians, econometricians, a wide variety of mathematicians and many engineering specialists. The list could easily be lengthened.

It is not surprising, therefore, that our modern information manager, like all generalists, must know a considerable amount about the theories, methodologies, tools, and applications of all of the disciplines concerned with information-handling. He need not be a specialist in anyone of them, however, and of course we will still need technical specialists in every one of the supporting information-handling disciplines because, like all technologies in our complex society, information technology has become increasingly specialized, technical, fragmented and complex. Accordingly, many different professions, approaches, techniques, and tools are involved in harnessing the new technology, with no single group enjoying a monopoly or preeminent position. If it were to be managed on a permissive basis, by a sort of benign or benevolent approach, less than the full ultimate value and potential of the information resource would be utilized to help achieve the organization's goals; the information disciplines, professions and vested interests would tend to maximize their own ends without necessarily considering how they fit (their role) into the overall organizational context.

THE INFORMATION DISCIPLINES

Which are the "information disciplines?" How do they relate to one another now? And what can be done to bring them together? In my view, probably there are eight or nine major planets in our "information solar system." (See Figure 3-5.) What each has in common is that data and information—or facts, figures and symbols—are their main subject-matter, concern and interest. In short, *information* is the common denominator of all of them. They are:

- computers, and associated automation technologies;
- the theory and practice of statistics and probability;
- communication and telecommunication;
- publishing, printing and replication;
- libraries and library science;
- microform and miniaturization technologies;
- the information sciences;
- the systems and management sciences; and
- the information arts.

Every one of these professions has been working to advance mankind's capability to collect, process, store, utilize and disseminate data and information more effectively and efficiently. Each is represented internationally and nationally, and sometimes locally, by professional, trade, academic and user groups. They are, by and large, individually integrated in a "vertical" sense. What is missing, in my view, are the horizontal bridges between these disciplines—forums, councils and mediums which encourage and promote more direct and intensive dialogues between and among them.

Figure 3-5 is a simple "mileage chart" matrix. Even though it may not be inclusive of all planets in the information universe, it is useful to highlight the collaborative and inter-disciplinary nature of the several

THE INFORMATION SOLAR SYSTEM

	COMPUTERS & AUTOMATION	COMMUNICATIONS & TELECOMMUNICATIONS	PUBLISHING, PRINT. & REPL.	MICROFORM & MINIATURE,	STATISTICS & PROBABILITY	LIBRARY SCIENCE	MANAGEMENT & SYSTEMS	INFO. SCIENCE	INFO. ARTS
COMPUTERS & AUTOMATION									
COMMUNICATIONS & TELECOMMUNICATIONS	Mass data trsfr Auto msg switch networking Real time control Satellites								
PUBLISHING, PRINTING & REPLICATION	Phototypesetting Automated morgues Tex processing Page make-up	Remote editing Multiple editions national papers Facsimile transm.							
MICROFORM & MINIATURIZATION	COM Direct text ret.	Video transmission document images	Micropublishing Microform report Condensed packaging collect.						
STATISTICS & PROBABILITY THEORY	Mini computing Random access Boolean algebra Linear program.	Real time control Network structures	Report generators	Ultrafiche microminia- turization retrieval					
LIBRARY SCIENCE	KWIC indexing Auto. catalog Machine-read. Biblio. search	Multiple facility access	Book catalogs Bibliographic systems	Microform holdings	Bibliometric analysis				
MANAGEMENT & SYSTEMS SCIENCES	Data base mgt Process control MIS SDA	Teletransportation Laser technologies	Process Control printing	Photomicro- graphy	Regression an. Monte Carlo Poisson Models/Simul.	Machine index. Auto. abs. & cat.			
INFORMATION SCIENCES	SDI Synth. lang. Cybernetics Machine trans.	Data reduction & compaction	Comprehensive & selective bibliographies	Holographic technology	Relevance & Access tech. Information Theory	Clearing houses Document centers	OCR Lg. capacity storage Info. stnds.		
INFORMATION ARTS	Computer graph. CAI Heuristic prog. Music scoring	Telelectures Teleconferencing Picture phones	Voice-Visual- graphic Video cassette	Micrography	Dimensional and contour projections	"Please Ask"	Info. as resource Info. budget	Knowledge mgt.	

Figure 3-5.

"information planets." All have one thing in common: data and information are the "raw material" with which they deal. Their input or output (or sometimes both) is information, and the products and services with which they concern themselves are informational. Acting singly, they have all developed important theories, concepts, technologies, methodologies, tools and applications that are now found virtually everywhere—in the pure sciences, the applied sciences, the disciplines, business, government, in the home and elsewhere. Some of the more illustrative of these are listed in Figure 3-5.

Acting in consort, they reinforce one another. In an inter-disciplinary mode, they are capable, potentially at least, of substantially increasing and accelerating their contributions to the resolution of some of society's problems. What is needed, it seems to me, is more intensive interaction between and among them, within some kind of harmonizing institutional framework.

In Figure 3-5, at each intersect is shown: a theory, concept, technology, methodology, tool or key application jointly developed and then applied to the pure sciences, applied sciences, the professions, business, government, the arts, in the home or in some other sector of society. The reader might, without too much difficulty, expand the matrix from a two-dimensional to a multi-dimensional one.

One of my contentions is that not enough of our energies, resources, creativity and imagination are now directed to an anticipatory, prescriptive course of action that would help us to fill in such a multi-dimensional matrix. Instead, interfaces are evolving in part along reactive, heuristic and empirical axes. In my view, both paths should be pursued simultaneously.

The multi-disciplinary definition of information implies that the computernik who aspires to be the information manager of the future must somehow break the shackles of hardware bells and whistles. The librarian who similarly aspires must go beyond the Dewey Decimal System and the card catalogue, and the paperwork manager, trained in time and motion studies, files classification schemes and records disposition schedules, must learn something of the arcane world of the economics of information, benefit/cost analysis, and the techniques for developing responsive, yet economical, information services. The gap will be easy for some to overcome; a few will jump over it quickly with hardly a ripple in their careers and personal lives. Others will stumble, but pick themselves up and, after establishing a new set of credentials, move on to become the information managers of the future. A few, inevitably, won't make it; for whatever reason, they will find the climb too difficult.

PLURALISTIC INFORMATION MANAGEMENT

The academic community seems to admonish us that it might be permissible to treat information as a resource so long as it is recognized that:

- people with knowledge are resources;
- people, not machines, organize knowledge; and
- since there are many different ways to organize knowledge in a democratic system, management of information must be pluralistic.

Duplication and redundancy may be considered as ways of assuring pluralism in democratic information systems. The commodity formulation of information neatly side steps the apparent dilemma of having to deal with information only as an abstraction—out of context to the real-life situations in which it is used—because context is what produces value for the commodity. Again, Baratz points out that organizing the information commodity to fit the context is a value-enhancing process. Information in context produces meaning. Organizing information for consumption by computer, in anticipation of later analysis and utilization, does not produce meaningful information, nor does the file system of a secretary give meaning to the content of her files. By the same token, the card catalog of a library and the filing system for books does not produce value for the contents of the library. The enhancement of value for information in context occurs only when the process of organization is compatible with the individual who is to use it. Value is decreased when the organization of the information does not meet the organized framework of the user.

TOO MUCH DATA?

Sir Stafford Beer, one of Britian's leading cyberneticists, is perhaps a bit more blunt and direct in differentiating data and information for us. He said: "Data, I want to say to you, are excrescence. Data are the very latest kind of pollution." Beer believes that we are not going to do anything at all about the management of information and knowledge toward the regulation of society as long as we think in data-processing terms. That is technologically easy. It is what the computer companies and the telecommunication interests would like us to do. Data are assuredly the great new marketable commodities of the 1970's. "But let me repeat," he says "data of themselves have no value." "What has value," he intimates, "is the machinery to transform data into information and the machinery by which that information may be used to energize society. Society has become a complex organism, and it needs a better nervous system. Managing the development of informational science and technology is this task."[10]

In short, Beer is complaining about what he calls informational overload. He continues: "The private citizen seeking knowledge is inundated by information which is virtually free. Yet, the publishing industry responds in the old mode—by selling him yet more. The firm continues to buy expensive market research, because that is what it has always done, oblivious of the fact that transactions of every kind can now be electronically monitored, so that data are in glut. Its problem too is one of procuring adaptive behavior, and no longer at all one of 'finding the facts.' As for the Government, there is really no dearth of securing information either; there is instead a problem of organizing information—across departmental boundaries and in time."

I would argue with Beer that information can still be considered a "free good." Have you tried dialing 411 lately? Or have you tried to add up the costs of collecting information demanded for a government report? Or filled out an income tax form? Henry brings to our attention an even more critical consideration. He says: "In the rubric of knowledge management, who *knows* what assumes more importance in the bureaucratic decision-making process than who *has* what. In the most profound sense of that overworked cliche, knowledge is power. Hence, we find ourselves studying the dynamics of such public policies as the Copyright Act, the Administrative Procedure Act, the Freedom of Information Act, the National Environmental Policy Act, the Fair Credit Reporting Act, and the Federal Advisory Committee Act, as well as the sundry agency policies dealing with computers, security, and citizen participation in organizational decision-making. The commonality in all these policies (as well as many others) is that they rest on the assumption that those with knowledge have power, and, as policies, they attempt to redistribute knowledge throughout the policy in such a way as to give a greater number of citizens more knowledge with which they can influence the policy-making process."[11]

Henry points out that, in essence, Beer's analysis represents a rejection of a hydraulic thesis of public policy-making from the standpoint of information theory. Beer contends that knowledge itself is distributed throughout a social network of "esoteric boxes." The esoteric box is "an identifiably social institution," such as a firm, a profession, or a social service, that is "internally autonomous and self-organizing and self-regulating." Each "esoteric box" constitutes a system closed to pressures from the "outside," and the "outside," in this construct, means all the other institutions and interests in society. The more the boxes "put up their shutters," the more the policy becomes atomized at an institutional professional level.

Weitzenbaum attacks vigorously the "mindless" computer as a counterproductive force that is leading us deeper into irreversible counterknowledge scenarios because we can't efficiently modify the knowledge held in data banks. He says:

> But even worse, since computer-based knowledge systems become essentially unmodifiable except in that they can grow, and since they induce dependence and cannot, after a certain threshold is crossed, be abandoned, there is an enormous risk that they will be passed from one generation to another, always growing. Man, too, passes knowledge from one generation to another. But because man is mortal, his transmission of knowledge over the generations is at once a process of filtering and accrual. Man doesn't merely pass knowledge, he rather generates it continuously. Much as we may mourn the crumbling of ancient civilizations, we know nevertheless that the glory of man resides as much in the evolution of his cultures as in that of his brain. The unwise use of ever larger and even more complex computer systems may well bring this process to a halt. It could well replace the ebb and flow of culture with a world without values, a world in which what counts for a fact has long ago been determined and forever fixed.[12]

For those like Beer and Weitzenbaum, efforts to match the capabilities of computers and information users are leading us into a thicket of problems unanticipated in the narrow efficiency-base model of information implicit in the discussion of treating information as a commodity. The debate over the legitimacy of exploring the developing area of artificial intelligence is the visible, public policy expression of this concern. Given the lack of fit between the ways in which computers and users process information, it is a very simple logical extension to attempt to produce computers which "think" (artificial intelligence). Yet many very significant ethical and legal issues undergird the search for more efficient information systems—not the least being how to build the concept of democracy into the machine.

Having therefore touched upon some of the political, economic, sociological, psychological, philosophical, semantic, and epistemological interfaces of the conceptual relationship between data, information, and knowledge, in the next chapter we will examine more closely exactly what we mean by information as a resource.

QUESTIONS FOR DISCUSSION

1. Give an example to illustrate the notion "one man's data is often another man's information." How about the reverse: "one man's information is often another man's data?"

2. Do you agree with the assertion sometimes made that "all information is context specific; no element of data or item of information has any meaning or significance 'standing alone'?"

3. A variation of the question preceding this one is "for information to be of 'value' or 'useful' it must be related to some purpose or result or goal." Do you agree or disagree with that hypothesis, and why?

4. In a recent survey, most respondents said they agreed that "data should be managed"; many respondents expressed approval that "information should be managed"; but only a very few were comfortable with the idea that "knowledge should be managed." What might explain this spectrum of opinion as one moves up the data / information / knowledge tree? Might this difference in viewpoint be a transitory phenomenon?

5. In the preceding chapter we asked for illustrations of "trade-offs" between "information-intensive" alternatives and "manpower-intensive" alternatives. What might be some trade-offs between "data-intensive" alternatives and "knowledge-intensive" alternatives? How might the variables of time, cost, and precision enter into such a trade-off decision?

6. Why might the Archivist of the United States of America contend that "all information is history?" Why might a computer programmer contend that "little information is history?" Is there a middle ground between these two "extreme" viewpoints?

FOOTNOTES

[1]Shannon, Claude E., *"A Mathematical Theory of Communication,"* (Bell System Technical Journal, Vol. 27, July, 1948) pp. 632–656. Information scientists generally credit Dr. Shannon for developing innovative approaches to define and measure information during his year as a research engineer at Bell Telephone Labs. The National Archives and Records Service of the U.S. Government bases much of its theoretical material used for communication workshops, and other training material, on Shannon's theories.

[2]Simon, Herbert, "*Administrative Behavior: A Study of Decision-making Processes in Administrative Organization,*" (2nd ed., New York Free Press, 1959). Dr. Simon's works are particularly helpful in illuminating the role of data and information in the decision-making setting.

[3]Baratz, Stephen S. Op. cit.

[4]Dunn, Edgar, Op. cit.

[5]Diener, Richard A. V., "*Value: Data, Information, Knowledge,*" paper presented at 6th Mid-Year Meeting, May 19–21, 1977, Syracuse University, American Society for Information Science. The essence of the argument I have with this author goes to whether information is treated in a personal context or an organizational context. If the former, then I have no problem with "unlimited, unbridled information acquisition"; but if the latter, I would say the organization should have a say in the limits, costs and other constraints on information acquisition because the individual's role is as a part of an organization, not as a free spirit or "private citizen."

[6]Caldwell, Lynton K., Op.cit.

[7]Berry, J. F. and Cook, C. M., "*Managing Knowledge As a Corporate Resource,*" (NTIS Document ADA-29891, May 28, 1976) pp. 1–9. These authors are to be commended for their "courageous" exposition of a difficult theme whilst in a bureaucratic setting in Washington, D.C., that may not have been fully sympathetic with their aims. I had the pleasure of exchanging views with them in 1976 and 1977 when they were developing their papers and I was employed at the Paperwork Commission.

[8]"*Toward A National Program for Library and Information Services: Goals For Action,*" (The National Commission on Libraries and Information Science, Washington, D.C., 1975) pp. 1–3. unquestionably, the libraries—both individually and as an honored institution—have a key role to play in information resources management. It is to be hoped the library community will continue to move forward aggressively, through forums such as the National Commission and the White House Conference, to push their cause in the highest councils of Government and the professions.

[9]Saracevic, Tefko, "*Intellectual Organization of Knowledge: The American Contribution,*" (Bulletin of the American Society for Information Science, Vol. 2, No. 8, March 1976) pp. 16–17. "The problem of quality," as Saracevic puts it, is squarely the challenge of the information resources management. Data Base Management, in contrast, addressed "the problem of quantity."

[10]Beer, Sir Stafford, "*Managing Modern Complexity,*" (The Management of Information and Knowledge, Committee on Science and Astronautics, U.S. House of Representatives, 91st Congress, 2nd Session, January 27, 1970) pp. 43–44. The parent work, a small yellow cover pamphlet of less than 100 pages, is somewhat of an "information classic" in its own right. It is well worth the modest purchase price.

[11]Henry, Nicholas, "*Bureaucracy, Technology, and Knowledge Management,*" (Public Administration Review, Symposium on Knowledge Management, Nov/Dec. 1975) pp. 572–576. Henry's exposition of the "information is power" theme is effectively done in the bureaucratic setting. Like Simon, he evinces a perceptive understanding of the shifting power base phenomenon, based on an admixture of strong personalities, economic power, technocratic power and an elitist, doctrinaire attitude of power figures.

[12]Weitzenbaum, Joseph, "*On The Impact of the Computer on Society,*" (Science, Vol. 176, 12 May 1972) pp. 612–613. This author raises a wide array of computer/technology/privacy/future of mankind issues that can and should be usefully debated. I cannot help but believe, however, that his "message" is much like the "late-in-life-turned-missionary" scientist who suddenly feels it is his poor Frankenstein (the computer in this case) that will ultimately be blamed for the demise of mankind—ergo, "I must sound the alarms before it is too late." I think he gives us too little credit. Consider computer fraud and embezzlement, consider wire tapping and electronic surveillance; man's ingenuity is surely keeping up with the machine!

4 INFORMATION RESOURCES —Typologies

This chapter examines approaches to the development of useful information classification schemes or typologies. No "all-purpose recipe" is put forward to be applied in cook-book fashion. Alas, other from Aristotle to John Dewey foundered upon those shoals. Although no single typology has yet been evolved that is clearly superior to the rest, nor is any likely to be soon, for our purposes we will, near the end of this chapter, put forward one approach which divides information resources into four major classes: sources, services, products, and systems. Within each class, sub-categories are identified. First, however, it will be instructive to review broader considerations relevant to our objective. What is central to this objective is not some Rosetta typology, but the *role of typology* in information resources management.

At least nine considerations are pertinent to a discussion of the utility of classification structures in the management of information. They include the use of classification schemes as:

- a finding aid;
- a means of illuminating and making explicit relationships between elements of data;
- an aid to the accurate representation of reality;
- a means of purifying data;
- tool to help reduce a body of data, documents, or literature to more manageable proportions;
- a key to help unlock hidden meanings and significance;
- a tool to help facilitate the transmission of meaning from transmitter to receiver;

- a simplification device to facilitate understanding and comprehension; and
- a conceptualization aid, given the inherent, hierarchical nature of knowledge itself in terms of successively higher levels of abstraction.

Let us take each of these in turn, classification schemes as a finding aid first. This area is perhaps the oldest and most obvious use of taxonomy that comes to mind. Typologies are fundamentally a method of organizing. It seems almost axiomatic to take the position that one or more typologies are indispensable to making sense out of what otherwise would be a jumble of meaningless data and information. Perhaps, in retrospect, we might believe that the very earliest of man's attempts to classify knowledge did not have "finding" as a central purpose, because then the quantity and quality of the extant body of knowledge (say, during Aristotle's time) may not have been unmanageable, but even Aristotle found information typology useful. He designed ten categories:

- substance
- quantity
- quality
- relation
- place
- time
- situation
- state
- action
- passion

A quick perusal of this list immediately reveals some resemblance to a major classification scheme in use today, that developed by Roget. Roget's scheme[1] uses eight classes, forty-three sub-categories, and a total of 1,040 separate headings:

Class One—*Abstract Relations*

I existence
II relation
III quantity
IV order
V number
VI time
VII change
VIII eventuality
IX causation
X power

Class Two—*Space*

I space in general

II dimensions
III structure, form
IV motion

Class Three—*Physics*

I physics
II heat
III light
IV electricity and electronics
V mechanics
VI physical properties
VII color

Class Four—*Matter*

I matter in general
II inorganic matter
III organic matter

Class Five—*Sensation*

I sensation in general
II touch
III taste
IV smell
V sight
VI hearing

Class Six—*Intellect*

I intellectual faculty and processes
II states of mind
III communication of ideas

Class Seven—*Volition*

I volition in general
II conditions
III voluntary action
IV authority, control
V support and opposition
VI possessive relations

Class Eight—*Affections*

I personal affections
II sympathetic affections
III morality affections
IV religious affections

By the time of the Renaissance, when libraries in both the New World and the Old World were beginning to overflow, simple bibliographic structuring and classification by author and by subject appeared to be direct, simple, pragmatic solutions of the problem. Information classification has come a long way since Aristotle's time, and even since Dewey's era. Figure 4-1, for example, which lists some "key word" entries for the noun "information" itself, gives us some appreciation of the magnitude and specialization of the information arts and sciences in the scheme of Government's largest documentation depository, the Defense Documentation Center.

IDENTIFYING RELATIONSHIPS

Next, classification schemes are essential if one is to correlate and collect similar items of information which are related to one another. This function is important for a number of reasons. First, it helps us to identify overlap and duplication among and between similar or identical items. Second, it helps specify and sharpen the full range of items among the universe of data, document, or literature holdings and thus helps us establish useful boundaries or delimitations (what the statistician calls "class intervals"). Intuitively, we may suspect what these relationships are, but until a classification scheme is developed, the suspicion remains only a suspicion. In addition to identifying duplication and overlap, the use of a classification scheme, in this context, also helps us to identify gaps or "missing" items of information in our classification sets and subsets

CLASSIFICATIONS AS REPRESENTATIONS OF REALITY

A third consideration is to view information typologies as a representation of reality. One might say that a useful criterion of the utility of classification schemes is the extent to which they serve as *an accurate* representation of reality. However, accurate or not, one of the fundamental purposes of information itself is to represent reality. The human mind cannot comprehend reality in an exclusively physical sense and hence must rely to an extent on abstractions. Since reality itself is a dynamic, changing concept, this would seem to argue for an information classification structure which itself has the flexibility to make corresponding changes in its own structure to mirror the changes in reality which it represents. The mathematician and the physicist

Information Acquisition
Information Acquisition Rates
Information Activities
Information Audit
Information Bandwith
Information Bank
Information Base
Information Center
Information Centers
Information Data
Information Data Flow
Information Display
Information Display Encoding Requirements
Information Display Requirements
Information Display Systems
Information Displays
Information Dynamics
Information Entry
Information Exchange
Information Exchange System
Information Exchange Forums
Information Extraction
Information Extraction Programs
Information Extraction Techniques
Information Feedback Paths
Information Field
Information Flow
Information Flow Problems
Information Input
Information Input Quality
Information Input Requirements
Information Link
Information Links
Information Management
Information Management Storage
Information Management System
Information Mapping Research
Information Matrix
Information Modulation
Information Monitoring
Information Organization
Information Output
Information Overlay
Information Problems
Information Processes
Information Processing
Information Processing Activities
Information Processing Devices
Information Processing Environment
Information Processing Equipment
Information Processing Measurement
Information Processing Neural Networks
Information Processing Problems
Information Processing Program
Information Processing Rate
Information Processing Software
Information Processing Support
Information Processing Systems
Information Processing Techniques
Information Processing Workload
Information Processor
Information Processor Testing
Information Programs
Information Rate
Information Repositories
Information Requirements
Information Resources
Information Retrieval
Information Retrieval Activity
Information Retrieval Devices
Information Retrieval Research Support
Information Retrieval System
Information Retrieval Systems Making
Information Science
Information Sciences
Information Sciences Identification
Information Sources
Information Storage
Information Storage Devices
Information Storage Requirements
Information Storage Retrieval

***Figure 4-1.* Defense documentation center thesaurus**

are perhaps the "luckiest" users of information typologies because the representations with which they deal are numbers and symbols, which may be extremely complex from an inter-relationship standpoint but which are comparatively simple in terms of conceptual representation. Management and operating reports produced by computerized management information systems in large corporations or government agencies are, by comparison, far more complex, because of the extraordinary difficulty in taking into account the large number of variables and their interrelationships in the "real worlds" which those reports are supposed to represent.

ELIMINATING INACCURACIES AND INCONSISTENCIES

Moving to the use of classification schemes as a purification process, many a systems designer of an information retrieval system and many a librarian have come to the conclusion that perhaps the most valuable purpose of their classification scheme was not so much to develop some aesthetically pleasing or elegantly appealing scheme, but to edit and purge obsolete, unreliable, incomplete, inaccurate, and untimely elements of data—in short, to prevent such data from getting into the retrieval system in the first place. In this sense, then, classification schemes implicitly set parameters and act as screens or sieves to filter the "pure" information from the "impure" information. If our scheme is too general, too many items "slip through" and may fall below our visibility horizon. Conversely, if we use too fine a net, we will catch too much, even data we should not be capturing. Both over-classification and under-classification are pitfalls to be avoided.

ELIMINATING INFORMATION OVERLOAD

Information classification schemes can also help us reduce to manageable proportions bodies of data, documents, or literature which might otherwise be too unwieldy. In effect, we break the problem down into smaller pieces. In so doing, we are implicitly helping to sort out the relevant from irrelevant, the pertinent from the non-pertinent, and the useful from the meaningless. Various studies in psychology and physiology have documented the capacity of the human eye, ear, and mind to grapple simultaneously with a rather limited number of variables. One of the simplest of these experiments has to do with the number of digits, for example, we are able to memorize and repeat with accuracy.

DECIPHERING MEANING

Another purpose of information typologies has to do with semantics, that is, they can be a tool to unlock meaning and significance. Perhaps the simplest example in this area is the notion of the thesaurus, which to most people suggests a collection of synonyms with some kind of an index. By bringing together words, ideas, expressions, and terms with similar meanings under a common heading, we are in a better position to discern shades of meaning of the terms in the group. Juxtaposing them helps us understand meaning and significance. Unlike a dictionary, a thesaurus does not seek to define a word in all its meanings and in one place. It deals with context rather than definitions. It starts with a meaning, not with a word, and sets the words which symbolize some aspect of that meaning in a context, somewhat like sentences in a book. A valid context exhibits the related aspect of the component words, throwing into relief those components of meaning which each individual term or word can contribute to the overall, governing idea. At the same time, senses and meanings which are ambiguous, irrelevant, or incompatible are suppressed.

SIMPLIFYING

Information typologies are also a means of facilitating comprehension through a process of simplification. The very process of ordering and labeling a finite number of words or terms or ideas into a limited number of classes or categories in itself simplifies the problem of comprehension. The index, catalog, bibliography, catalog, and directory are among the best examples of this purpose of classification. We could, for example, use the telephone company's yellow pages even if it did not have an index. But its usefulness is enhanced by the addition of an index, which serves to limit the total number of initial access categories by cross-referencing words and terms in common usage that may be used as substitutes, synonyms, or analogous words to selected ("controlled") key index terms.

THE HIGHER ORDER MENTAL PROCESSES

Finally, the use of information typologies can be considered an aid to conceptualization because such schemes help move data and information from the more abstract media and expressions to the more concrete and perceptual media and expressions, thereby helping the cognitive processes to operate more efficiently. The faculty of the mind to deal with ideas is more efficient in understanding and comprehending streams of information if they are channeled through the conscious, sentient pathways than if they are channeled exclusively in the context of ideas and abstractions in the milieu of the cerebrum. Schematizing disordered and disarrayed data and information into some kind of taxonomy eliminates many anomalies, much randomness, and a great deal of indiscriminate and extraneous data and information.

EARLY ATTEMPTS AT CLASSIFICATION

A review of approaches to the technical problems of designing and developing classification schemes informs us that, in recent times, two major divergent branches have appeared in archival and library science that affect knowledge and information classification. First, Melvil Dewey, in the 1870's, began to develop a decimal classification scheme which, to this day, bears his name. The second major thrust was developed by Charles A. Cutter who believed that the decimal scheme advanced by Dewey was too inflexible. He introduced alphabetical notations into his system and developed a more evolutionary kind of scheme. Guthrie points out that the basic order for classifying information—both literature and data holdings—has most often been assumed to be hierarchical[2]; that is, documents have been acquired under various topics, and then subtopics, and then sub-subtopics. However, the problem of cross-referencing between and among two different overlapping hierarchies was implicitly ignored in this approach. Since relationships within a given cycle are important, there has been strong resistance to destroying or ignoring these relationships. Guthrie points out that it is the amateur who, "when faced with a records problem, breaks up an established linear relationship in favor of a new system of headings."

A more recent authority, Mortimer Taube, who worked with the Atomic Energy Commission, developed a technique for determining "uniterms" (or "descriptors") for documents. These uniterms could be arranged in combinations as desired, thus allowing searchers to indicate which documents they desired by stating which combination of terms they were interested in searching. The virtue of this approach is that with the advent of modern information-handling technologies, such as the computer and microfilm, much of the inquiry, search, and identification chore can be handled automatically, or semi-automatically, by machines. Through a synthesis of the research done by Taube, S. R. Raganathan and Frederick Jonker, many modern information storage and retrieval systems and methodologies have been developed.

A SYSTEMS APPROACH

Adrian McDonough uses a systems approach classification scheme, oriented to the resolution of typical problems to be solved by management in either the private sector or the public sector. He articulates the following fifteen main headings in his systems approach classification, saying "they can act as the points for assembling the knowledge of the systems field":[3]

1. major approaches to system studies
2. sequence in problem studies
3. sequence in data processing
4. verbal (literal) level of systems
5. graphical level of systems
6. mathematical level of systems
7. computer level of systems
8. criteria classes
9. equipment
10. supplies
11. documents and records
12. organization of systems department
13. background disciplines
14. connectors
15. management systems literature

Figure 4-2 identifies the McDonough scheme in more detail, to the sub-category heading level. Under the coding scheme built into his classifications, it is possible to sort out the various concepts and tools and relate them to their uses in specific management problem contexts. Perhaps the scheme's main utility is that it provides concerted approaches to the analysis of "real" management problems. He divides those management problems into five broad categories: general, verbal, graphical, mathematical, and computer-related. This scheme also provides an inventory of criteria coded to particular generic management problems. Selections can then be made from these classifications, and their combinations, to provide both a general structure and the supporting materials for, for example, courses to be taught in business

100 EXTERNAL ENVIRONMENT?
- 110 GOVERNMENT?
  - 111 LAWS?
  - 112 REPORTS TO?
  - 113 TAXES?
  - 114 LICENSES?
  - 115 PENALTIES?
- 120 ORGANIZED LABOR?
  - 121 LIAISON?
  - 122 CONTRACT NEGOTIATION?
  - 123 GRIEVANCES?
  - 124 ARBITRATIONS?
  - 125 MEDIATION?
- 130 MARKETING (CON-(CONSUMER)?
  - 131 COMPETITION AND PRICING?
  - 132 TRADE ASSOCIATION?
  - 133 ADVERTISING?
  - 134 MERCHANDISING?
  - 135 RESEARCH?
- 140 COMMUNITY?
  - 141 LABOR SUPPLY?
  - 142 NUISANCE?
  - 143 TAXES?
  - 144 PARTICIPATION IN COMMUNITY AFFAIRS
- 150 SUPPLIERS

AND SO ON

200 SEARCH AND SELECT OBJECTIVES?
- 210 FORECASTS?
  - 211 SIGNIFICANT AREAS IDENTIFICATION
  - 212 TRENDS?
  - 213 NEW AREAS?
  - 214 EXTRAPOLATION POSSIBILITIES AND LIMITATIONS?
  - 215 BIAS?
- 220 MARKET SHARE?
  - 221 MARKET VOLUME?

(SUBCATEGORIES OMITTED BELOW 221)

300 ORGANIZATION?

400 FINANCE AND ACCOUNTING?

500 PHYSICAL FACILITIES?

600 PRODUCTION PLANNING AND CONTROL?

700 PERSONNEL?

800 MATERIAL?

BY PERMISSION, ADRIAN MCDONOUGH, *"INFORMATION ECONOMICS AND MANAGEMENT SYSTEMS"*

Figure 4-2. **Goal management problems classification**

subjects and in management systems. Similar use can be made of the classifications by a systems designer.

McDonough coined the term "affinity factor" to express various relationships among different parts of his classifications. In effect, the affinity factor is the bridge that allows us to transform the relatively static classifications into a working tool to assist in selecting, spelling out, and solving dynamic management problems. For example, under his scheme, the term *taxes* would have redundant locations in several broad, generic headings, but the coding scheme would allow pulling together the various management problem contexts in which taxes play a role. These context situations can then be profiled by a combination kind of coding.

THE CONTROLLED THESAURUS

A more conventional approach, perhaps, of the problem of classifying information resources is the use of the controlled thesaurus of index terms. This is the classic approach used by historians, archivists, librarians, and records managers in ordering literature and document holdings. For example, take the problem of indexing the contents of the *Federal Register,* the official publication of the Federal Government in which agencies publish various kinds of rules, regulations and other information (e.g., scheduled meetings) which affect the public at large. The vocabulary used by Government agencies often differs substantially from that of the layman. Therefore, it becomes necessary to develop a controlled vocabulary of terms so that both the layman and information professional may efficiently search the contents of the *Register* for the needed information. Indexing terms are needed to describe the specific agency regulations as well as those general administrative provisions common to all agencies which are published in the *Register.* A further complicating factor is the variety of users of this publication.

Indexing terms are needed to express and organize the often-technical regulatory concepts under research terms familiar to the lay-person. Under the *Federal Register* typology, 19 broad subject matter headings are developed (see Figure 4-3). Then, for each index term in the control thesaurus, the use of this index term under each of these 19 headings is cross-referenced. For example, the very first term which appears in the thesaurus of indexing terms published by the Office of Federal Register, March 7, 1977, is the word *accounting.* The word accounting appears in two of the major headings out of the 19, namely 02, which is Commerce, and 08, which is Government. Like all thesauri, this scheme is not immutable, and the Office of the Federal Register which is responsible for updating the thesaurus of indexing terms, periodically requests public comment as well as official comment on the accuracy, timeliness and continued semantic validity of the terms in use.[4]

Accounting (02, 08)
sa Uniform System of Accounts
xx Business and industry

Acreage allotments
see Marketing quotas and acreage allotments

Additives
see Food additives
Fuel additives

Adjustment assistance
see Trade adjustment assistance

Administrative practice and procedure (08)
x Practice and procedure

Adult education (04)
x Continuing education
Extension and continuing education
xx Education

Advertising (02)
xx Business and industry

Advisory committees (08)
[Use only for documents on the management of advisory committes within an agency]
x Committees

AFDC
see Aid to Families with Dependent Children

Affirmative action plans
see Equal employment opportunity

Aged (13)
sa Medicare
Supplemental Security Income (SSI)
x Elderly
Senior citizens

Agricultural commodities (01)
sa *Specific commodities*
Commodities exchanges
Crop insurance
Fruits
Grains
Marketing quotas and acreage allotments
Oilseeds
Price support programs
Surplus agricultural commodities
Vegetables
x Commodities
Crops
xx Agriculture

Agricultural research (01, 17)
xx Agriculture
Research

Agricultural statistics (01)
x Statistics
xx Agriculture

Agriculture (01)
sa Agricultural commodities
Agricultural research
Agricultural statistics
Farm loans
Farmers
Fertilizers
Food relief programs
Foods
Foreign agriculture
Forestry
Irrigation
Migrant labor
Pesticides and pests
Range management
Rural areas

Aid to Families with Dependent Children (18)
sa Public Assistance Programs
x AFDC
xx Child welfare
Public Assistance Programs

Air carriers (19)
[Organizations operating passenger or cargo carrying aircraft]

see refers to authorized terms; x refers from terms not used; sa refers to more specific or related terms; xx refers from broader or related terms. Numbers in parenthesis refer to subject category listings following alphabetical listing of terms.

***Figure 4-3.* Federal register thesaurus**

A COMMUNICATIONS APPROACH

In contrast to the McDonough approach, which develops a typology broadly based upon a management problem-solving context, and the more conventional approach to information typology discussed above using the example of the *Federal Register,* Dr. Joseph Wilkinson puts forward another typology based on the assumption that information needed by managers is mainly conveyed through messages. Under the Wilkinson scheme, which is graphically portrayed in Figure 4-4, each message, for example, or report is classified on the basis of eight characteristics:[5]

AN ORGANIZATIONAL MISSION APPROACH

Still another approach to information resources classification was proposed by Charles E. Bosley in 1973. Bosley emphasized the need to classify information on the basis of organizational units and their assigned mission, as well as the operational functions in which those offices may be engaged. For example, he points out that, in the case of the Bureau of Sports, Fisheries and Wild Life of the Department of Interior, the function served by that unit is "Natural Resources Management." But some of the information stored by that unit in its information systems and data banks is described as "Research Data on Chemical Compounds," so the use of this information is classified, not under "management," but under "general/data." On the other hand, information systems in personnel offices, for example, are classified as "administration/personnel" in all cases. Bosley lists seven major conclusions in his analysis of the Federal use of information technology:[6]

- In the Federal Government as a whole the only standard use of information technology appears to be for administration.
- Though most large bureaus in the Federal Government make some use of information technology, as many as one-third do not use it extensively.
- Federal agencies develop information technology uses largely on their own initiative, often working with units in other offices sharing the same functional interests and purposes.
- Approximately one-third of all Federal information systems

Characteristic	Typical Categories
1. Purpose	Operating report Control report Planning report Stewardship report Legal compliance report Motivational report Proposal report Action report
2. Scope	Firm-wide report Divisional report Departmental report Sales territory report
3. Conciseness	Detailed report Summary report ("key item" report) Exception report
4. Occurrence	Scheduled or periodic report Demand report Triggered report
5. Time Horizon	Historical report Short-range forecast report Long-range forecast report
6. Presentation	"Hard copy" report "Soft copy" computer display Oral report (possibly with visual aids) Narrative report Narrative report Graphical report Tabular report
7. User	Report to management Report to owners Report to employees Report to governmental agencies
8. Operating Function	Accounting report Production report Marketing report

*By permission, Dr. Joseph W. Wilkinson

Figure 4-4. **Reports-oriented information typology**

include case files of private information about citizens, businesses, or private organizations.
- Safeguards for protecting private information are most often arranged by each agency on its own initiative.
- Eighty percent of the information in Federal automated systems is customarily used by government and its special agents only.
- Most information which is used by organizations serving the public is in the form of general data or reference materials.

INFORMATION RESOURCES

For our purposes, we shall divide the term "information resources" into four major classes. We shall then subdivide each class into two or more categories, and in a few cases, we may need to drop to a third level—the subcategory.

First, *information sources.* An information source is an individual or an organization—a place—which furnishes needed information and data to users. For our purposes, we will not identify a specific document, per se, as a source, but rather as an information product. Thus, the information source might be considered the interrogatives "where" and "who": From where and from whom can I obtain the information I seek? Examples of information sources of a business executive, might include a personal secretary, special assistant, boss, peer, subordinate; an office library, a technical information center, or a computer; the financial, marketing, production or sales department; and so forth. The publisher is also an important source of information. Figure 4-5 illustrates some very different kinds of information sources.

Next, *information services.* An information service is a helpful activity provided users to assist them in meeting their information needs and requirements. Among traditional information services are: public assistance bureaus in airports and train stations; publications offices; library reference services—how to look for information, or actually locating information for the seeker; consulting and planning services; micrographic services; abstracting and indexing; searching and tracing; current awareness activities; selective retrieval services; and so forth. The information service, then, is the interrogative "what": What means do I select to seek what I'm looking for? Figure 4-6 is a list of selected information services which are commercially available.

Moving to the third class—*information products:* an information product is a helpful commodity provided users to assist them in meeting

Information Sources

1. Public Libraries
2. School Libraries
3. Research Libraries and Centers
4. Office Libraries
5. Information Analysis Centers
6. Information Dissemination Centers
7. Clearinghouses and Exchanges
8. Referral and Abstract Services
9. Book Publishers
10. Serial Publishers
11. Map Publishers
12. Management Consultants
13. Computer Centers and System Centers
14. Museums and Archives
15. News Media Stations and Companies
16. Government Agencies
17. Ombudsman Services
18. Professional Societies and Trade Associations
19. Telephone Companies (information)
20. Documentation Centers
21. Information Bureaus
22. Statistical Centers
23. Education and Training Centers
24. Public Information Offices
25. Community Relations Offices
26. Travel Bureaus
27. Historical Associations
28. Market Research Firms
29. Conferences and Symposia
30. Records Centers and Depositories
31. Special Book Collections
32. Magnetic Tape Libraries
33. Audio-Visual Libraries
34. Phonograph Recordings Libraries
35. International Information Networks
36. Consumer Information Bureaus
37. Minority Information Centers
38. Employment and Job Assistance Centers
39. Drug and Alcohol Rehabilitation Centers
40. Vital Records Registries
41. License and Permit Offices
42. Passport and Visa Offices
43. Patent and Copyright Offices
44. Visitor Centers
45. Trade Fairs
46. Traffic, Weather, Special Events Bureaus
47. Lost and Found Departments
48. Buy and Sell Bureaus
49. Veterans, Students Assistance Centers
50. Regional Resource Libraries

Figure 4-5. **Information sources**

Information Products and Services

Accounting & bookkeeping
Actuarial services
Adding & calculating machines & supplies
Addressing & lettering
Advertising services
Aerial photography & surveys
Analytical services
Answering services
Association management services
Audio-visual equipment & supplies & services
Auditing
Automatic data processing
Automatic electric typing
Automatic handwriting machines
Blueprinting
Bonded messengers
Book dealers, printers, & publishers
Broadcasting
Brokerage information
Bulletin & directory boards
Business forms, systems, & consultants
Buy & sell exchanges
Buyers information service
Cablegrams
Calligraphers
Calling, paging, & signaling
Carbon paper
Cartographers
Cassettes—sound & video tape
Catalogue compilers
Certified public accountants
Charts
City & town guides & maps
Clipping bureaus
Communications systems, equipment, and supplies
Composition, offset printing
Computation services, equipment & supplies
Conference recording, services, & consultants
Convention services & facilities
Copying & duplicating
Correspondence services
Credit reporting
Delivery services
Demonstration services
Display designers & producers
Economic & social science research
Educational consultants
Encyclopedias & dictionaries
Exhibit handling
Facsimile transmission
Ghostwriting services
Government information
Graphic designers
Information bureaus
Information retrieval systems & equipment
International conferences
Investment counseling
Job information
Keypunch services
Lecture bureaus
Legislative research
Library research & services
Lithographic supplies & equipment
Magazines & periodicals, subscription services
Mailing lists, machines & services
Management consultants
Maps
Market research & analysis

Figure 4-6. **Information products and services**

their information needs and requirements. The conventional distinction made between products and services in private industry is used here, within our information resources context.

And finally, an *information system*—the last of our four major classes of information resources—is the structured process or procedure by which basic data or information is collected, organized, and distributed to users. Basic data collected in an information system is often referred to as inputs, and the reports and other products generated from the system as outputs. Also, the totality of information streams moving to and from a user is also sometimes referred to as an information system. It would perhaps be more useful for our purposes to call this latter situation, however, the total information system. The system, then, is the interrogative "how": How do I process the information? Clearly information systems are very valuable information resources even though they are, in effect, means to ends, the ends, of course, being our information products and services. By the same token, so are information sources a means to an end.

In summary, then, two of our four major classes of information resources are means-oriented: sources and systems. The other two are ends-oriented: products and services. In the end, the four terms are partially overlapping. To avoid confusion, careful attention must be paid to the particular context in which the terms are used. Some ambiguity is virtually inevitable in any event.

It would seem clear that, confronted with such a wide array of information resources, the organization would do well to make some attempt to control them. The practitioner of the systems approach might well tell us that we need an information resources management system. Indeed, in a prior work, I pointed out that the systems approach was an extremely promising approach for control of the increasing proliferation of information and data.[7]

It is important to remember here that information classification is a living, dynamic concept. As new discoveries are made and as we proceed through the four stages of the fact's life cycle, data becomes progressively metamorphosed into information and data and information both become transformed into the body of knowledge. This is a continuous process, and because it is continuous, our approach to classification must also be periodically reviewed in the light of changing "external realities." The hallmark of a good classification scheme is, in part, its ability to react flexibly and efficiently to changing realities. Schemes which are too rigid and inflexible constrain rather than assist. The modern information-handling technologies offer considerable promise in helping classification methodology in this area. Certainly with the move from hard copy forms and documents to "soft" media, such as computerized data bases, at least the efficiency-oriented problems of additions, deletions, and changes to the classification structure should be materially abated.

THE STANDARD BUDGET CLASSIFICATIONS OF THE U.S.—AN EXAMPLE

Functional classifications have been used for many years to portray the different categories into which programs are aggregated by the Federal Government, regardless of which agencies manage and administer those programs. Budget system designers have long since stopped trying to construct a single scheme that would meet all possible uses. Historically, budget and related financial data have used the appropriation accounts as the basic building block for the budget classification task. Appropriation accounts are the "packages" the legislature uses to authorize the executive to spend monies for specified purposes. The problem is that the appropriation account structure itself is patterned after this historical organization of the committee structure of the legislature. Those committees do not necessarily "match" the national, State or local priorities and major program aggregations. Moreover, the committees are slow to redefine their respective roles and authorities.

In August, 1976, the U.S. General Accounting Office published a report which examined alternative proposed changes to the standard Federal budget classifications (the "Functional Classification Scheme" as it is called). As there is no one "best" way to approach the problem of developing the budget classification typology, what is of interest to us are the criteria used by the GAO for making its proposals.[8] The approach was to propose changes in the present functional category structure "only when they will alleviate problems." Changes were recommended based on three paramount criteria:

1. Highlighting major ongoing areas of national concern. For example, energy, which had been combined under a single heading with natural resources and the environment, was broken out into a distinct category of its own since it had clearly become a major national priority.
2. Separating functions containing programs with divergent purposes, where feasible. For example, the present structure combines education, training, employment and social services

in one function. GAO separated these four major families of programs because of their divergent objectives. The President's recommendation to establish a separate Department of Education, split from the existing Department of Health, Education and Welfare, gave further impetus to this recommendation.

3. Aggregating functions and subfunctions (the scheme is multi-tiered into two levels) on a more consistent basis. Here, for example, GAO recommended expanding the present "interest" function (i.e. interest earned and interest paid in a financial sense) to include other activities related to financing the Government and retitling it "Financial Operations of the Federal Government."

The budget classification problem is one of the annual exercises in typology in Washington, D.C., and it is anything but an "academic" matter. Indeed, millions of dollars are invested in the gigantic information systems which process budgetary, accounting, planning, and programming data at both the Federal level and at agency level. Beyond the relatively simple question of how much money it is going to cost to modify these expensive automated systems, there are other, more substantive considerations of far greater import. For example, whether certain personnel salary and benefit expenses are broken out or buried in some other designation, determines how much visibility they will get before a wide public, media and Congressional audience. The President is thus able to emphasize, or deemphasize certain categories of expenses by his decision on where to lump them in the classification system.

Certainly changes in categories affect documents, forms, reports, records, computers, files, and the whole array of data, document, and system infrastructures. Changes in major proportions cannot be effected simply with a wave of the wand.

In the late 1960's the Office of Management and Budget studied the problem of reconciling the traditional appropriation accounting classification scheme with "newer" PPBS schemes which were output-oriented, based on program structures. The contractor assigned the chore came up with a proposal for using "entity programs" as building blocks, on the theory that, in the end, data would have to be aggregated and reaggregated in many different ways. If the basic building block unit could be defined at the outset of the cycles, it could be "carried through all of the information systems" with a new set of descriptors "hung on" at each stage to facilitate reaggregation. In theory, at least, the idea seemed to make sense because it did follow a "systems approach" and was a form of compromise between two "armed camps"—the appropriation account crowd, which counted among its supporters the Congress, certain elements within GAO, and old line "budgeteers" in the agencies; and the PPB crowd, which was composed of the "new wave" of program budget types, agency management analysis personnel, computer and systems analysis staffs, and related groups.

In the end, the building block approach was rejected. There is room for argument as to why. Some believe that the cost of changing the information system machinery to accomodate the reforms was exorbitant. Others were simply uninterested in the problem; there was no "felt need" for effecting changes in this area (after all, who but a computer analyst is interested in classification schemes?). Still others saw the study as a power play of the President to control the budget more closely. The Congress, at that time under criticism from many quarters for failing to assert its leadership during the accelerating Vietnam War, perhaps felt that the appropriation accounting scheme was an effective brake on Executive arrogation of power and influence. Since it was rooted in the committee structure, this meant that there was more or less a direct, "one-to-one" relationship to the operating level of agencies. Any changes in the scheme might destroy or seriously impair this relationship.

My purpose in citing this example here is to underscore the fact that classification schemes are not simply matters of "administrative convenience," as the efficiency expert might have us believe. As in the Budget Classifications of the United States Government, such "routine" considerations often relate directly to matters of substance and power relationships. The classification designer who fails to take this consideration into account runs the risk of stepping right into the middle of a battleground and getting fired at from all sides. What may have begun as a simple exercise in matrices and interstitial analysis ends up as an extremely serious organizational confrontation involving, in the case in point, the country's most powerful institutions.

Not every classification designer may be treated to these kinds of fireworks, however. So let us conclude this chapter by recapitulating a few simple rules for typology construction:

1. Any classification scheme should be viewed as a dynamic, not a static, information management tool. Additional flexibility can be built into most systems by developing a multi-tiered system involving secondary and perhaps tertiary classifications.
2. Classifications are only as good as they illuminate problems for top officials; they are not for the purpose of making life easier for data-handling technicians by compartmentalizing

information into neat little pigeonholes.

3. In large organizations with long-standing traditions and heavy investments in information handling infrastructures, classifications will, in the end, involve a process of consensus and compromise. Top management would do well to instruct its classification system overseers to recognize that there is no "higher order" body of knowledge that can be tapped for clues as to just what the "right" system will be. In all but the very simplest classification problems, such an attitude is misguided.

QUESTIONS FOR DISCUSSION

1. Why do semanticists and lexicographers often consider the mathematician "lucky" because symbols are his language, whereas other scientists and professionals must use words?

2. Why isn't it practical to develop some kind of monolithic, immutable classification scheme for the categorization of knowledge and information, thereby "solving for all time" the problem of consistency, compatibility and redundancy which librarians, computer systems analysts, catalogers and others grapple with every day?

3. How might a librarian "over-classify" the document and literature holdings under a given subject category? What are the consequences of such overclassification? How might holdings be "under-classified?" What are the consequences of underclassification?

4. Syntax is often defined as the harmonious arrangement of words to form phrases, clauses or sentences. A sentence may be grammatically correct, but syntactically deficient. What problems does syntax cause for computer-controlled typesetting?

5. In early hierarchical classification approaches, the problem of cross-referencing was often ignored. How did the "uniterm" idea advanced by Mortimer Taube help to get around the cross-referencing problem?

6. "Pleonasm" means the use of more words than may be necessary to define a subject or give meaning to a word; in a sense, deliberate redundancy. Why is this concept important to taxonomists, classifiers and catalogers?

7. Debate continues on the relative merits and demerits of using controlled thesauri to manage a given set of data or information instead of "free indexing" or an uncontrolled thesaurus. What are the factors

that should be taken into account by an author/designer/composer in deciding which way he or she should proceed?

8. Data Element Dictionaries (DEDs) have recently come into extensive use in both industry and government, and yet the problem of standardizing names, terms, definitions and symbols in large organizations is still a very difficult and real problem. Why? If we assume the DED is the "technology" needed, why might there still be barriers?

FOOTNOTES

[1]"*Roget's International Thesaurus*" (Thomas Y. Crowell Company, Third Edition, 1962.) The challenge to the thesaurus preparer, of course, goes to the very core of our chapter topic, but, happily, at the individual and organizational "level" we are not confronted with such an awesome task. Nevertheless, the character of the task is essentially the same. Dictionary-makers and thesauri-preparers are the first to attest to the dynamic quality of their profession.

[2]See a very good review of these early schemes by Chester L. Guthrie, Chapter 6, Federal Contributions to the Management of Records, in "*Federal Contributions to Management,*" Brown, David S., (ed.), Praeg. 1971, pp. 126–152.

[3]McDonough, M. Adrian, "*The Information Economics and Management Systems,*" (McGraw-Hill Book Co., Inc. 1963) pp. 158–170. This author must be credited with a truly seminal contribution to information management. While the general thrust of this work lies in the need to "reclassify" the white collar office worker from the "non-productive column" to the "productive column," the need to treat information as a commodity is also central to his hypotheses.

[4]See *Federal Register*, Vol. 42, No. 44, Monday, March 7, 1977, "*Thesaurus of Indexing Terms—Request for Public Comment.*" The "challenge of the *Federal Register,*" like the Thesaurus, lies ultimately in its pragmatic utility as a decision-aiding, problem-solving tool. The fact that its primary subscribers are lawyers, information specialists and Washington, D.C. bureaucrats, does not speak well for its effectiveness to the average citizen as a finding aid. Considerable work needs to be done to refashion this important public document before it comes close to realizing its full potential. The same may be said for its Canadian counterpart, *The Gazette.*

[5]Wilkinson, Dr. Joseph W., "*Effective Reporting Structures,*" (Journal of Systems Management, 1 November, 1976) pp. 38–42.

[6]Bosley, Charles E., "*Federal Use of Advanced Information and Communications Technology,*" (Appendix 4, Preliminary Report issued by Congressional Research Service, Library of Congress, October 30, 1973.) This important report should be in every information specialist's library.

[7]See "*Budget of the United States Government, FY 1979,*" available from the Superintendent of Documents, U.S. Government Printing Office. Three or four companion documents are available, including the Budget Appendix, The Budget In Brief, and The Special Analyses.

[8]See GAO Report entitled "*Mission Budgeting: Discussion and Illustration of the Concept in Research and Development Programs,*" PSAD 77-124, dated July 27, 1977.

5 THE INFORMATION RESOURCES MANAGEMENT SYSTEM

The Information Resources Management System can be viewed as a framework within which to accomplish the management of data resources in an orderly and systematic fashion. Without the system, the process might proceed, but in a disjointed, ad hoc, and difficult-to-control fashion. I said earlier that the challenge of the system is to marshall data and information resources and use them effectively and efficiently in the service of man's decision-making and problem-solving needs. The system, then, challenges the designer, the user, the data suppliers and providers, and others with a role to play to work together to insure that the system is a positive force and not a cause for obstruction, delay, procrastination or disincentive.

The information resources management system is a very special kind of system, and we will at the outset differentiate it from other information systems. After discussing semantic and substantive aspects, the two key dimensions of information management—the communications process and the management of "hardware" used to handle data—will be discussed.

Next some guideposts to help in the design of such a system, as well as some pitfalls, will be listed. The experiences of some large organizations will then be reviewed to see where problems are encountered and what might be done to nip them in the bud.

Finally, considerable attention will be given to the information process itself, in flow-chart fashion, because such an understanding is essential to the organic construction of the information resource management system. Later chapters will take up each stage of the resource process, beginning with planning information requirements. Appendix B should be consulted where necessary.

Let us review some definitions first. The term *information system* is most often defined at two different levels. At the highest level, it is often taken to represent the combined network of all communication methods within the overall organization. At the lowest level—and as most commonly defined—the term is used to define a single network of information-processing steps associated with a particular operation or set of related operations. The phrase *information-processing steps* is taken to embrace the successive stages of collection, recording, processing, transfer, storage, retrieval, dissemination and, in some cases, disposal.

Next, the term *resource management system* includes all methods and procedures for collecting and processing information *on a particular resource* (i.e., men, money, machines, or what is germane to our subject here, information itself) and formating that data in a manner which is useful for management. In the jargon of both business and government, very often the phrase "men, money, and machines" is used as a convenient shorthand phrase to refer to resources used by organizations to accomplish their missions. But information itself is usually left out, unfortunately.

Bearing these key terms and their definitions in mind, it may be useful next to review what we are *not* talking about here. With respect to the term *information system*, for example, we are not talking about one-time, nonrecurring collections of data and information. A one-time report, for example, although it might cover such subjects as crisis management, research and development management, intelligence management, marketing management, or investment management, is an information *product or service*. The key word is *one-time*. A reporting *system* is certainly an information system. Instead, by the term *information resources*, we include all information sources, services, products, and individual information systems which are functionally oriented to some aspects of the organization's operations and activities. For example, we *would* include under this definition of information resources all personnel information systems, payroll information systems, inventory information systems, program management information systems, marketing information systems, manufacturing information systems, and so on. It is central to our understanding that we recognize that we are concerned both with the substance and the content of each of these functionally oriented information systems and with a profile of their identity, location, purpose, use, and other key attributes. But it will not be crucial to understand the organic functioning of each of these individual information systems; we need merely to see and understand where they fit in our overall scheme of information resources management.

This latter point has given rise to no end of confusion. As soon as one begins to talk about information resources management to certain audiences, the dilemma of distinguishing between information substance or content and information *on information* confronts us. The information scientist has a nice phrase for this distinction. He refers to "information on information" as the information meta-system or simply metadata.

WHY DO WE NEED AN INFORMATION RESOURCES MANAGEMENT SYSTEM?

So much for semantics and definitions. Why do we need an information resources management system? There are a number of reasons. First, in today's modern organization, information resources are scattered, compartmentalized, fragmented, and diffused throughout headquarters and subordinate units. Indeed, any organization which takes information resources management seriously finds it absolutely essential, as a first step in bringing its resources under control, to conduct a thorough, systematic, and comprehensive inventory of its information resources. Only after we have such a base line of detailed data on hand, profiling each information source, service, product, and system, can we undertake a rationalization and begin the long and difficult task of constructing some kind of management system. Let us be clear. Some might take the position that we need only to add up all of the organization's information systems and then label that collection "the information resources management system." Not only does that approach get us nowhere, it simply won't work. What it does is present a hodgepodge of incompatible, inconsistent, and overlapping information streams. Those streams must be carefully juxtaposed to uncover overlaps and duplication, both at the macrodata element level, and at the microdata element level.

TWO PRIMARY DIMENSIONS

To go further with information resources management, we must understand that it has two separate and distinct dimensions. One concerns the management of the information *process*, the other the management of the information *resources used in the process.* The first dimension relates to the assurance of the adequacy of information as it is needed for organizational decision-making, analysis, and communications. The second dimension relates to the various kinds of resources which an organization needs, space, equipment, personnel, and so on, in support of the information process. In short, the management of the information *process* concerns itself with how well the members of an organization use data resources and supporting information technologies to support decision-making and analytical purposes. There we are concerned with the relationships between information collected, the uses to which data are put, and finally how valuable the information is to helping the organization achieve its end-result purposes. See Figure 5-1.

On the other hand, the management of data *resources* concerns itself with such considerations as:

- the six organic attributes of information: scope, measure, subject, time, source, and quality (all discussed in greater detail later);
- the efficiency with which data handling hardware and software are employed;
- the effectiveness with which data handling hardware and software contribute to the information process (and ultimately the communications process).

INDIVIDUALS VS. ORGANIZATIONS

A number of problems for both these two dimensions can be identified in modern organizational settings. Many of them involve the subject interplay between individual goals and organizational goals. For example, in the case of the data resources, one difficulty is the tendency of the data-generating sources, services, and systems to produce too much data for too many individuals in the organization.

Another problem is the fact that organizational information-processing possesses many of the same characteristics as individual information-processing and also displays some unique characteristics. First, there is no unique "self" in an organization. It is made up of the coordinated activities of all of the organizational members. Since individual goals, values, and so forth differ, it is almost trite to say that the organizational viewpoint is not merely a composite of individual viewpoints. This results in the development of both formal and informal information-processing flows, systems, and so on which

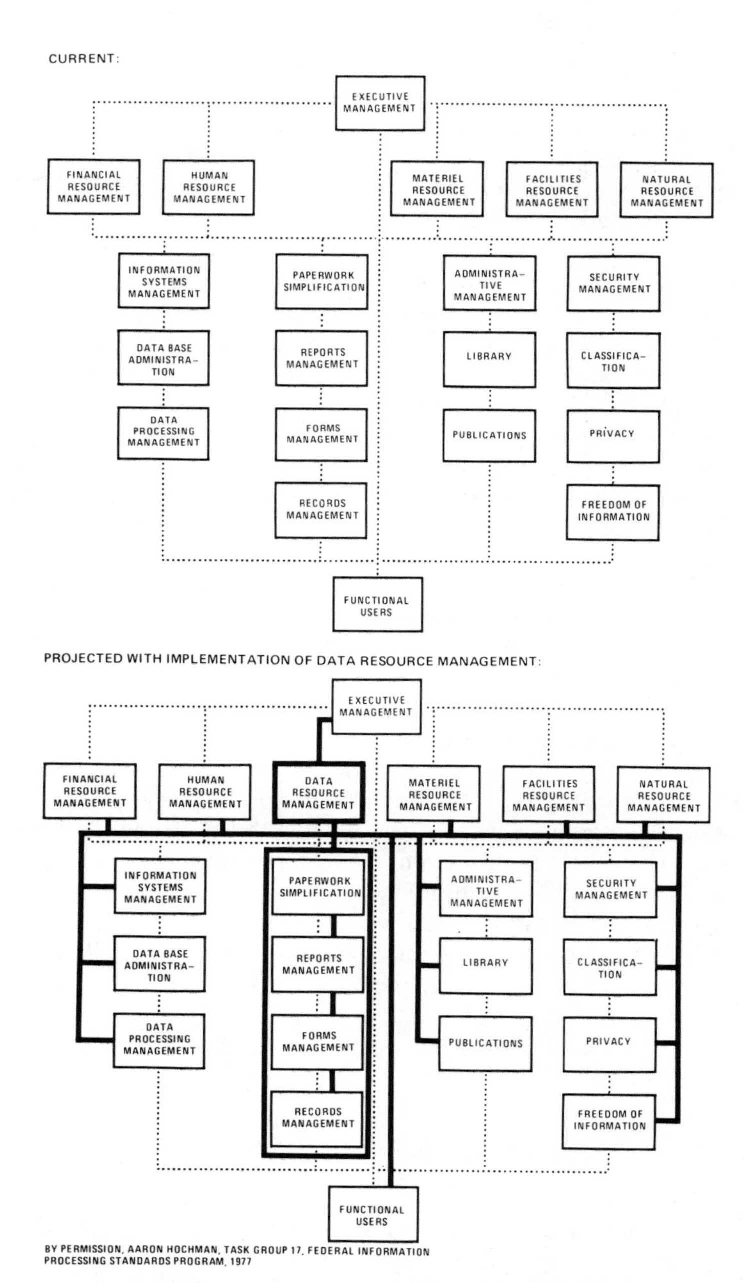

BY PERMISSION, AARON HOCHMAN, TASK GROUP 17, FEDERAL INFORMATION PROCESSING STANDARDS PROGRAM, 1977

***Figure 5-1.* Resources management environment**

sometimes complement and reinforce the formal processes but oftentimes do not.

Many would say that one basic function of information management in organizations is to help "manage" conflict—reduce it to manageable proportions—and mobilize support for its resolution. Organizational information-processing can be structured and consciously designed with certain limits, just as individual information processing can. Formal and structured modes of information processing are helpful when the organization's internal and external environments are relatively stable. However, the formal information systems of an organization may be dysfunctional when these environments are dynamic, that is, when missions and goals are in a state of radical flux or the organization is tumultuous because of changing key personalities or long standing policy conflicts.

Because of this subtle interplay between individual and organizational information-processing, development of the information resources management system in an organization requires attention to several key factors. First, there is the need to focus on the quality of the interaction between individuals and the kinds of symbolic data used in the organization. For example, how well do individuals in the organization process and use different kinds of data? To what extent do they have adequate knowledge and training to use, manipulate and communicate data to others and to assimilate or search for new types of data when necessary?

Second, there is the concern with how well messages and other data are communicated in the organization. Does relevant information, for example, get passed around easily in both the formal and informal systems? Third, to what extent is information processing in the organization coordinated among members and managers? For example, do individuals share information readily and easily in the organization? Or is there a great deal of unnecessary duplication and overlap of information-processing in the separate units? Finally, what is the relationship between data collection, use, and value in the organization? To what extent is information collected used? Does that which is used result in value?

OBJECTIVES OF THE SYSTEM

The last set of considerations and their interrelationships—collection, use and results—leads us to a discussion now of developing the system. The first step, of course, is to identify its objectives. One Federal agency lists four objectives:

- First, to provide managers at all levels within the agency with data to assure resources are obtained and used effectively and efficiently in the accomplishment of the agency's objectives;
- Second, to provide information that is useful in the formulation of objectives and plans;
- Third, to provide data to support program proposals and requests for funds; and
- Fourth, to provide a means of assuring that statutes, agreements with Congressional committees, and other requirements emanating from outside the agency relating to resources, are complied with.[1]

Whether or not we fully agree with this set of objectives, it seems clear that we must deal with the management of information resources at different stages in the information life cycle, and at each stage the requirements are slightly different.

PPBS AS A "MODEL"

Although the *practice* of PPBS (Planning-Programming-Budgeting System) has fallen somewhat into disfavor in recent years, its *foundation* in the Government's financial management system remains. Undeniably it is a financial resource management system and by virtue of that fact alone warrants our attention.

The concept has four or more parts, depending upon how far one wishes to go in tracking a resource. Typically, however, all resources, including information resources, must be dealt with in financial contexts, at a minimum, in four phases or stages: planning, programming, budgeting, and accounting. Occasionally one sees added to that list two more stages, evaluating and auditing. A primary goal of resource management systems, then, is to integrate these four (or more) stages in such a way that one can track the cost of resources as they are planned and used at each stage and the values the resource consumptions contribute to the achievement of the organization's goals (i.e., profit, welfare, services, or whatever). As has been mentioned earlier, information, unlike other resources, is not normally "consumed" in the process of its use. However, it does, in many cases, obsolesce with time.

PPBS illustrated, then, that any system developed for the management of resources must:

- provide for the accurate and complete comparison of actual resource utilization with planned resource utilization;
- hold managers accountable for the efficient and effective use of resources entrusted to their custody;
- define commonly used terms and abbreviations in standard language and using standard representations and codes, to provide crosswalks between different subsystems;
- clearly relate inputs to outputs;
- carefully weigh the value of the benefits expected from the use of the resource against the costs incurred at all stages in the resource life cycle: acquisition, enhancement, utilization, and disposition; and
- minimize the information needs of decisionmakers consistent with the effective and efficient achievement of the organization's goals and objectives.

DEVELOPING THE SYSTEM

Now let us get more specific concerning the design and development of the information resources management system. Aaron Hochman of the Office of the Assistant Secretary of Defense, identifies a half dozen "fundamental management principles" in the development of an information resources management system.[2] First, he reminds us that an improvement in one facet of management does not necessarily improve total management. The key factor in this principle is recognition of the end-objectives of the organization as opposed to the end-objectives of subordinate management programs and organizational sub-elements. An information resources management system must be keyed to the primary objectives of the organization rather than merely responding to a compendium of subordinate objectives.

Second, the effectiveness of functional mission performance is directly related to the effectiveness of the data and information management. Information resources management provides critically-needed access to required information and reduces the time and effort required to find such information. Such reduction in time and effort contributes to increased efficiency of the system users in performing their mission assignments. Collaterally, the availability of required information permits its reutilization and thus avoids the necessity for duplicative data procurement and/or development.

Third, the effectiveness of information resources management involves efficiency in providing the data customer with the information required, on time, and in a form that can be understood without unnecessary effort. The purpose of the information resources management system is to provide necessary information support services to system users. The system customer's acceptance and use of the system is contingent upon the responsiveness of the system to users' needs. Such responsiveness is directly related to the facility of accession, timeliness of retrieval, and usefulness of the information provided. It is well recognized that the user of an information retrieval system will tend to avoid use of the system if retrieval requires any significant level of work to be performed by the user.

Fourth, information is a critical resource and deserves the same kind of management disciplines as are employed in the management of other resources. Data and information are fundamental elements of any system, whether it is a management system, a weapon system, or a data system. Data and information are subject to the same life cycle events as other resources (e.g., requirements determination; design; development; identification; cataloging; acquisition; storage; maintenance; utilization; and disposal). Data and information are not normally expended when used, and in this sense, they provide a potential for reutilization not common to other resources. It is this reutilization potential that dictates the application of data resource management, particularly in an environment where the costs of doing business are overwhelmingly dominated by the cost of human resources which, in turn, are the "consumers" of data and information.

Fifth, information can be managed on either a commodity or system-oriented basis, or a combination of both. Commodity-oriented management is essentially concerned with what the data are, independent of application. System-oriented data management is primarily concerned with how the data are applied. Information resources management provides the critically required correlation of the substantively different forms of data management.

Finally, computers are intended to be labor-saving devices. The amount of effort expended by the human in relation to the computer must be kept to a minimum. In short, the maxim should be: "say not what you can do for the computer, but what the computer can do for you."

PROBLEMS AND PITFALLS

Edgar S. Dunn helps point out pitfalls in the design and development and use of information resources management systems by pointing out a number of deficiencies in the Federal information resources management system.[3] Although his focus is primarily on the Federal

Statistical System, his criticisms can be constructively viewed in our broader context. For example, he points out that a serious obstacle to the full utilization of information resources is the absence of "any clearly defined reference function." The reference function, he points out, has generally been thought of as a responsibility of the document centers. To the extent that an agency attempts to provide occasional reference assistance, "the task falls to an individual whose primary mission is defined very often in terms of the publication mission. The inadequacy of this service is also traceable to the fragmented nature of the records of the Federal Statistical System, resulting from divided responsibility for their generation and maintenance. The reference problem is made especially complex because of the decentralized character of the Federal statistical program. No agency has been in a position to perform a reference service for the total file."

Another deficiency of Federal information resources management which Dunn points out is the failure of the Federal Statistical System to permit the association of data elements and what he calls "data sets" in a manner that would permit the identification and measurement of interrelationships between and among interdependent activities.This deficiency has been partially overcome in a few vital areas where we need to trace and analyze the performance of the economy, by the establishment of special programs to bring together data sets in the form of national accounts, special index series, etc., "but it remains a debilitating constraint for most uses of data for analysis and planning. This is true for virtually all levels of use and for all purposes. It is a problem that plagues the research analyst inside and outside of the Federal Government who, for example, are engaged in building models of the economy in the interest of analyzing and projecting the major dimensions of economic growth and stability. It has been the principle obstacle to the administration's attempt to build a post-attack reevaluation and recuperation model."

Dunn also calls our attention to the inherent conflict between archival needs and records management needs. He points out that this was a problem that interested the Ruggles Committee "and from which they proceeded to the broader issue of file management. The statistical agencies are primarily concerned with producing data publications. They often leave their records improperly documented for further processing and analysis. Worse still, they have allowed useful records to be destroyed. These things occur because the existing system has no standards for identifying the files significant for preservation or for assuring essential levels of file documentation. It provides no financial or organizational mechanisms for their maintenance. The decisions about the significance of archives is left to functionaries with little knowledge of their value and who must allocate funds for their documentation and preservation in competition with agency missions defined by previous policy in more restrictive terms and considered primary by agency personnel."

SYSTEMATIC VS. AD HOC APPROACH

One thread running through much of the foregoing discussion is the need to develop the system systematically, and comprehensively, instead of piecemeal. For example, periodic publication of some kind of hard-cover, bound and stitched volume in lieu of flexible and updatable machinery, has several deficiencies. That approach is what might be called the ad hoc approach, rather than the systems approach, to information resources management. Under the ad hoc approach, sporadically generated directories are often out of date by the time they are printed. Where an attempt is made to establish an updating and maintenance capability, changes are received so frequently, and in such large numbers, as to render such capabilities marginally effective at best. Second, such directories, despite adjectives like "company-wide," "national," "comprehensive," and so forth, are, in fact, restrictive in one or more ways. It often turns out, for example, that they contain purely quantitative data and exclude narrative and qualitative data; or they include administrative and business-type data and exclude scientific and technical data; or they deal with secondary source materials and avoid or ignore primary source materials entirely; or they address higher order systems and leave out lower order systems; or, finally, they are preoccupied with automated and computerized systems to the virtual exclusion of manual systems and files.

There are other criticisms of the ad hoc approach. For example, a typical "product" of the ad hoc approach to information resources management is the development and distribution of single publications. Single publications, by definition, do not provide desirable servicing features such as full or partial text abstracts of selected source context material. Perhaps an even more serious criticism of the ad hoc approach is that the all-important capability of human intervention and interaction with the data files and records is missing.

COUNTERPRESSURES

Historically when one reviews case histories at the Federal level where the option to proceed with the comprehensive development of an information resources management system approach was at least theoretically feasible (if not always politically feasible) one sees that a strong economic argument was often a counterforce. In the case of the Atomic Energy Commission and the National Aeronautics and Space Administration, for example, in the first decade of their existence, no single, agency-wide inventory of information resources was ever undertaken.

Such a course of action was considered in the highest management counsels of those agencies but officials contended that the cost would have been prohibitive. If pressed closely, they also indicated that, while the economic argument may have, in the end, been the most persuasive one, there were also problems in the realm of information technology, information handling and retrieval methodologies, in particular. These, in turn, boiled down to problems of standardized formats, uniform definitions for data elements, and similar considerations. In their view, an information resources management system constructed in the first decade of the existence of those agencies would have amounted to nothing more than a skeleton framework, with no interconnection between the organs and the muscles.

Another agency, the Environmental Protection Agency (EPA), found itself in late 1970—the year it was created—in a similar dilemma but EPA decided to undertake a comprehensive inventory of its information resources—both technical and nontechnical. As a result, for the first time in recent memory, there was created a single focal point at the Federal level to which the user of environmental data could go to acquire the one-stop service capability created as a result of this inventory. The system:

- provided substantive data and information directly to the user/inquirer;
- referred the user/inquirer to a secondary source of information as a supplementary service to providing direct information products and services; and
- responded to the user/inquirer in accordance with pre-determined parameters, such as priority of need, scope of information required, modes and media of response formats desired, and so forth.

In short, the EPA comprehensive inventory was able to function as a central switching point linking together, eventually, the entire network of environmental information resources. Under this concept, EPA did not "sit astride" the flow of information queries. Rather, the exchange mechanism acted as a communications switching device to speed direct contact between users/inquirers and the producer/sources they sought.

THREE INFORMATION WORLDS

At this juncture it would seem useful to reemphasize that the information resources management concept brings together three major "information worlds" which traditionally have been divided and separated. The first information world is the literature world of libraries and archives. The second is the "hard copy" document world of information centers, clearinghouses, documentation centers and record centers. The third information world is the "soft copy" data world of computers, telecommunications and automated information systems which deal with "perishable" data.

A key variable which distinguishes these groups is the time frame in which the information is collected and stored. Another is the storage medium. Thus, libraries and information centers deal largely with books, periodicals and journals, documents and technical reports, films and film strips, and other selected materials. Modern facilities provide a wide variety of microform media, document and referral activities and services, and personalized search methodologies. The time frame in which this information is collected and stored is largely historical. Books, for example, usually take several years to prepare, and the research is therefore from six months to several years out of date before the book is eventually published. Serials take less time in preparation, but they are also outdated to a degree at the time of publication. Equally important, the various tools used to search and access this literature are also to a degree obsolete at the time of publication. These include bibliographies, abstracts, directories, indices, and various reference guides. Conversely, "soft data" information resources deal largely with current information in capsulated form ("elements of data" and "items of information" are the two generic phrases most commonly used). Recall we introduced the data/document/literature triad in Chapter 1.

The significant point being made here is that three sets of data must be integrally linked in the same conceptual framework to maximize the utility of the information to the user. This hypothesis rests upon the observation that many users do not know in advance of their search whether the information they seek is in "hard" or "soft" form. Of course the scientist working in his laboratory day after day, week after week, year after year, does become familiar with both the primary and secondary sources of information in his particular speciality. But as one moves away from this elite researcher to businessman and Government officials, it surely must become apparent that such foreknowledge becomes increasingly rare. Consequently, an extraordinary amount of time is lost pursuing widely disparate search methodologies in geographically distant and remote locations and involving the time and efforts of a wide variety of information specialists. This creates enormous cost, not to mention lost opportunities, missed actions, and so on.[4] The reader may wish to review Figure 1-4.

THE PROBLEM SOLVING CONTEXT

In an earlier chapter we previewed the iterative, algorithmic process of transforming raw, unevaluated data into "processed" information and eventually the knowledge base. It was pointed out that results cannot always lead to the conclusion that information does or does not "have value." Sometimes we go off on the wrong track by misidentifying the problem, the information needed, and how to apply it. Let us pursue that process now in greater depth because it directly bears upon our broader chapter purposes, in the context of the information resources management system.

There are several decision points in a problem-solving or decision-making process that determine the value, non-value, or negative value of information. These decision points and possible outcomes are shown in Figure 5-2. The proper decision, assessment, or action at each point determines the positive value of information. A final result that is positive requires that the outcome from each decision be positive. A positive result from any decision point can move to the next point and be turned into a negative outcome. Once a negative outcome is reached in the process, all subsequent decision outcomes will tend to be negative or value-neutral to produce a final result that is not value-positive.

The negative path can only be reversed by repeating the step which started the negative series of events. For each step to produce a positive outcome, the result of the preceding step must be positive.

Briefly, these steps or decision points and alternatives are as follows:

1. *Identify the problem.* The first, and essential step, is to identify the problem accurately and completely. The terms *objective* or *goal* are often used interchangeably with the term *problem* in this context. If an objective or problem is not identified, none of the remaining steps or decision points will occur, and the objective or problem will remain unknown. However,

a problem can be identified correctly or mis-identified. An identified problem can be properly identified in the next decision step, or it can move from the positive side of the ledger to the negative by being mis-identified. An identified problem or objective may also result in an undefined problem in Step 2. Subsequent steps can be based on an undefined problem that produces final results of counter- or neutral-value. The same holds true for a misidentified problem or objective.

2. *Define the Problem.* Even though a problem may be identified, it must be adequately defined before it can be fully understood and subsequent action taken to resolve it. The same is true of an objective or goal. Clear definition must follow identification, if positive results are to be achieved. A mis-defined problem or objective will establish a false premise for subsequent decision steps and result in a final negative or non-value outcome.
3. *Assess the Problem.* After a problem has been identified and defined properly, its magnitude, character, and consequences must be assessed before appropriate steps can be taken to apply a solution. A properly assigned problem offers the opportunity for developing and applying a solution of equivalent offsetting value. A mis-assessed problem can result in solutions that are greater than required (uneconomical) or smaller than necessary (ineffective or inconsequential).
4. *Define the Information Needed.* We now come more specifically to the Information Resources Management task, but of course we had to set its role into a broader problem-solving context first. After a problem has been identified, defined, and assessed, there is usually a need for more information to provide a better understanding as well as conceptual basis for the design and development of appropriate alternative solutions to the problem. The information definition process is concerned with defining that information which is relevant to the problem or objective. The definition step is regulated by the problem assessment step. If mis-assessed, the variety and quantity of information defined may result in an overload or an inadequacy. Information definition, in turn, regulates the definition of the specific data needed—its kind, quantity, quality, character, and so forth. When irrelevant information is inadvertently defined, related data will not be pertinent to the problem or objective. The objective of the information definition step is to adequately define necessary and relevant information. "Necessary" deals with the magnitude of the

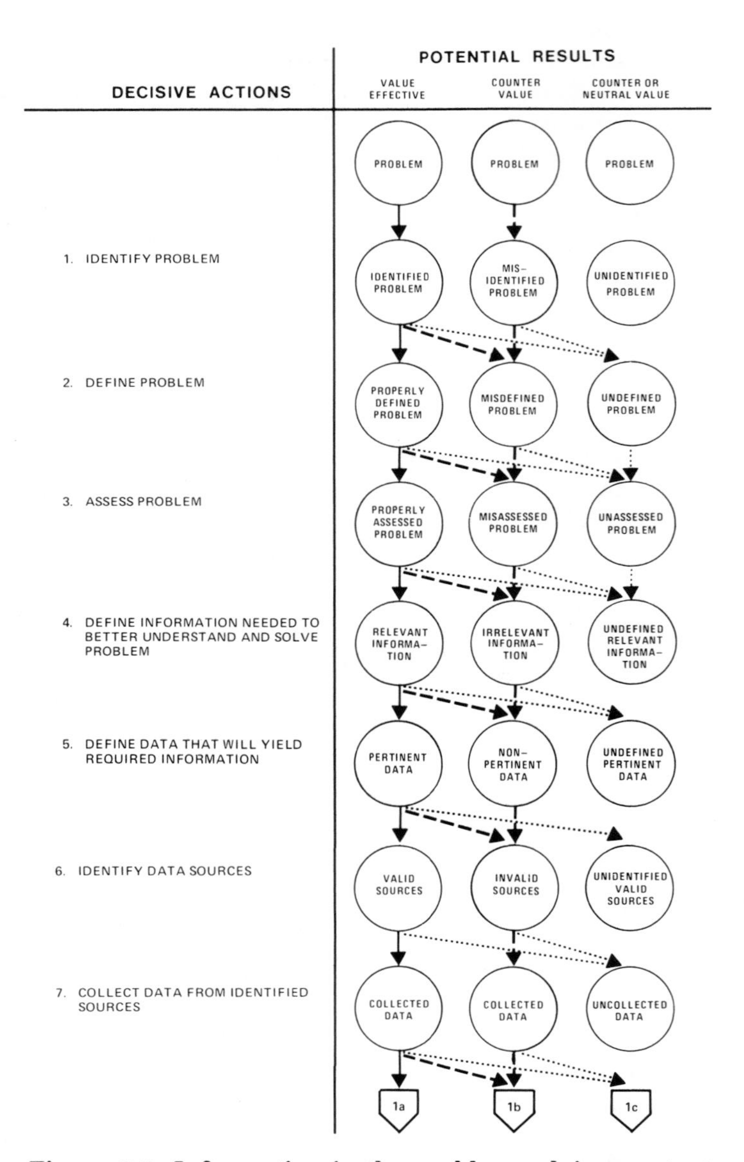

Figure 5-2. **Information in the problem-solving context**

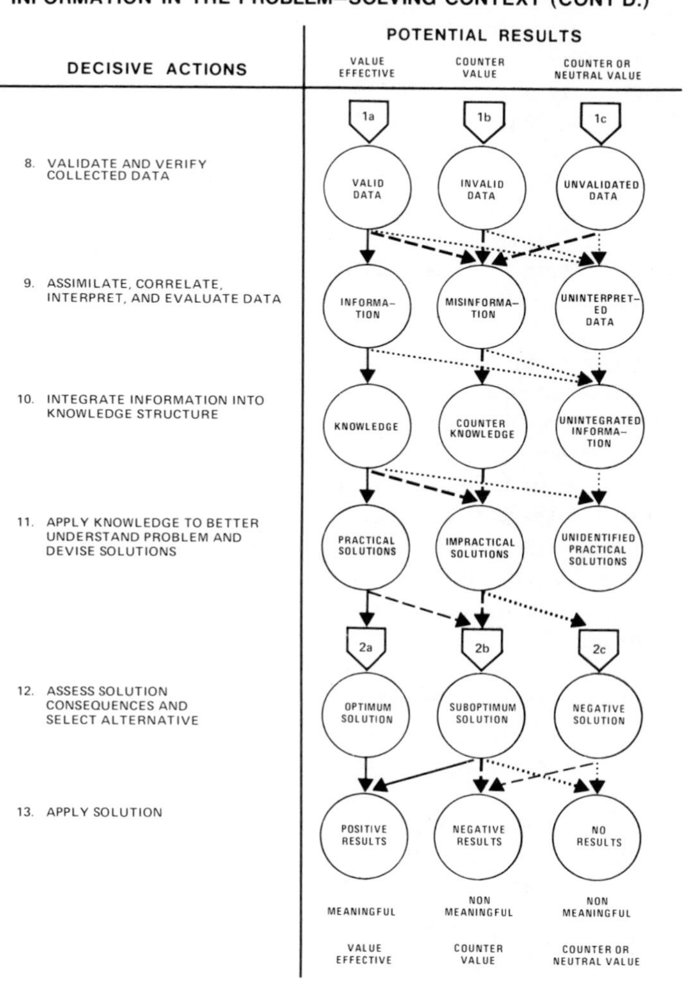
INFORMATION IN THE PROBLEM–SOLVING CONTEXT (CONT'D.)
DECISIVE ACTIONS
POTENTIAL RESULTS
VALUE EFFECTIVE
COUNTER VALUE
COUNTER OR NEUTRAL VALUE
1a
1b
1c
8. VALIDATE AND VERIFY COLLECTED DATA
VALID DATA
INVALID DATA
UNVALIDATED DATA
9. ASSIMILATE, CORRELATE, INTERPRET, AND EVALUATE DATA
INFORMA-TION
MISINFORMA-TION
UNINTERPRET-ED DATA
10. INTEGRATE INFORMATION INTO KNOWLEDGE STRUCTURE
KNOWLEDGE
COUNTER KNOWLEDGE
UNINTEGRATED INFORMA-TION
11. APPLY KNOWLEDGE TO BETTER UNDERSTAND PROBLEM AND DEVISE SOLUTIONS
PRACTICAL SOLUTIONS
IMPRACTICAL SOLUTIONS
UNIDENTIFIED PRACTICAL SOLUTIONS
2a
2b
2c
12. ASSESS SOLUTION CONSEQUENCES AND SELECT ALTERNATIVE
OPTIMUM SOLUTION
SUBOPTIMUM SOLUTION
NEGATIVE SOLUTION
13. APPLY SOLUTION
POSITIVE RESULTS
NEGATIVE RESULTS
NO RESULTS
MEANINGFUL
NON MEANINGFUL
NON MEANINGFUL
VALUE EFFECTIVE
COUNTER VALUE
COUNTER OR NEUTRAL VALUE

problem or objective. "Relevant" deals with the subject and substantive relationships.

5. *Define the Data.* Now we will try to be more careful in differentiating between data in a technical sense and information. Information is derived from data. This decision step defines that data which will produce the necessary, relevant information. Even though only relevant and necessary information may have been clearly defined in the preceding step, this step can result in the definition of non-pertinent or unnecessary data, since relationships of data to information are not always clear. There is again the danger of defining data that will overload a correlation and interpretation process and thus subsequently cause an information inadequacy.
6. *Identify Data Sources.* After data that will yield the required information has been defined, the proper sources of such data must be determined. Unreliable sources can produce invalid and misleading data. Even though pertinent data may have been defined in the preceding step, collection from an invalid source can shift the positive sequence of events into a negative pathway and outcome.
7. *Collect the Data.* After pertinent data and valid sources have been defined, data are collected. The collection process can result in the partial collection of data required or the collection of erroneous data. Even though the data may have been adequately defined, it is possible that such data is not readily available from identified sources or, for that matter, from any source. The request may then result in best estimates or possibly even guesses. It is therefore necessary to coordinate data requests with intended sources prior to initiating collection. Some data may have to be dropped from the requirement, and other defined data may have to be replaced by an equivalent substitute.
8. *Validate and Verify Collected Data.* There is a potential for error and omission in all collected data. Data must, therefore, be edited, validated, and verified before it is used. Valid data is considered to be that which is complete, accurate, and reliable, and, in fact, representative of the reality it is supposed to represent. Invalid data, if detected, can oftentimes be corrected or at least removed from the collection without too much difficulty. Removal or omission will not necessarily, then, render the remaining data invalid. The significance of an item of invalid data, if omitted, may, on the other hand, sometimes render the rest of the data invalid or unusable.

In some circumstances, the identification of invalid data, and its inclusion with valid data, can still provide a high degree of utility for the entire collection.

9. *Assimilate, Correlate, Interpret, and Evaluate Data.* Information is derived from data through the process of organizing, correlating, interpreting, and evaluating collections of related data. Inadequate or improper correlation and interpretation can produce mis-information. The process, as well as the data itself, is critical to the results. Too often it is assumed that if the right data is collected, the use processes which follow will proceed along the appropriate pathways.
10. *Integrate Information into Knowledge Structure.* Information may have intrinsic or potential value. However, its true value is fully realized only when it improves human knowledge, understanding, and well-being, and this knowledge then is effectively applied to the resolution of problems and the achievement of objectives. Mis-information, on the other hand, can result in a real setback—"counterknowledge" is the term sometimes used. The negative consequences of counter-knowledge are greater than those that may arise from lack of knowledge in the first place. At least in the latter case there is the opportunity or opening for improving understanding and knowledge. However, the former involves "knowing things which are untrue." The behavioral scientist and the psychologist can tell us how difficult it is to unlearn things which were learned incorrectly. This involves serious resistance, and therefore counterknowledge can often lead to indecision and inaction because the unlearning is painful, embarassing, humiliating, and generally awkward to deal with. Accordingly, this step in the process is one of the most critical. If preceding steps have produced positive outcomes, there is the potential for a positive knowledge outcome from this step. However, mis-information derived from invalid data, and mis-defined problems resulting in irrelevant information requirements, will result often in counterknowledge. To some extent this can be avoided by a certain amount of "preventive maintenance," if the results from preceding steps are rigorously and critically reviewed and questioned, rather than blindly accepted and integrated into the knowledge structure.
11. *Apply the Knowledge.* The ultimate value of information is realized when knowledge is applied to practical, optimum solutions, and these solutions or actions are implemented with positive results. In this step, then, knowledge is applied to

better understand the problem or objective, and possibly to redefine it with greater precision and accuracy, and iterate the process again up to this point. If adequate, however, we can begin the process of devising alternative solutions. Impractical solutions result from counterknowledge, or the improper application of knowledge in understanding the problem and potential outcomes of solutions.

12. *Assess Solution Consequences.* Practical alternative solutions are assessed here to determine which solution or action will offer optimum results relative to costs and other constraints, for developing and implementing.
13. *Apply the Solution.* The ultimate outcome from these series of decisions and actions is realized when solutions are applied. The most desirable outcome for solution of problems or achievement of objectives is positive results. Positive results are dependent on value-positive information. However, information can produce negative or value-neutral results where subsequent decision stages result in negative outcomes or where there is indecision and inaction with no outcome. As the old saw goes, "doing nothing is deciding." In the latter situation, results may remain dormant for a long period of time or they may deteriorate. Some may contend that there is nothing wrong with "a solution running around looking for a problem" either, and therefore the third possibility—an eventual positive outcome—should be considered.

SUMMARY

All of the preceding material may seem to many to be tedious, overly precise and somewhat redundant. Perhaps so. But the designer of the information resources management system would do well to keep the overall flow continuum in mind as he or she begins the task of designing a new system, or evaluating an existing one for the purpose of plugging loopholes and strengthening its responsiveness. The fact is, I believe the single, most important reason why information resources are not used as effectively as they might is because we've not taken a "longitudinal" approach to closing the gap between raw data flows and positive, sought-for results. Too many backwater streams are the result of failing to ask the hard questions: who is really using this information and for what purposes (and, by the way, one doesn't get the answer to that question by asking "tell me why you need the information" but rather by asking "show me how you use the information.")

This is what the *system* really involves. Otherwise, we would simply start data flows and let the data find its own "water level." Sometimes it may, without our intervention. But many times I would suggest, it will not. An Information Resources Management System gives us a better chance of getting the right data to the right people at the right times.

QUESTIONS FOR DISCUSSION

1. In theory, at least, an Information Resources Management System might be designed to manage *either or both* the information *process* (communication) or the information *resources* which are needed to support the information process (i.e. equipment, software, people and so on). Many believe there is a direct link between the two. That is, the quality of the data resources, the efficiency with which they are employed, and the skill and expertise with which they are applied, all contribute directly to the quality and effectiveness of the information process. Do you agree? Give examples.

2. Pursuing the question above, do you believe that the communication process itself can be "managed" in the same way a production supervisor, for example, manages an assembly line. Or an inventory control superintendent keeps track of tools in a tool crib? Support your position and illustrate with examples.

3. An important and useful distinction can be made between information *efficiency* and information *effectiveness*. Compare and contrast these two ideas and give examples of each. For example, if we succeed in reducing the unit cost of reproducing one sheet of paper on a reprographic machine, which (if either, or both) of the two concepts are we dealing with? Or, if we hold our information flows and data bases "constant" but achieve greater output productivity (e.g. more cars off the assembly line per hour), which do we have?

4. Sometimes information can be said to be the *critical* resource in an enterprise or endeavor; sometimes it is less important, but still essential; and sometimes information plays virtually no role whatsoever. Give an example of a business or commercial activity for each of the three categories. Give an example of a government agency. Give an example of a professional activity.

5. Modern management theorists, engineers and others sometimes use the phrase "systems approach" to mean that an organization is a kind of system, and the decisions and goods made at one state, in one department of the organization, are usually not end-products for sale,

but serve as inputs to another stage or department. An information system, therefore, might be said to be a conglomeration of sub-systems. Assuming some merit to that thesis, what "lessons" does it portend for information system designers?

6. The "use typology" put forward by the text depends, ultimately, on the organization's ability to differentiate between information used to *operate* a program (or directly support the manufacture of a product) and "all other information" needed to administer, manage, evaluate and control the program or product. Do you believe that capability is both theoretically and practically feasible? Support your contention with illustrations.

7. It is sometimes argued that one serious defect with an Information Resources Management "systems approach" is that very often decisionmakers and problemsolvers *simply don't know what information they need in the first place.* They want, rather, "to find out what is there" so as to narrow down the range of courses of action, alternatives and paths on which to proceed. Therefore, if one can't specify one's information needs in advance of the collection, with precision, doesn't the whole idea of "managing" information fall apart? Comment on this line of argument.

8. "Need to know" and "nice to know" are two short-hand phrases which have often been applied to situations where information users attempt to justify information to higher authorities. Do you believe such a distinction is a real one or simply rhetoric?

FOOTNOTES

[1]Department of Defense Directive Number 7000.1, *"Resource Management Systems of the Department of Defense,"* (August 22, 1966). The Department of Defense was one of the first Federal agencies to establish a central information management control office to deal with the information explosion. They must be given much of the credit for shifting the control focus from control over information handling hardware and software to control over the articulation of information requirements. They recognized early that the problem of overlap and duplication throughout DOD could not be dealt with exclusively through greater standardization of data element codes and communications symbols, but would have to back up to the "front end" of the process and zero-in on the early planning processes.

[2]Hochman, Aaron, *"Principles and Concepts of Data Resource Management System Development,"* (Undated paper) (and in communications with the author who directs the DOD Logistics Data Element Standardization and Management Office, ASD (I&L), Alexandria, Va. 22332) pp. 91–98. At about the same time the Commission on Federal Paperwork was developing its themes with regard to information resources management, an important task group operating under the aegis of the Federal Information Processing Standards program of the Institute for Computer Science and Technology of the National Bureau of Standards, Task Group 17, was hard at work on a companion theme: data resource management. Two draft volumes were ultimately produced and when this work was being completed, these volumes were under draft review. They were, volume 1, *"Executive Guide to the Management of Data Resources,"* preliminary draft September 20, 1977, and *"Guidelines for the Management of Data Resources,"* preliminary draft, same date. Interested persons may obtain either volume, or perhaps a final publication, from Mr. Hochman, chairman of Task Group 17.

[3]Dunn, Edgar S. Jr., *"Social Information Processing and Statistical Systems—Change and Reform,"* (A Wiley-Interscience Publication, 1974) pp. 206–220. Dr. Dunn unjustly received much of the brunt of Congressional and media criticisms when the debate concerning the National Data Bank received so much attention in the late 1960's. His writings on this subject continue to deserve the close and serious review of scholars and others interested in the "right to privacy vs. the public's right to know" arguments.

[4]Horton, Forest W. Jr., "Interdisciplinary Approach Sought for Information Management," (Information Action, 9th Year, No. 1, Feb. 1977) pp. 1. The case for a multidisciplinary approach to information resources management is set forth in this short article.

6 PLANNING INFORMATION REQUIREMENTS

We are here moving from structure and process to substance. Preceding chapters have set the stage, provided a framework, introduced a concept, attempted some key definitions of crucial terms, and spelled out the role of the systems approach. All this leads to the topic at hand, the substance of information. The first step in the process is the planning of information needs and uses or, as the chapter heading suggests, the planning of information requirements.

Planning, defined in perhaps an oversimplified way, is the process of deciding what action should be taken in the future. As some authors define it, planning is the futurity of present decisions. The distinction between planning and forecasting is essentially that the forecaster makes no attempt to influence the future, whereas the planner does. For example, people forecast the weather but they do not attempt to plan it—except perhaps for experiments in cloud seeding. Planning can only be successful as an integral part of the decisionmaking process, and the only way that planning can be a part of that process is through the three-step management cycle (planning, programing, and budgeting).

Programs must be based on plans; budgets must be based on programs; actual results must be measured in terms of plans (expected results); and feedback must be used to modify the initial plans. I said in an earlier work that, if programs and budgets flow from decisions on sources, people, policies, and strategies *other* than those embodied in agreed-to plans, then planning will inevitably be considered peripheral to the mainstream of the organization's operations. If, on the other hand, programs and budgets are a product of approved plans, then the planning department will be treated with respect, and the planning function will be accorded the status of an organic, essential organizational element—not a frill or a luxury.

AUTHORIZATION TO COLLECT INFORMATION

An integral part of the program planning process is identification of the information that will be needed to support the program. In government, the first requirement that must be met is information expressly identified in the legislation which authorizes the program, along with additional information required to operate it. This type of information requirement may be reviewed by higher levels of management in the organization. At the middle level—the program level—the program manager and the planning staff may determine the types of information that may be useful for management of the program, as well as for use by higher organizational management. Figure 6-1 summarizes this schematic flow, whereas the detailed information flow process in Government is an overwhelming complex process, as Appendix B demonstrates. Undoubtedly informed observers of the information process would criticize this material for being greatly simplified, shortened, and streamlined! Moreover, there are innumerable variations of this idealized, schematic portrayal. Nevertheless, there are several reasons for including the detailed information flow in Appendix B:

- to give the reader a general feeling of the enormity and complexity of the information process, including a substantial amount of real, or at least potential, redundancy;
- to identify key "leverage points" where controls may strengthen the management of the flow process itself as well as the uses to which the information is being put; and
- to underscore that this entire process, unlike other resource flow processes such as those controlling the use of human resources, material resources (i.e., inventories), and real property resources (e.g., office space, plant space, and laboratory space), *is not now covered by any kind of systematic, integrated, policy and procedural doctrine.*

To return to the first step, the legislative authorization, the essential question in this definition is: "Can we anticipate everything that might be asked about the program?" In government, unfortunately, there

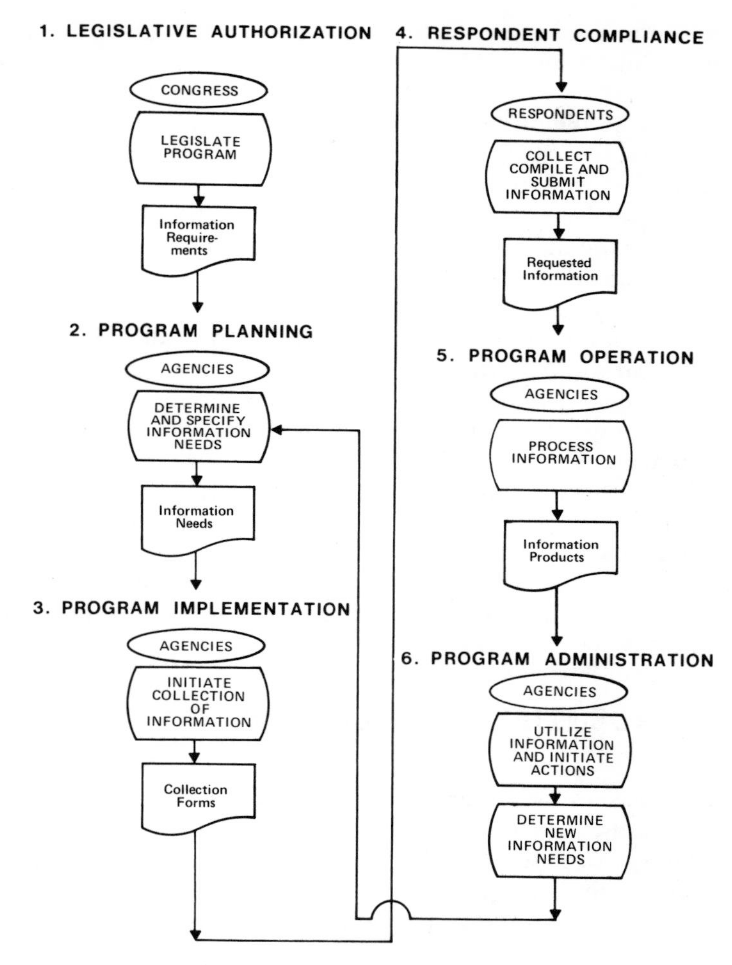

Figure 6-1. **Information flow**

is an overriding concern for "not knowing" and thus looking bad to the legislature, superiors, peers, and subordinates. In private industry, the concern of course is with increased risks and missed opportunities.

Certainly one unarguable hypothesis is that a clear definition of the problem, a clear articulation of the organizational goal, a clear understanding of resource availabilities, limitations, and constraints, and a clear idea of how the information will be used in decision-making together should lead us on a path that results in fewer information requirements.

Ronen and Sadan remind us that the Government's cost of collecting the information it needs is clearly more amenable to quantification than is the cost to private industry of responding to Government's requirements. However, the benefits of the information "elude any numerical analysis." "To be able to do so," these authors write, "we would have had to ascertain how the data are used, how they effect the decisions, and what is the ultimate impact of the decision changes (resulting from the information)." These authors point out that through a "group consensus—generating process, prominent users of national data representing both the public and private sector, sitting in committees (such as the Data Improvement Committee) register, through their voiced demand for data, the implied benefits of the information. And the more insistently and persuasively they argue for additional data, presumably the greater their perception of the benefits. In the absence of a mechanism whereby costs and benefits can be accurately determined, the consensus device may be the optimal solution. At least it seems to be the only feasible device. In other words, the loss resulting from the nonanalytical determination of cost and benefit through the consensus mechanism, could well be exceeded by the cost of attempting to accurately measure the costs and benefits. Nonetheless, it seems that the process could be improved."[1]

IDENTIFYING FULL AND TRUE COSTS

The Commission on Federal Paperwork very early determined that it was absolutely essential to strengthen and improve the processes by which the information requirements of Government are determined and weighed against the expected costs and burdens that the collection of such information would impose on respondents in private industry and the public in general. One important effort undertaken by that body was the development of information planning guidelines by a joint Commission-National Bureau of Standards task group. That group identified six key steps in the determination and formulation of data and information requirements to achieve approved program goals and objectives. These six steps were:

1. Review established and approved program goals and objectives; pinpoint statutory parent authority;
2. Identify key decisions needed, program outputs to be produced, and information products to be generated (how information collected will be actually used);
3. Conduct an "alternatives assessment" of various options open

to satisfy established information requirements;

4. Estimate and make explicit the total cost expected to be incurred for each alternative considered in step 3 above; consider both internal Government costs and the costs to be borne by the public (external cost); break costs into the three major phases of the program life cycle: planning, operations (implementation), and evaluation;
5. Select the preferred alternative after weighing benefits against costs; and
6. Prepare an Information Plan for inclusion in the agency's overall Planning, Budgeting and Programming documents; include in the plan: an analysis of impact on the economy as a whole; an analysis of impact on affected respondent group(s); generic classes of data to be collected and maintained; assignment of specific responsibilities to named individuals and organizational units: A value/burden analysis that takes into account both "external" (publicly borne) costs as well as "internal" (Government borne) costs; and the capacity of respondents in the private sector to furnish the data or information requested; and, finally, a time-phased Implementation Plan that sets key milestones and benchmarks for the completion of each major event (decisions, outputs, and information products).

INFORMATION IN THE DECISION-SETTING

Many studies have pointed to a correlation between the kinds of decisions which an information user must make and the nature of the information he needs and uses. For example, some authors have attempted to construct "decision sets" or "decision modules" and functionally relate these to the supporting information sets on which they depend. Decisions—at least the so-called "go/no go" kinds of decisions—are relatively tangible "products" which are generated from the consumption of information. Quantification of risks, or measurement of missed opportunities, is far more difficult to identify, observe, and determine, but a great deal of research by information scientists and system scientists centers on risk theory, or "risk and uncertainty" theory as the subject is sometimes called. This line of reasoning begins with the question: "What is the penalty of not receiving accurate, complete, timely, and relevant information?"

Another key consideration of information use in the decision setting is that less emphasis should be placed on the technical structure of the information system and correspondingly more emphasis should be placed on the behavioral attributes of information users. The central idea here seems to be that, by studying and analyzing the behavior of users, clues can be obtained to needs and uses—clues which are useful to the information systems analyst because they take into account personal qualities and idiosyncracies usually ignored by exclusively "hardware" approaches to information system design. Some individuals, for example, use very little information. The intuitive individual uses information only as a casual check upon his intuitive abilities. More often than not he does not seek corroborative evidence, unless the penalty of misusing the information—making a wrong decision, taking a risk, or missing an opportunity—is extremely grave. Another class of information user, whom we might call the "information hoarder," never seems to get enough information. One might argue that such individuals probably make very little use of the information they hoard. Nevertheless, their life styles—the pattern of their day, their work habits, their choice of friends—are all heavily influenced by at least an apparent need for information.

In sum, almost every task in operating a government program, or manufacturing a product in private industry, requires the collection and processing of information. The cost of information resources used represents a very substantial fraction of the total costs. Data costs also usually represent a significant burden on the individuals and organizations from whom the information is collected. It is in the consideration of alternative ways and means to satisfy information requirements, in the first instance, that the manager has options available to him in several areas. His choice of options can significantly affect the total costs to the organization.

WHERE ARE WE HEADED?

Before getting any further into the anatomy and physiology of the information requirements planning process, it may be well to reveal where we are headed. Bluntly, why do we plan information needs, and what will we do with the information once we get it? One direct and simple use of such information will be the development of a management tool to allow managers to ask the question: Why is Product B twice as "information and paperwork-intensive" as Product C? Or, in government, why does Program B require twice as much information and paperwork handling resources as does Program C?

In Figure 6-2, we see that it is possible to construct a simple ratio of information costs to total costs. We might call this, simply, the "Information/Paperwork Intensity Ratio." We see in Figure 6-2 that

1. *THE "FORMULA"*

$$\frac{\text{INFORMATION} + \text{PAPERWORK COSTS}}{\text{TOTAL PROGRAM COSTS}} = \text{INFORMATION/PAPERWORK INTENSITY RATIO}$$

2. *THE INTENSITY . . . WHERE TO ANALYZE*

PRODUCT	*RANKING*	*INFORMATION/PAPERWORK INTENSITY RATIO*
B	1	(1:3)
C	2	1:6
A	3	1:7
D	4	1:8 why?

3. *POSSIBLE TRADEOFFS IN BUDGET REVIEW*

Between Information Resources and Other Resources

- Ratio of Information Overhead to Direct Activities of the Program (or Product)
- Information Intensity of Program (or Product)
- Source of Intensity (e.g., People Systems vs. Hardware Systems; Complex Directives)
- Frequency of Data
- Quantity of Information Collected

AMONG INFORMATION SOURCES

- Existing Information vs. Newly Developed Information
- Intermediate vs. Originals
- Derived vs. Absolute/Specific
- Summarized vs. Detailed

***Figure 6-2.* Planning information requirements**

if we are successful in planning information requirements, we can then, as we will see in the next few chapters, both cost and budget those requirements.

Of course ratios, per se, tell us very little. They do, however, give us a *point of departure, a strategy, a pathway upon which to proceed,* to then begin asking the more relevant and pertinent questions. In short, they help us ask better questions, rather than give us answers. Let us return now to the planning process, after having "lifted the curtain" a little on where we are headed.

THREE PRIMARY ACTORS

The roles of three primary "actors" are central to any discussion of planning information requirements, whether in a Government or private industry or some other context. To make the context of what follows as broadly applicable as possible, the nouns used are generic:

- the *collector* of the information. In private industry, this would be the operating unit (e.g., a plant, an entire division, a product line, or whatever); in government, the agency at Federal, State or local level;
- the *provider* of the information. In private industry, again, this would be the unit which furnishes the information to a sister unit, under some kind of transfer pricing or charge-back procedure; in government, the agency which furnishes the information to a sister agency, under some kind of interagency billing agreement; the provider, in the case of the government, could be the public—a citizen, a business, or other;
- the *organization as a whole.* In private industry, the proprietor, partnership, or corporation as a whole; in government, the level of government—Federal, a State, or a local unit of government.

Options and alternatives to minimize information needed by managers should be considered at each stage of data planning. At each stage, steps should be taken to reduce or eliminate excessively costly collection. We will come back to these three actors. But first, let us zero-in, microscopic fashion, on the information requirements process itself. In preceding chapters we looked at the information process in a somewhat telescopic fashion, that is, peering outward to see how information resources fit in the broader scheme of things. We saw that information needs, ultimately, relate back to statutory prescriptions, at least in the case of government, and to corporate goals in the case of the private industry sector. In Figure 6-3 we continue our examination with a more detailed scrutiny of the information *requirements determination* process, proceeding from the premise that there is indeed, *some* kind of need, but its shape and form is as yet indeterminate and amorphous.

As we proceed to examine the information flow process, we quickly must stop at point "K" in Figure 6-3 because an understanding of

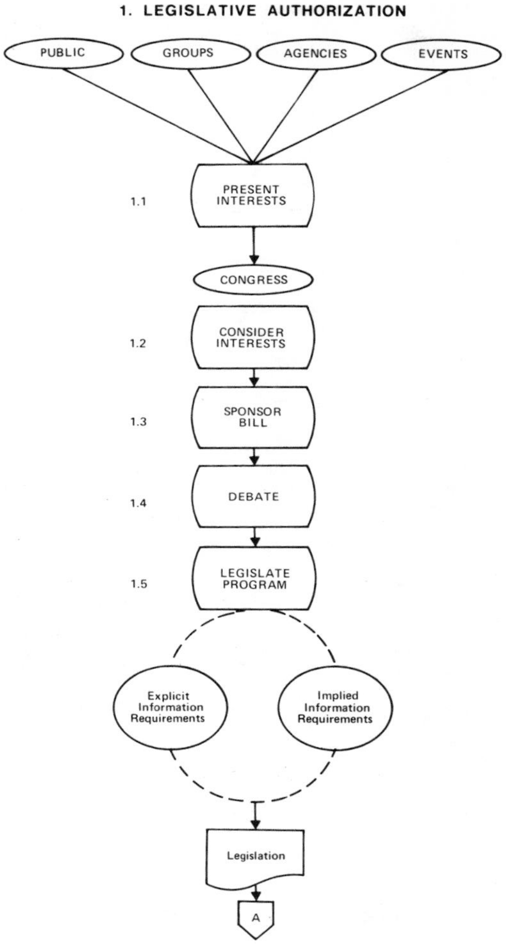

Figure 6-3. **Determining information requirements for use with Appendix B**

information needs requires first some discussion of the anatomy and physiology of information. We promised earlier to move into the laboratory and will do so now, under the heading the "six attributes of data." Oftentimes writers will reduce the six factors to three or four, such as "timely, accurate and complete." Sometimes relevancy is added. We suggest those attributes are partially responsive to our needs, but we must go further.

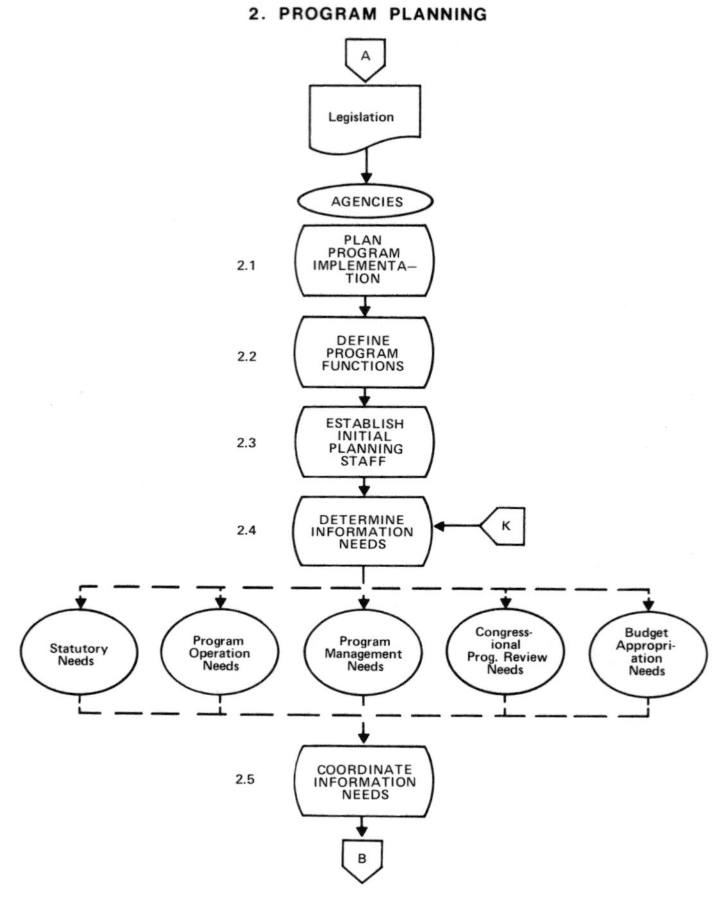

Figure 6-3. (Continued)

SIX ATTRIBUTES OF DATA

In considering alternative information options, it is useful to consider choices in the context of six fundamental attributes of data itself;

- subject;
- scope;
- measure;
- time;
- source; and
- quality and precision

The manager's freedom to explore these options is constrained to

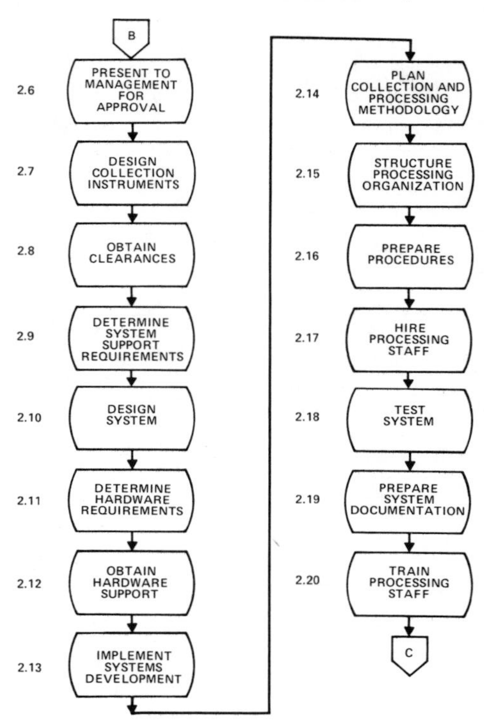

Figure 6-3. (Continued)

various degrees of organizational goals and objectives. In what follows each of the option areas will be defined and illustrated with examples showing the manager's range of discretion.

Subject and Scope. The first attribute, *subject,* refers to a particular event, person, place or thing. For example, the subject attribute of a particular set of data might be *employees.* The second attribute, *scope,* defines, bounds and circumscribes the subject attribute and acts as a kind of modifier or limiter. In a sense, scope might be considered a sub-part of the subject dimension. Continuing with our example of a set of data dealing with employees, the scope attribute might be *position titles, tour of duty, names and addresses, retirement eligibility,* and so on.

The attribute of *scope* connotes the extent or comprehensiveness of information about an event, person, place or thing. The information may range from the least comprehensive, namely, just the fact of the

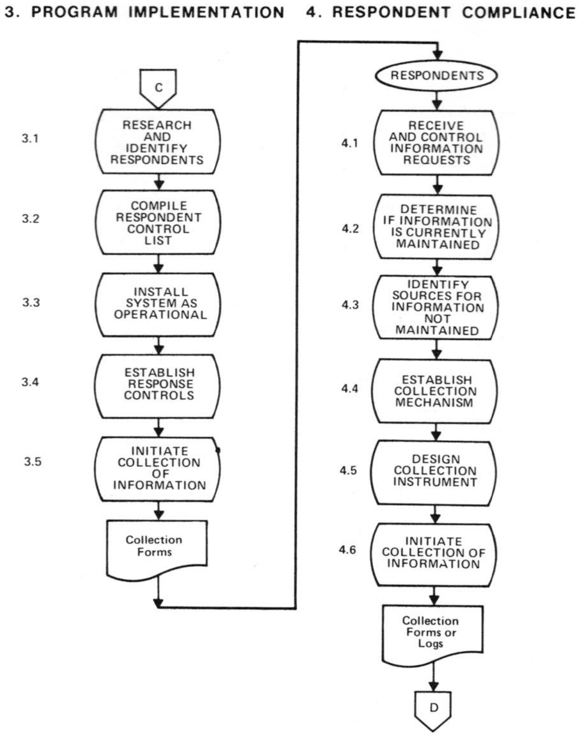

3. PROGRAM IMPLEMENTATION

C

3.1 RESEARCH AND IDENTIFY RESPONDENTS

3.2 COMPILE RESPONDENT CONTROL LIST

3.3 INSTALL SYSTEM AS OPERATIONAL

3.4 ESTABLISH RESPONSE CONTROLS

3.5 INITIATE COLLECTION OF INFORMATION

Collection Forms

4. RESPONDENT COMPLIANCE

RESPONDENTS

4.1 RECEIVE AND CONTROL INFORMATION REQUESTS

4.2 DETERMINE IF INFORMATION IS CURRENTLY MAINTAINED

4.3 IDENTIFY SOURCES FOR INFORMATION NOT MAINTAINED

4.4 ESTABLISH COLLECTION MECHANISM

4.5 DESIGN COLLECTION INSTRUMENT

4.6 INITIATE COLLECTION OF INFORMATION

Collection Forms or Logs

D

Figure 6-3. (Continued)

existence of the event, person, place or thing, or it may include any of the characteristics. For example, a Federal program dealing with energy conservation may only require information regarding whether a barrel of oil exists in some stockpile somewhere. On the other hand it may require information as to size, shape, weight, viscosity, sulphur content, age, ownership, purchase price, and so on.

Measure. The third attribute, the dimension of *measure* defines the unit of count or measure in which the subject is conventionally expressed. For example, in the case of employee data, a number of different measure units are possible: *persons, man-years, man-hours, male or female,* and so on. Some measure attributes may be considered the same if they have a common denominator and are convertible. For example, man-years and man-hours can be the same where they share a common denominator of 2,080 hours representing one man-year. (Other standard multipliers are, of course, possible).

Time. Next, the attribute of *time* identifies a point in time, or a

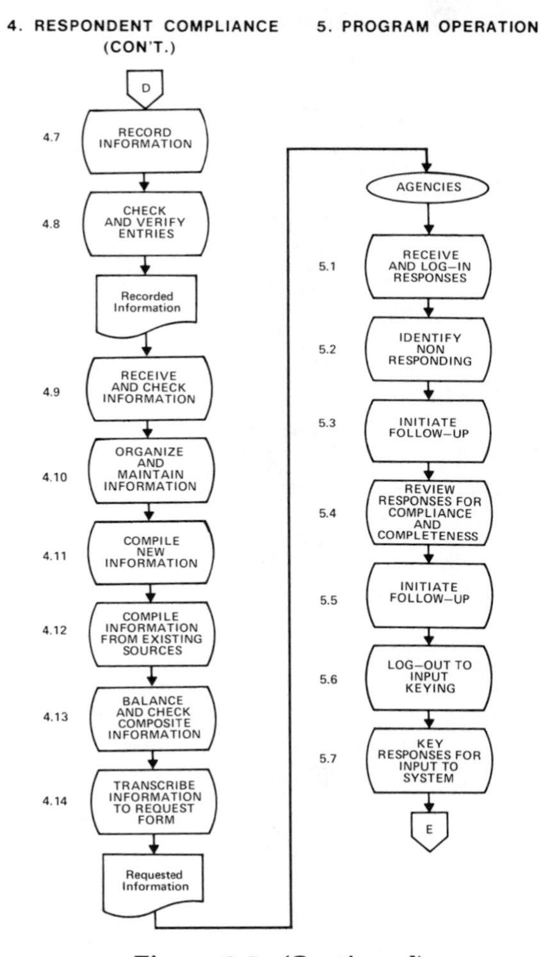

Figure 6-3. (Continued)

time span, represented by the data. Some examples of the time dimension are: *end of calendar month, fiscal year, fiscal quarter, calendar years,* and so on. An example is the time lag allowed in reporting. This is typically called the "as of" date. The information may be reported "as of" the end of the last quarter or "as of" an hour ago. In the extreme, real-time reporting may be required (e.g., location of aircraft in a holding pattern at a precise time).

Source. The *source* attribute identifies the origin of the data and, in a sense, acts as a scope and subject limiter. Data source identification has two other values. First, it is an indicator of reliability and ultimately

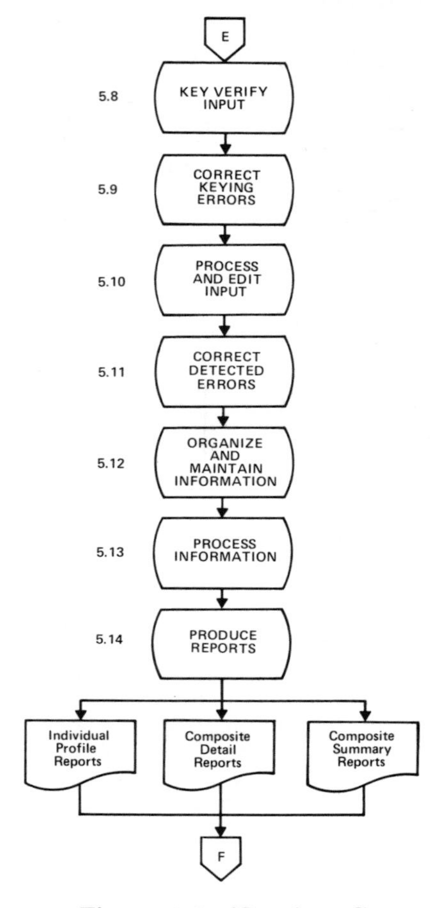

Figure 6-3. (Continued)

of the utility of data for a given use. Secondly, identification of the source of the data is essential to prevention of duplication. Examples of the source attributes include: *company files and records, almanacs and encyclopedias, personnel dossiers, official Government reports, academic treatises and dissertations,* and so forth. Generally, there is a direct correlation between the specificity of the source identity and the utility of the data; that is, the more specific the source identity, the higher the data utility. Conversely, the more general the source, the more ambiguous and difficult the problems of interpretation.

Quality and Precision. Finally we come to the *quality/precision*

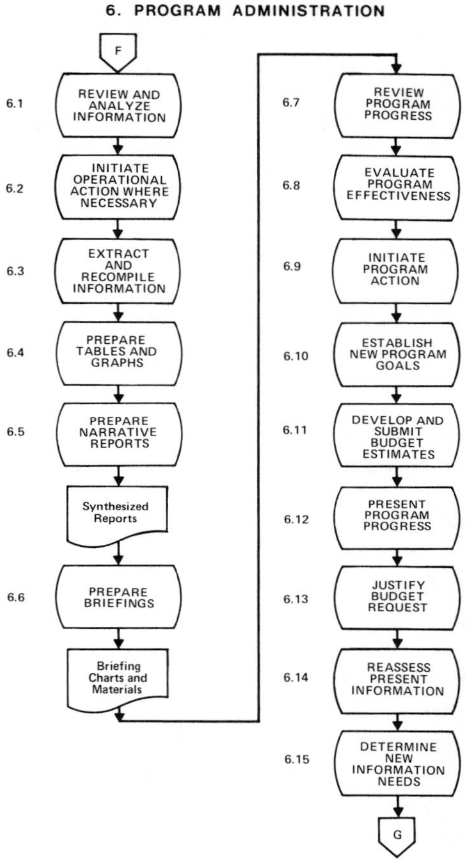

6. PROGRAM ADMINISTRATION

F

6.1	REVIEW AND ANALYZE INFORMATION
6.2	INITIATE OPERATIONAL ACTION WHERE NECESSARY
6.3	EXTRACT AND RECOMPILE INFORMATION
6.4	PREPARE TABLES AND GRAPHS
6.5	PREPARE NARRATIVE REPORTS
	Synthesized Reports
6.6	PREPARE BRIEFINGS
	Briefing Charts and Materials
6.7	REVIEW PROGRAM PROGRESS
6.8	EVALUATE PROGRAM EFFECTIVENESS
6.9	INITIATE PROGRAM ACTION
6.10	ESTABLISH NEW PROGRAM GOALS
6.11	DEVELOP AND SUBMIT BUDGET ESTIMATES
6.12	PRESENT PROGRAM PROGRESS
6.13	JUSTIFY BUDGET REQUEST
6.14	REASSESS PRESENT INFORMATION
6.15	DETERMINE NEW INFORMATION NEEDS

G

Figure 6-3. (Continued)

attribute, which embraces a number of components, including accuracy, level of detail and uniformity. Quality addresses the basic questions of credibility, reliability and validity, whereas precision deals with error tolerance, either in the original collection, or in gathering, or in value estimation and significance interpretation of the data, or in all three of these steps.

Accuracy deals with required correctness of the information. This may range from "triple checked and audited," to a +/−10% or similar tolerance. In some cases errors can be acceptable if their numbers and magnitude will not significantly affect the results desired.

Level of detail deals with the "fineness" of the information. In some cases numeric data may be needed with precision to many decimal places (e.g., parts per million of smoke for air pollution measurements). In other cases data reported to the nearest hundred may be acceptable (e.g., estimates of numbers of tourists visiting National Parks each year).

Uniformity deals with the amount of formating required in the reported data. In extreme cases the data must be reported in exactly the format the government requires (e.g., filling out an application form which will be keypunched). In other cases a handwritten paragraph may be acceptable (e.g., contractor's experience resume).

The foregoing discussion of the six attributes of data have set the stage for a clearer articulation of information needs. What must appear obvious to us now is that there are important and undeniable trade-offs that we must address between and among these attributes before we can definitively state our information requirements. The layman knows intuitively that the attributes of time and cost, for example, are directly interchangeable with accuracy and precision. Thus, with each information-related decision and problem, the office worker with access to the telephone must ask himself or herself: Can I make a rough estimate, a judgment myself, or should I corroborate my estimate with another source? How much time do I have to make the decision or solve the problem? And the busy houseperson who wants to call his or her neighbor may decide to use the telephone directory or alternatively call the information operator. As everyone knows, calling the information operator is becoming expensive, and, once again a benefit: cost dimension must be considered. And so the examples are endless.

When we move to a more technical and hopefully "scientific" treatment of the problem, the same principles are involved, but our matrix of trade-off permutations and combinations is much larger. We can, and must, for example, trade scope with time, alternative units of measure with one another, and cost with all of the attributes, not time alone. Instead of dealing with these permutations piecemeal, or in a purely theoretical view, let's look at them "systematically," in the context of an organization's problems. An organization—any organization—must consider options.

COST IMPLICATIONS OF THE OPTIONS

It is necessary, in assessing the relative worthiness of various competing options, to consider the cost effects of shifting program information requirements. For example, a typical cost curve for all of the options faced by government in collecting data from the public is shown in Figure 6-4. There is usually some point (A) which represents the minimum level of the option which could possibly be accepted

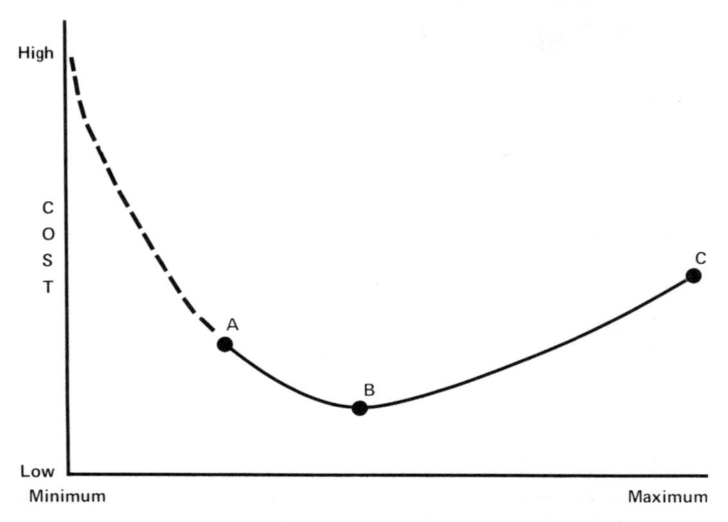

Figure 6-4. **Typical government cost/burden curve**

by the government agency, or by any "collector," whether in government or elsewhere, referring back to our discussion of the three "actors."

Extra work may be required within the agency at point (A), however, to make the data useful (e.g., handwritten or free form data must be put into the proper forms by clerks). Point (B) is the optimum point for the collector. Data reported with this scope, accuracy, etc., are exactly matched to the collector's system for using the data. Data reported with scope, accuracy, etc. beyond point (B) tend to become more expensive for the collector to process (e.g., must be summarized for managers to use).

Recall our second "actor" was the provider or respondent. The provider's typical cost curve for responding to a requirement is shown in Figure 6-5. It starts at (Y), where no data are being collected, and rises toward (Z) where everything possible is being collected. In the extreme case (Z), the provider may even have to go elsewhere to collect data not ordinarily required to support his own operations and business.

BENEFIT/VALUES VS. COST/BURDENS

Returning to our organizational setting, in considering which "preferred" options to choose, the manager *must carefully consider and weigh the cost implications of the options on both his own operation*

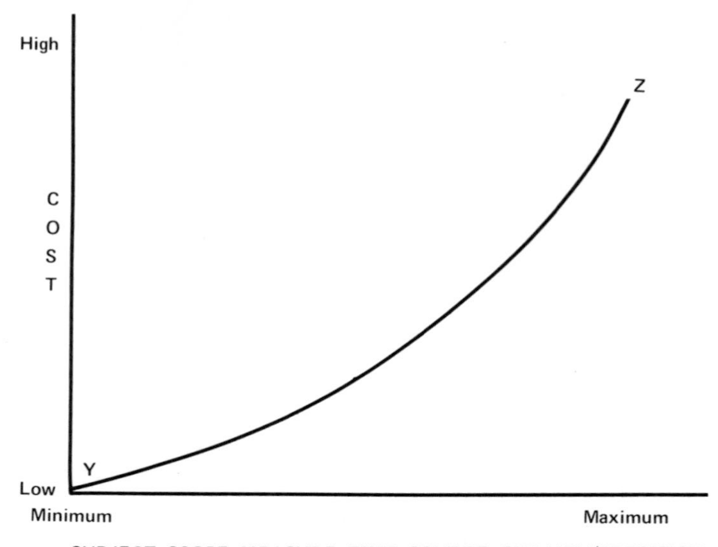

Figure 6-5. **Typical respondent cost/burden curve**

and on the organization as a whole. There are three possible interactions of the two curves. These are shown in Figure 6-6. First, the collector's curve, ABC, is shown as before the curve YZ1 shows a situation where the provider's costs rise very rapidly with an increase in any of the options. Provider's cost at B are excessive. Even at A they are far out of proportion with the collector's costs. There is no point in this situation where the provider can meet the collector's minimum requirements except at prohibitive cost.

Next, with curve YZ2 there is point Q where the provider's costs are more nearly in line with the collector's costs. This is not necessarily the least cost situation for the collector, *but there can be justification for the organization as a whole absorbing more of the data costs in this situation.*

Finally, with curve YZ3 provider costs go up very slowly and are always well below the collector's costs. In this case the manager is free to choose point B to minimize his own costs.

SELECTING THE PREFERRED ALTERNATIVE

There are two principal timeframes in which the manager should react to the situation described above. In the short-term he should

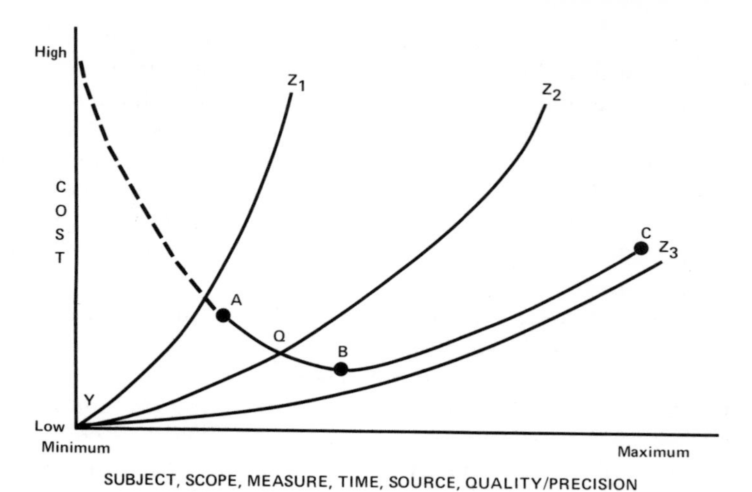

Figure 6-6. **Government / respondent cost / burden relationships**

try to select the option which is the least burdensome from an overall standpoint. This may mean the collector's costs are higher relative to the provider's costs, in some situations. In the longer term, the manager should focus his information R&D efforts on three areas:

- to reduce direct costs by developing more effective methods and techniques for handling data at all option levels;
- to extend the organization's ability to accept information in the low end of the option area (to avoid the situation where the provider's curve and the collector's curve do not intersect); and
- to seek methods for reducing the provider's costs in areas where improvements will reduce overall costs, and especially where improvements will also reduce costs.

In the absence of overriding policy or similar constraints, the top manager would normally select the preferred option which *minimizes the overall costs to the organization as a whole, even in instances where the collector's costs (for example, to an internal division) may be somewhat higher than the provider's costs.*

Curves may be plotted in terms of political and social costs as well as in terms of direct and measurable economic costs. A weighting scheme to bring the various curves into line with each other could be developed in consultation with appropriate budget, planning, and other managers.

After the manager has completed a review of the fundamental

organizational goals and objectives, considered the information options and alternatives from the standpoint of broad information requirements, he is on firmer ground as to why information is needed, what purposes it is authorized to serve, and who are the providers, collectors, and users of the information. Next the manager requires complete "profiles" of what is needed in the way of specific items of information to satisfy objectives. These profiles should be sufficiently explicit so that they can be used later during information system design and for improvement of input forms and products.

Profiles should specify input types, the depth of detail necessary, and other matters, such as sources and timing. There are many kinds of "profiles" of major information needs that might be articulated. Certainly any for-profit organization must have a good handle on its cost inflows vis-a-vis its outflows. One of the headings below, then, goes to cost implications. There is also fairly widespread agreement that any organization, profit or not-for-profit, must learn to separate the wheat from the chaff. In some of the management literature this admonition is often referred to as "Management by Exception" or simply "Management Reporting." Beyond these considerations, we must know about workload and operational bottlenecks. All of these considerations may seem too "management oriented" to the scientist and professional. I apologize for having to pick examples selectively and confess I am leaning heavily to the organizational rather than individual context once more.

CURRENT INFORMATION

A first consideration should be to look at the immediate needs for current, up-to-date information. Most managers rely on certain "key data indicators" for this purpose. Such material is often kept within arm's reach. It usually has been developed out of past crises rather than from a general plan. Its value is very great, although it is not always recognized as part of the established information system. Key data indicator information may deal with such things as, for example, daily bed occupancy and turnover by some or all of the wards in a hospital or, in government, the number of passports applied for yesterday, the number processed thus far this month, and the unprocessed backlog.

Each activity in a program has a potential for producing a number of key data indicators. Policies for developing a rational and responsive system of key data indicators can be summarized as follows:

General Criteria for Selecting Indicators

(a) Limit objectives to providing advance information and to serving for cross-checking and trouble-shooting purposes.
(b) Choose those key data which are consistent (or easily relatable) as to time and content.
(c) Use only those data which can be obtained at minimum or no additional cost. (much key data can be obtained as a by-product of a necessary process, such as receipt, recording and routing of new applications, nurses' daily ward reports, and similar activities).
(d) Avoid data which require several processing steps or which call for clerical judgment.

More Specific Guidelines

(a) Keep the level of difficulty of selecting data no greater than the capacity of a new employee after basic training.
(b) Assure that data are unrefined, highly reliable, and up-to-date. (Remember, some progress reports, supposedly up-to-the-minute, may contain feeder data covering 90 to 120 days!)
(c) Obtain key data from gathering points which have already been established to perform normal processing activities.

The purpose of these policies is to obtain key data quickly, inexpensively, with a minimum of bias, and as reliably and automatically as possible. There are many media other than "hard copy" which can be useful for obtaining key data indicators, if appropriate. These include telephone, wire, messenger, computer-to-computer, and even more sophisticated media, such as facsimile transmission or cassettes—machine language or verbal recordings. The general policies discussed above apply also to selecting a medium. It is especially important that:

(a) the media selected work readily with normal procedures, and
(b) that the media selected be cost-effective.

There are some warnings which should be heeded when obtaining key data indicators by word-of-mouth. For example, there are situations wherein information is obtained through the "eyes and ears" of trusted lieutenants. Some managers hold early morning coffee breaks during which certain staff members are expected to pass along their observations and speculations on operations and situations likely to affect the manager. Sometimes staff meetings are used for this purpose. Generally speaking, this type of key data input is both inefficient and dangerous. It is not orderly and consistent. It is fraught with individual judgment and bias. A better use of staff meetings and individual consultations is for planning, policy making and difficult decision-making. It is good policy to avoid unstructured, word-of-mouth key data input.

INFORMATION ON CRITICAL SITUATIONS

An important part of a manager's information, which is often overlooked in developing an information resource, can be categorized as "Significant Events." There are problem situations, crises, cases which are "hot-to-handle" (because of personal, social, or economic problems), and other unusual occurrences. "Outsiders" are almost always involved to a substantial degree. For this reason, if for no other, "significant events" reporting is necessary.

In general, managers have felt that critical situations, being unpredictable, cannot be reported in a systematic manner. This is an error. There are practical, workable methods by which significant happenings, emergency problems, and difficult situations can be recognized early and be reported so that timely action can be taken.

General policies and guidelines to obtain timely and accurate information on critical situations are stated below:

(a) Turn first to those elements in your operations which process new cases or projects (applications, claims, entitlements, adjudication, etc.). Make it a policy that operating personnel bring to the attention of their supervisors any case or project which does not fit established norms because of delays, confusing data, complaints, personalities, or other problems.

(b) Second, require operating personnel who process older cases and projects to report those which have reached certain significant phases or have encountered abnormal difficulties.

(c) Third, if there are established complaint groups, have these people provided with instructions similar to those given to processing personnel, as regards to critical situations.

(d) Fourth, provide supervisors with training and instructions so that appropriate cases will be reported to you, and all cases will be taken care of without undue delay.

Unlike key data indicators, which concern normal processing, "Significant Events" reporting calls for use of judgment on the part of senior clerks and supervisors. In fact, this type of reporting provides the manager with a measure of the level of judgment being exercised in his program.

OPERATIONAL REPORTING

Regular, established reports on operations have been considered to be the backbone of most information systems. These reports include statistical and financial data, trend analyses, information considered to be of value to the administrative history of an activity, or similar materials reflecting the administration of a program and events likely to affect its management. Too often, the accumulation of monthly, quarterly, annual and other reports becomes monolithic in structure and overwhelming in quantity, as far as the individual manager is concerned. Among the problems encountered in Operational Reporting is a tendency to attempt to provide for all information needs. Realistically speaking, such an attempt cannot but fail.

For example, Operational Reporting often tries to provide key data indicators. This effort is almost always too little, too late, and off the mark as far as many of the managers are concerned. It is seldom geared to the needs of the individual manager. In other words, operational reports are awkward, expensive, and nonresponsive media for key data indicators. The same can be said of information on critical situations. Operational reports cannot provide for the rapid response needs of managers. A reasonable proof of these observations can be found in the amount of specialized data being collected by most successful managers, independent of, or supplementary to, the operation reports.

Operational reporting can impose onerous requirements on clients as well as internal personnel. Many a special report or lines in a regular report required from clients are used only for statistical or financial summaries in an operational report. Usually, with a little thought and imagination, similar but more useful information could have been developed from data at hand.

As a matter of policy, input from clients should be held to that minimum needed and not sought solely to provide data for reporting on operations. Another weakness of operational reports, frequently, is their failure to coordinate with the general records, sometimes called the data base, of the organization. In general, records (manual or machine) contain the best and most complete information on activities. Information in records which are conveniently available and structured along functional lines can be used and referred to by operational reports, but they should not be duplicated in function or even extensively summarized.

The foregoing comments are, indeed, critical of operational reporting. However, there is a real need by managers for good operational reporting, especially to provide statistical and financial trends essential to an individual manager's operations and to provide summaries on general activities from time to time.

Basic policy to assure good, responsive operational reporting is to view such reporting in terms of the entire scope of information resources available to managers. It should be used only for purposes for which it is best suited. Operational reporting should not attempt to be the single source of processed information. Specifically, to achieve the objectives of the basic policy, the guidelines given below should be followed.

(a) Ascertain which trends are essential to know and therefore needed by a manager. (A manager will usually find that he needs fewer, but sharper, statistical and financial trend data.)
(b) Require operational summaries only of specific value for planning, formulating policy, and budgeting.
(c) Avoid overlapping with other information resources.
(d) Provide for a review of submissions by clients, to eliminate input for operational reporting. (Clients provide base data for program services; operational reporting should begin when operations begin—subsequent to client input).

A SUMMING UP

Planning information requirements is no different from planning other resource needs. As when we are deciding on personnel, or how many dollars, or how much space, deciding how much and what kind of information we need confronts us with pitfalls and opportunities remarkably similar. If we are careful, and look circumspectly at trade-offs, using a knowledge of the six attributes of data, our requirements should be defined more sharply and with greater utility and specificity. Therefore, when the actual data begins to flow, our expectations of what we *should* be getting, and what we *in fact* are getting, should match more closely.

But planning is, at bottom, a dynamic process, as are all of the other management processes and the intuitive, heuristic processes as well. Our information requirements are not immutable; they do not "stand still." Instead, they change with time, with circumstances, with shifting priorities, with changing opportunities and with new risks that must be taken into account. Therefore, our processes for planning information requirements must take this dynamic character into account. That is why management theorists are so fond of talking about "closing the feedback loop." The example which by now is almost an overworn cliche, is the air-conditioning thermostat. The thermostat as we all know, is self-regulating when it works. But as we found in the energy crisis, turning the thermostat off and opening the windows may be impossible in our walled-in, glassed-in society. In building after building, we've found the windows simply won't open! I believe there is a lesson here for information system designers. Make sure we can still open the windows and let some fresh air in; after all, in the end a self-regulating device may be self-defeating.

QUESTIONS FOR DISCUSSION

1. Planning for information may be said to embrace both the substance of information needs and the resources needed to collect, handle, store, process, use and disseminate the information. Again, then, the dichotomy between the information process, and the information resources, is posed. Should we plan for the two simultaneously? In tandem? In short, how do relate the planning *function* to two different kinds of needs: a process and a resource?

2. Some authors make a distinction between *strategic* planning and *tactical or operational* planning. The former concerns itself with the truly crucial elements of the organization's livelihood—its distinctive market niche, growth, return on investment, product lines, and so on—while the latter is concerned with means for achieving those ends and "housekeeping" matters. In the context of this chapter's focus—planning information requirements—what kind of an information product or service might be needed by an insurance company, for example, for strategic planning purposes? What kind of product or service for operational planning? Extend the question to other kinds of industries and activities.

3. Can a professional inventor ever "plan his or her information needs?" How about a composer; artist; or author? Is there any difference in the *processes* by which the information needs of professions which tend to be creative and innovative are satisfied, versus more prosaic work and endeavor? If so, what is the character of that difference? (Note we are not here talking about the quality or substance of the information itself, but the systems and procedures by which the data

is collected, handled, stored, used and disseminated).

4. One important technique borrowed from the business and financial worlds that the information planner can use is the "Make versus Buy" technique. That is, at what point is it cheaper to produce information needed in-house, rather than purchase it from outside the organization. What factors should go into the make/buy calculation? Select information products and services across a range of the market spectrum (e.g. a single periodical at the one extreme, or one-time survey purchase, to a multi-million dollar, highly complex technical information system).

FOOTNOTES

[1]Ronen, Joshua and Sadan, Simcha, "*Corporate Financial Information for Government Decision-Making,*" (A research Study and report prepared for the Financial Executives Research Foundation, 1975) pp. 7–12 and pp. 100–111. This document was of special use to the Commission on Federal Paperwork's Study of "Segmented Financial Reporting." It appears as one of a very few authoritative works which probe the interface between government's insatiable appetite for data and industry's boundless reservoir of data.

7 INFORMATION BUDGETING

Existing budget classification schemes do not adequately illuminate how budget funds are expended. The primary reason in my view is that existing schemes are oriented to the needs and character of an industrial society and do not take into account the radical changes which have taken place in the last two decades in the post-industrial work place or the office. As we have progressed to increasingly automated modes of handling information in the post-industrial society, corresponding changes have not taken place in the way organizations account for, budget for, and manage the funds which they use.

When the Commission on Federal Paperwork tried to determine, in the aggregate, paperwork, information and communication activity costs to the Federal Government, it was unable to do so because such costs simply were not captured in this way and summed in the Government's financial accounts. Existing accounting and budgeting schemes both understated the full magnitude of such costs and in many cases mis-characterized their nature and relative importance. Only a few examples are needed to make the point.

For one, take the mail operations of any organization. Traditionally, "mail" is viewed by the accountant and management analyst as bundles of letters, documents, reports, publications, and a certain amount of "junk mail" which enters the organization every day. It is sorted and pigeon-holed into boxes for later distribution to the various components of the organization. The key "mail unit of measure" involved is the *document* or multiples of documents. In any event, productivity and accounting controls over mail operations are typically oriented to the handling of documents—their receipt, sorting, collating, recording, registering, organizing, storing, retrieving, reorganizing, packaging and so forth.

The came the computer and communication advances of the Fifties and the Sixties, and we entered the Information Age. "Mail" quickly became a somewhat ambiguous notion. Is data and information transmitted over high speed telecommunication lines to be considered "mail?" Is information moved instantaneously and directly from a buying organization's computer to a selling organization's computer, via magnetic tape transmission, "mail?" A few organizations have made this data processing transition smoothly and have taken the necessary decisions and actions to transform their old accounting labels and approaches to new ones. Perhaps "mail" was redefined as "communications" and an effort made to reidentify and recapture the full costs associated with this new accounting activity, *communications.* But most organizations didn't bother; they tried to limp along. To this day, in many cases, we are operating with buggy whip accounting and budgeting classification concepts in the Information Age.

Mail is but one example; another is Reproduction and Printing. Here, once again, there have been radical changes in the very character of the processes involved. For example, where the computer's output leaves off and the "formal printing activity" begins becomes hazy. The line is indistinct. Why? Because, once more, the nature of the operations being performed has been fundamentally transformed from what it was less than a quarter century ago. The move has been to *data and information processing* in a world where "printing" is no longer some isolatable, distinct operation "at the end of the line." Rather, printing and reprographic operations take place *as an integral and sometimes inseparable component of integrated data processing systems.* Is it any wonder, then, when budget officials are pondering requested budgets to defray the costs of operating enormously expensive central printing plants, they fume and sputter when such requests, they know full well, understate the specific character and magnitude of the total organizational printing budget? Because so much of the cost is hidden and buried throughout many overhead and direct accounts, "printing is only one, and sometimes the smallest account." A big chunk of such cost is carried under "data processing" labels.

All of this begs the question: of course there is a certain overlap between the newer data processing budget line item and the more traditional accounting categorizations with which the organization deals such as mail, printing, and telephone. But so what. We could go on with a discussion of the "telephone" classification. But I hope the point has been made. Suffice it to say that *budgeting for information not only helps us manage our information resources more efficiently and effectively, but helps us take a giant stride toward "rationalizing" our overall accounting and budgeting classification schemes and purging them of obsolescent traditions and approaches.* It should, thereby, help reduce a great deal of overlap and ambiguity among accounting designations.

A program for recycling data and information takes on renewed importance and priority as we consider the implications of the zero-base budgeting concept discussed in earlier chapters. Recycling data and information is a natural and logical outgrowth of the concept of treating information as a resource, and reusing, renewing, and replenishing information resources is essential if zero-based budgeting is to succeed. We cannot usually just throw out expensive data investments when Congress decides a program has outlived its usefulness; we must take into account salvage value.

In acknowledging that we have entered the Information Age, changes must be effected in accounting and budgeting concepts, classification schemes, approaches and tools to assure that top management officials know how much money is being spent, for what purposes, where, and by whom. Let us see now what those changes are.

TWO DIMENSIONS

We can say that there are really two dimensions to information budgeting. One, the more direct and obvious dimension with which we've been dealing, is the idea that information budgeting should *help us to manage our information resources more efficiently and effectively by identifying such resources accurately and completely and presenting them in accounting and budgeting formats which are useful to managers and others for resource allocation and other decision-making purposes.*

The other dimension, equally important but less obvious, is that information budgeting also should put us on a path that, at best, will "clean up" what in many organizations is a rather chaotic accounting and budgeting situation. That is, improving our controls over information resources implies *improving controls over all of our resources.* Certainly the organizational head, line management officials, and staff accountants would all agree that one of the underlying purposes of an accounting and budgeting system is to assure that resource planning and utilization is accurately and completely portrayed. The system should answer the questions: For what purposes is the organization spending its monies, and what is being achieved?

We've tried to point out that, when important costs get buried in overhead and hidden in other places ("other services"), not only are information resources ineffectively employed, but human, physical, material and other resources are also "abused and misused" to the extent that there is not a good picture of what is going on in the organization. After all, as we've pointed out elsewhere, information is not "just another resource;" it is the key resource, the common denominator that welds together all of the resources. If information itself is not accurately costed and budgeted, how can we expect the other resources to be efficiently managed?

HIDDEN AND BURIED COSTS

Traditionally, in government as well as private industry, information and data costs have been fragmented in both administrative overhead and direct program or product costs. They are thus hidden from evaluation and analysis. One result has been to obscure the rising cost of information and data-related activities; another has been to mask the effective and efficient consideration by top management of alternative trade-offs between information resources and other resources.

To manage data and information, component costs must first be extracted from existing accounting categories and then combined to institute effective controls. Budgeting is not the only tool for managing information as a resource, but it certainly is one of the most important tools. It is possible, for example, to develop an "information line item" in the budget. We would proceed to:

- First, identify and extract component data and information cost items and figures; in this regard, see the next chapter on Information Accounting;
- Second, construct the total information costs for each product or service (or in government, for each program); and
- Third, conduct various analyses, such as relating costs to value; identifying cost information and data-intensive aspects of products or programs and identifying opportunities for cutting information-related costs. For example, the information intensity ratio approach we discussed.

Many costs related to the collection, processing and dissemination of information are not obvious because they have been traditionally placed under the budget category "other services" or else they have been buried in overhead accounts. It is for this reason that, to budget for information, one must first predefine the cost accounting structure for information, a procedure that is discussed at length in the next chapter.

One of the benefits of treating information as a manageable resource is that company top officials can hold each subordinate level and each department head accountable for the efficient and effective use of the information resource. Some internal organizational elements are already primarily "data handling" in character. See Figure 7-1, for example. Product and program department heads demand information and data services from these central service elements. They should be charged for those services, just as they are charged by the personnel department for personnel transactions processed. In most companies some kind of charge-back procedure is already employed for services rendered by central computer centers, communication centers, and printing plants. However, the aggregate cost of the products and services received from these organizations are usually built up from an almost

Organizations which are "Data Handling" in Character

1. Computer Centers
2. Printing and Reproduction Services
3. Mailrooms and Message Centers
4. Libraries and Information Analysis Centers
5. Reports Control Offices
6. Communication and Telecommunication Centers
7. Statistical Services
8. Record Centers and Repositories
9. Clearinghouses and Information Referral Centers
10. Data Centers and Documentation Centers
11. Paperwork Management Offices

Activities which are "Data Handling" in Nature

1. Design and Development of Information Systems, Statistical Data Systems, Data Bases and Statistical Series
2. Records Creation, Maintenance and Disposition
3. Reports Creation, Maintenance and Processing
4. Data Base Management
5. Development and Maintenance of Directives and Instructional Materials
6. Development and Maintenance of Training and Educational Materials
7. Docket and Dossier Creation, Maintenance and Disposition
8. Stenographic and Court Reporting in creating records which are printed and filed (e.g. administrative, legal, medical, financial)

Figure 7-1. **Illustrative data handling organizations and activities**

perfunctory compilation of the "big three" expense categories: salary costs, equipment costs, and material costs. At no point is the *value* of the information usually estimated and priced, much less a net "cost of information sold" figure computed.

WHICH ACTIVITIES ARE "DATA HANDLING?"

In addition to the conventional data products and services which are produced by central information service organizations for internal consumption, there are a whole array of information activities which are essentially "data handling" in character and which are undertaken by a widely disparate range of both staff and line units within the parent organization. Oftentimes these fragmented and compartmentalized units are *not* identified as a major, central information service organization like "personnel" or "supplies." For example:

- the creation, maintenance, and disposition of records;
- the creation, maintenance, and processing of reports;
- the development and maintenance of directives and instructional materials;
- the development and maintenance of training and educational materials;
- stenography and court reporting in creating records which are printed and files (administrative, legal, medical and financial); and
- docket and dossier creation, maintenance, and disposition.

So, the first step is to go through the overall organizational structure and identify, not just the obvious major information handling organizations, such as the Computer Center, the Central Library, and the Main Printing Plant, but within each major organizational sub-division, those functions and activities which themselves are data handling in character. For example, in the list above, responsibility for files and records may be, literally, anywhere on the organizational landscape. Sometimes, there is no records person at all. But as organizations get larger, particularly organizations which tend to be paperwork-intensive, the function of records management sooner or later takes shape. It may at first just be "another duty assigned" to someone's position statement. Then one person may have to devote full time to managing files and records. Eventually larger and larger units become established, until in our very largest corporations and government agencies, entire records departments become necessary.

Next, we must cost out these activities, where we may have found them. In some cases the cost may be already readily ascertainable as a "line item" in the budget. In other cases it may be hidden or buried in overhead or program accounts.

When we move to the final step of computing the actual cost of these various activities, we must eventually go to basic chart of accounts:

- personnel compensation and benefits;
- equipment acquisition and lease;
- material and supplies;
- office space acquisition and rentals;
- related contractual services; and
- other financial services.

We will pursue this procedure of costing more exhaustively in the next chapter. Suffice it to say here that the cost of the total information line item is built up and developed on the principle that, in addition to a salary, everything an employee requires to do the job of creating and processing data and information should be counted as a cost, regardless of physical format, handling medium, location in the organization, or location in the master chart of accounts. See Figure 7-2.

AN ACTION-FORCING MECHANISM

Until now, managers and organizations have not looked upon data as a manageable or budgetable resource and tried to package the data resource as a line item in the budget in the same way we've traditionally packaged human, physical, financial and even natural resources. As a result, we've never had what some might call an "action-forcing mechanism" to hold managers accountable for the efficient and effective use of the data resource.

For example, can anyone imagine that a manager might hire, transfer, promote or fire his human resources in any manner he chose? Hardly. There is a well established and detailed set of rules, guidelines, sanctions and even rewards which tell us exactly how we should accomplish those actions. Come budget time we are told precisely how to define, measure and count bodies. We are directed to tally both positions authorized and on-board, as well as man-years, by a host of variables—organizational sub-unit, expense class, permanent

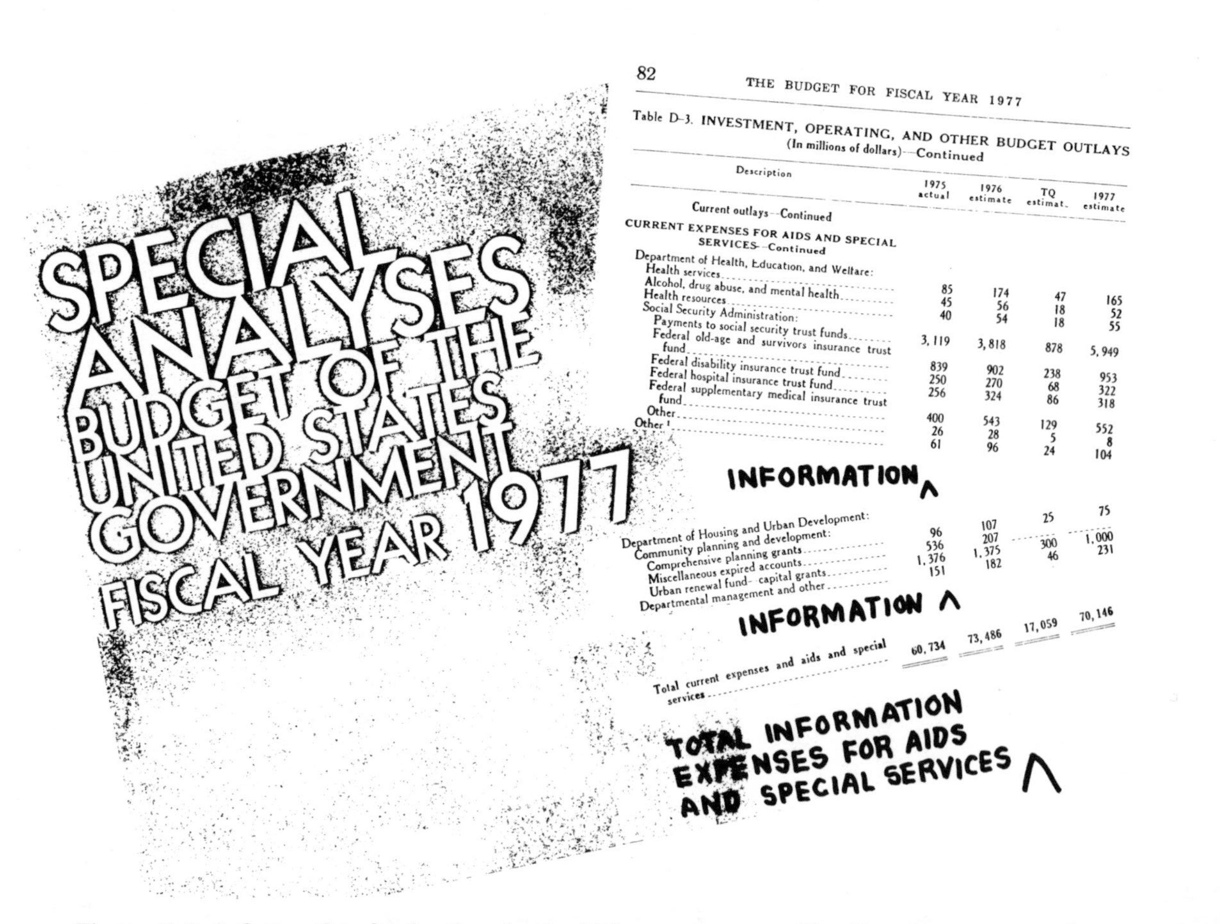

82 THE BUDGET FOR FISCAL YEAR 1977

Table D-3. INVESTMENT, OPERATING, AND OTHER BUDGET OUTLAYS
(In millions of dollars)—Continued

Description	1975 actual	1976 estimate	TQ estimate	1977 estimate
Current outlays—Continued				
CURRENT EXPENSES FOR AIDS AND SPECIAL SERVICES—Continued				
Department of Health, Education, and Welfare:				
Health services	85	174	47	165
Alcohol, drug abuse, and mental health	45	56	18	52
Health resources	40	54	18	55
Social Security Administration:				
Payments to social security trust funds	3,119	3,818	878	5,949
Federal old-age and survivors insurance trust fund	839	902	238	953
Federal disability insurance trust fund	250	270	68	322
Federal hospital insurance trust fund	256	324	86	318
Federal supplementary medical insurance trust fund	400	543	129	552
Other	26	28	5	8
Other [1]	61	96	24	104
Department of Housing and Urban Development:				
Community planning and development:				
Comprehensive planning grants	96	107	25	75
Miscellaneous expired accounts	536	207	----	----
Urban renewal fund—capital grants	1,376	1,375	300	1,000
Departmental management and other	151	182	46	231
Total current expenses and aids and special services	60,734	73,486	17,059	70,146

Figure 7-2. **Information budgeting in the U.S. government: The line item approach**

vs. temporary, and on and on. The Civil Service Commission in the Federal Government has a whole body of doctrine that pulls together all of these rules. At each successive level of government, there are corresponding counterparts of doctrine.

Can anyone imagine that the accountable property officer would allow us to requisition as many fancy chairs, tables, desks or typewriters as we wanted and use them for whatever purpose we wanted? Of course not. We have in this area tables of allowance and authorization schedules which prescribe standards, criteria and formulas for exactly how many of which of these commodities anyone is entitled to. The General Services Administration in Federal Government, like the Civil Service Commission, has promulgated over a long period of time a detailed body of doctrine in the area of managing and accounting for the use of assigned real and personal property resources.

The analogy can be extended to the financial and natural resources as well without straining our imaginations too much. Certainly when it comes to financial resources the rules of the game are perhaps even more inflexible and immutable, and the penalties and sanctions for misuse of public funds are even more severe.

Why is it, then, that not only is there no central, cohesive body of doctrine in the data and information resource area, but we don't always do a very good job in giving our officials informal guidance on a fragmented basis—a little bit for computers, a little bit for designing information systems, some for microform, some for reprography and so on. In few cases do we have policies, much less procedures, to guide officials in such areas as selecting possible handling media alternatives on a cost-effective basis or weighing the expected benefits of a new or upgraded information system against the total capital and operating investments costs.

PRINCIPLES OF BUDGETING

Let us look more closely now at some fundamental concepts and principles of budgeting, again relying heavily on our non-information resource analogies to get a clearer handle on how information budgeting would work.

In government, for its so-called operating programs, costs must represent the value of resources consumed or used. Budgetary guidance tells the agency budget chief that:

- for procurement and manufacturing programs, costs should represent the value of materials received or produced;

- for capital outlay programs, costs for public works should cover the value of work put in place, and costs for loan activities should represent assets acquired;
- quantified performance indicators and productivity indexes should be used to the maximum extent practicable to supplement narrative justifications, to show the outputs, manpower and cost per unit of output, total costs, and productivity trend data; productivity indexes should be based on the volume of product or services produced for use outside the organization, with due allowance for differences in the nature of individual products or services;
- measures of input may be based on the amount of manpower alone, on manpower costs, or on a more comprehensive measure of resource inputs which includes non-labor costs;
- programs must be identified in part on the basis of the adequacy of their accounting base and be related to administrative control and operations of the agency.

Clearly, none of these fundamental principles and concepts excludes the feasibility of considering information as one of the resource inputs necessary to produce an output. Indeed, if one looks closely at the official budgets prepared by those Government organizations which are exclusively "information handling" in character, such as the Census Bureau and the major statistical agencies, it readily becomes apparent that data and facts—in essence—are the "raw material" inputs, and organized and evaluated tables, charts, graphs, indices, and various other formats are the refined "output."

BUDGETING WITHIN A STATE

Kerker points out that the relationships of the overall State budget to the information "line item"—the value of data, and the cost of obtaining it—is a complex matter.[1] In the State of New York, where he is a budget officer, Kerker mentions that the problem lies not in the failure to adhere to established communication paths, but in what is communicated. That is, instead of the debate between budget officials and information managers centering on the value of the information to decision-makers, or on the cost of obtaining it, or on the consequences of not having it, it revolves around the details of running data processing installations. Instead of budgeting for outputs, the uses to which information is put, *we budget for inputs.* We budget for data processing activities, per se, not for information management. In another way of speaking, data processing is dealt with as some kind of abstraction, "standing separate and apart from the central programmatic, managerial and decision concerns of the agency."

Kerker points out that the prospects for change appear to be good because of the fiscal crisis recently confronting the State of New York. State agency heads are "increasingly having to make Hobson's choices among alternatives which seem equally unpalatable" and then, faced with budget ceilings, meat-axe decisions. In the end, Kerker lays down a challenge to the information manager by pointing out "indelicately" that he will not rise to the top of the organization unless he proves that his knowledge of his own field, data and information management, offers some substantive hope that the organization can achieve its goals more efficiently and effectively. Until now, budget officials are unpersuaded by perennial budget meetings with computer center directors who are still talking about megabytes, nanoseconds, and new minicomputers.

ZERO-BASE BUDGETING

The experience of the State of New York is not unique. Indeed, President Carter must have had a similar experience when he was Governor of the State of Georgia, or else his current Administration would not have pushed the highly touted "Zero-Base Budgeting" (ZBB) concept so hard. While it is true that much of the current "sunset" and ZBB impetus seems to be coming from dissatisfied and disgruntled legislatures and executives bristling over the unbridled growth and proliferation of new programs in the public sector, and at all levels of government—Federal, State and local—I contend that skyrocketing information costs are a big, if not the biggest fraction of the "unbridled cost of Government." To be sure inflation has taken its toll and is to some extent responsible. In a number of cases old Government programs are outmoded and simply aren't working; they must be replaced by new ones. Perhaps the fundamental goals and ideas behind the legislation were good, but somewhere along the line the idea got lost and bureaucracy took its place. It is here that we see the crucial importance of harnessing information costs, and information budgets are one critical tool we must have.

Government bureaucracies cannot grow without information. That would be like trying to culture bacteriological growth in a sterile medium. To grow, bureaucracies must have information. Information is the food of bureaucracy. The richer the diet, the greater the growth. If we turn the information faucets off, the growth dwindles and eventually dies. As bureaucracies get richer, they buy computers and expensive communication devices. Soon they are able to engage in what some have called a "stupendous bureaucratic chatter." Let us see if ZBB will help.

Zero-base budgeting proceeds from the premise that no program or product or service is sacrosanct. That is, each year, or alternatively during a limited number of years, say two or three, the fundamental purposes and goals of each program or product are placed under the microscope. In the light of current organizational priorities, economic conditions, resource constraints of all kinds, and the needs of competing programs, each program is reviewed. Many, if not most, of the programs stand the test of careful scrutiny, with perhaps minor modifications in funding and resource levels. They will probably be continued. But a significant minority, perhaps 10–15 percent, can expect to have their resource funding levels significantly curtailed, and an even smaller minority, perhaps 5 percent or less, are expected to go under. That is to say, by virtue of some combination of factors identified above (changing priorities, resource constraints or changes in underlying purposes and goals) this minority of programs will be phased out over a period of time—perhaps two to five years.

As more experience is gained with this concept in Government and industry, undoubtedly these rough percentage estimates will be refined. There is no way at this time to predict what the percentages may eventually turn out to be, but clearly there are some fundamental presumptions underlying organizations' desires to move in this direction. They are:

- a new set of choices confronts all organizations periodically, perhaps no less than every three to five years, but no more than seven to ten years;
- renewable and replenishable physical and natural resources appear to be decreasing in absolute terms if not in relative terms;
- although this country appears to be moving toward zero population growth, the same cannot be said for the rest of the world; and
- new risks and opportunities are continually presenting themselves, causing a rethinking of strategies, tactics, courses of action, management systems and management schedules.

Another factor which seems to be at work in the move to zero-base budgeting in the progressive disenchantment of the Congress, the news media and the public with the "budget game." The "budget game," as it is known in Washington, D.C., has the following characteristics:

- "the closer the better" is the unwritten rule; that is, agency commitment is based on spending precisely what is authorized—no more, no less;
- rewards are based on how effectively the above rule is carried out; the closer the budget officer gets, the higher the reward;
- end-of-the-year crush, last-minute buying is the hallmark of the budget game because managers are afraid that if they don't spend the money they have been authorized they will lose it;
- top-management doesn't like to see unspent money at the end of the fiscal year either, because Congress will then believe that agency management has been at worst devious, and at best inefficient; neither Congress nor the President really want to let the cat out of the bag; both find it more useful to play the budget game because they can blame one another.

INCREMENTAL BUDGETING

Under the incremental budgeting approach, the "going rate" principle is followed. That is, it is assumed that budgeted expenses for the coming year will be no less than for the preceding year or some average of the preceding years. This problem then is simply how much to add to the base line already established. Under the zero-base budgeting approach, a new "going rate" will be renegotiated each year at several levels:

- between individual programs and product lines and the overall organization;
- between line management and top management; and
- between plant, department and division management and headquarters.

Now it is clear that if we move (or perhaps when we move) to zero-base budgeting, none of our resource categories will escape budgetary scrutiny. Human resources, physical resources, financial resources, natural resources and *information* resources *all* will be carefully analyzed for the purpose of determining obsolescence, program goal fulfillment, or program goal irrelevancy. When and if any one or some combination of those three factors are encountered, action will be taken to cut back funding levels and scope.

Now, it is not too difficult to turn a desk or chair or typewriter back in to the accountable property officer for reissue, nor is it very difficult to turn over excess square footage of office space or laboratory space for reutilization since there is usually a shortage of available space. Accounting regulations make it crystal clear that any excess funds will be deposited to the appropriate financial accounts, and the environmental movement has seen to it that we are heavily committed to a wide range of programs to recycle our natural resources. Whether we are talking about energy resources such as gas, oil and coal, or endangered species of wild life, a body of doctrine has already been developing over the past decade that is based on the recycling principle. Papers and bottles are two common examples that come readily to mind. More exotic are programs to recycle solid waste in one form or another.

Again, though we are not so crass as to call them "recycling" programs, nonetheless it is perfectly clear that relocation programs that address the human problems faced by government employees, for example, due to base closings, outplacement programs which address similar problems for employees of agencies which go out of business, and an array of training for career employees in depressed or obsolete skill categories are only three important examples of "recycling people."

In the public sector we cannot simply discard information systems on a benefit-cost basis alone. There are important constitutional, statutory and other requirements for data collection, maintenance, retention and distribution which serve the national purpose beyond strictly cost-benefit grounds. Under any program for recycling data, a number of these alws, rules and regulations may need to be updated with the advent of zero-base budgeting. Indeed, such a review would seem absolutely essential if we are to capitalize on this huge data investment. Clearly we cannot simply jettison data systems which become obsolete and are no longer cost-effective. Rather, a carefully devised program should insure that data in the hands of an agency about to be cut back—like physical and material resources—be "advertised," "circulated," and made available to agencies which may have a need for such data but which—unlike the losing agency—are not faced with the need to dismantle their data investments.

BUDGETING IMPLICATIONS OF ADMINISTRATIVE STYLES

Another important approach which can be taken to the problem of budgeting for information is to look at information budgetary needs in the context of administrative styles. Different organizations and different key decision-makers employ a variety of styles. Their information needs, therefore, differ correspondingly. Implicit in these different styles are certain basic assumptions about information and its role in the budgetary process or, even more fundamentally, its role in the overall organization. These assumptions, in turn, influence the ways in which information about data resources might be collected and used by an organization in its budgetary process. See Figure 7-3.

One author approaches this line of attach by focusing on a classic discussion in public administration which compares and contrasts incremental styles of decision-making with comprehensive forms.[2]

INPUT VERSUS OUTPUT ORIENTED APPROACHES

Under the incremental approach, sometimes called an input-oriented approach, the basic orientation is to use whatever information is available. Here it is assumed that information is always partial and incomplete, and the incremental method tries to make the most out of what is relatively accessible. New information is not introduced

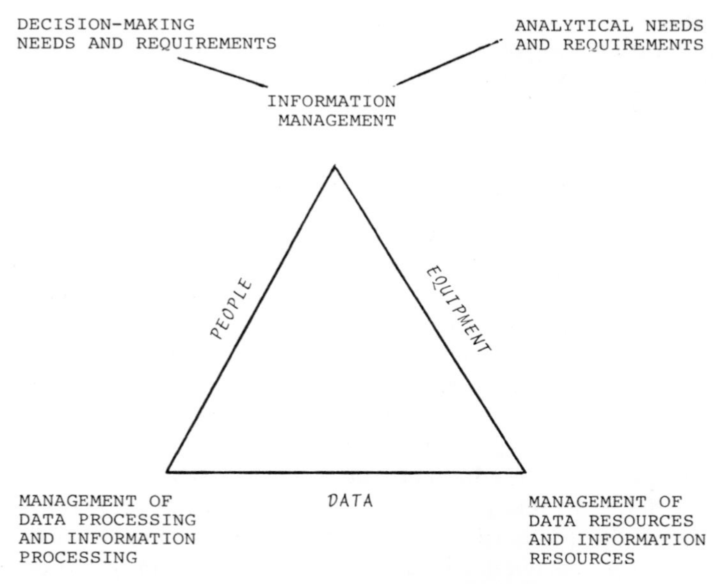

Figure 7-3. **What is information management?**

except when various organizations and individuals involved in the decision-making process feel that additional kinds of information might make a difference in the informal bargaining process. In the context of the budgetary process, this approach tends to focus on "tangible" resource accounting, defined in numbers of personnel, funds expended for the purchase of supplies and equipment, and so forth. The aim of the decision-making and information process here is decidedly retrospective and control-oriented.

By contrast, the output-oriented approach is based on the assumptions that the decision-maker needs all of the relevant information he can obtain and that it is at least theoretically possible to somehow obtain all of the data relevant to a decision. New information is developed, not as a result of the pressures and problems involved in the bargaining process, but as a result of conscious, systematic search. Information collection and use reflect a prospective, programmatic, and output-oriented bias. For example, advocates of such an approach place heavy emphasis on the need to identify program and organizational objectives and to tie information requirements to these objectives. This approach supports a style of decision-making which tends to be more formal and explicit and which devotes specific attention to the systematic definition of information needs and requirements. Rather than being control-oriented, the output-oriented approach tends to place heavy emphasis on planning and performance evaluation, not simply on accountability for tangible resources expended.

Marchand develops four modes of information resources budgeting; two each for the two major approaches discussed above. Let us review them briefly.

THE INCREMENTAL MODE

The Incremental Mode of budgeting is defined as an input-oriented approach, which aggregates the costs of resources in general, easily-comprehended categories for use by decision-makers. The categories of resource accounting generally tend to lump together the tangible expenditures of the organization for personnel costs, equipment costs, supply costs, and so on. The focus of the incremental decision-making process tends (and this is crucial to this approach) not to be on what has been spent, but on what is being requested. Thus, decision-making does not demand detailed information concerning resource expenditures, since the focus of the budgeting process is on changes at the margin, that is, on what additional resources are being requested and not on how past resources have been expended.

The Incremental Mode raises several significant problems about the ability of the organization to account for its data resources. For one, the object-of-expenditure categories traditionally used tend to obscure rather than highlight significant data resource expenditures. For another, the cost accounting, or cost reporting, systems developed to support this approach do not pick up major aspects of major resource expenditures, or do so only very indirectly. Thus, it is difficult, if not impossible, to assess what expenditures are being devoted to various kinds of information handling and production tasks.

THE ADJUSTED INCREMENTAL MODE

Marchand calls the second sub-type of his input-oriented class of budgeting approaches the Adjusted Incremental Mode. This variation of the incremental mode was developed to compensate for a possible major deficiency in the incremental mode, the tendency to "lump" together all costs, such as data processing, into one line-item. However, this can obscure some important considerations. For example, in many cases data processing terminals are both physical (geographically) and organizationally separate from the main computer (mainframe). The costs of the operation of the terminals may therefore be included in other organizational overhead budgets as part of their "administrative support" costs. The full and complete cost of data processing for the organization as a whole, therefore, may be significantly understated in the account of very important activities. Other examples could be cited in the printing and reprographic, microfilm, library and other areas. Under the Adjusted Incremental Approach, a separate data processing line item would be established for each cost center. It would therefore be feasible to aggregate the separate data processing costs for each cost center, and the central computer facility, to come up with more precise estimates of the actual costs of data processing in the organization as a whole. Another approach might be to set up a cost accounting system for the use of the central computer facility and on-line resources in each unit or program within the organization. In this case, the computer facility would not be regarded, then, as a "free good" within the organization.

As with the Incremental Approach, there are some pitfalls here too. For one, a major problem arises precisely because of its input-oriented bias. Despite the fact that the line item approach can be adjusted significantly to account for data resource expenditures in terms of personnel, supplies, equipment, and so on, such an approach may reveal little concerning the relationship between information expenditures and information value. The Adjusted Incremental Mode, therefore, tends to be a kind of "scorecard" approach aimed primarily at fiscal accountability. In short, a line item budget, used exclusively without other formats, may indicate very little concerning the relationship between data collection, data use, and data value.

Another problem lies in the fact that this approach is retrospective in its focus; one cannot easily relate past performance to any new or changing use of data resources. The line item approach, then, is of only limited utility as a data resource planning tool, since there is no attempt made to link programmatic goals and needs to actual expenditures and costs.

THE COMPREHENSIVE MODE

The first of the two sub-types of Marchand's output-oriented approaches is the Comprehensive Mode of Budgeting. Instead of focusing on traditional resource inputs exclusively, here the attention is on the relationship between the use of resources and the outputs or results which are achieved. The Comprehensive Mode is based on the assumption that assessment of data resource expenditures must be linked to the use of information to advance organizational or sub-unit goals and objectives. Thus, the only appropriate way to assess data resources is to define the relationship between the *uses* of information and the processes of decision-making and analysis to go on within the organization. In doing so, one inevitably focuses on the outputs of data resource utilization, not simply on inputs; that is, one moves from a preoccupation with information efficiency to a concern with information effectiveness for decision-making and analytical needs.

The Comprehensive Mode differs considerably from the Incremental Modes in that we would proceed more from a "top-down" vantage point. First, we would define, as explicitly as possible, the relationship between organizational and program goals and objectives and information needs and requirements. Then we would define the key types of decisions needed to reach these goals; translate the decision-making needs into information requirements—both substance and format; and then move to an assessment of alternative ways of meeting the information requirements.

However, there are some problems here too. First, this mode of data resource budgeting can be very costly in terms of information and time. A large public organization, for example, may simply be unable to devote the resources to such a task. Second, this approach may be politically unacceptable for two significant reasons. For one, such a mode of budgeting may demand a degree of centralization of organizational control that is incompatible with the organization's structure and traditions. The Comprehensive Mode is an "integrationist" mode of planning and control which, either implicitly or explicitly, will demand centralization of authority and resource control. Additionally, the Mode requires that organizational objectives and decision-making processes be clearly defined. In many organizations, such a demand for precise definition and transparency may be too high a price to pay politically. A third objection might be that the Comprehensive Mode may be methodologically inappropriate; that is to say, such a degree of formal definition may simply not be compatible with the existing state-of-scientific-knowledge.

THE VALUE/USE MODE

Finally, we come to the last of the four sub-types, the Value/Use Mode. Like the Comprehensive Mode, it too is output-oriented. The aim here is twofold: first, it is directed at integrating the cost of data resources with their use; second, it focuses on the key areas where information is of value for the organization. In contrast to the Comprehensive Mode, no assumption is made that, before one can identify problems of data resource use, one must understand comprehensively the organization's objectives, decision-making process, and information systems. The thrust here is to take a gradual approach to assessing the connection between data use and data value. It differs from the Incremental Modes because it is an output-oriented approach; that is, the key problem is to assess whether information that is collected is used and whether what is used is of value to individual decision-makers in the organization.

The Value/Use Mode is based on coordination, rather than the integration of the Comprehensive Mode or the "permissiveness" of the Incremental Modes. It assumes that the appropriate response to the "do your own thing" style of data resource management implied in the Incremental Modes is, not total integration, but a more appropriate degree of coordinated use of data resources in line with the needs of diverse individuals and units within the organization. Thus, the Value/Use Mode aims at (1) identifying the demands or needs for information in the organization; (2) identifying the supplies of information and data in the organization; and (3) closing the gap between the demands/needs for information and the supply of information and data resources.

Methodologically, one begins here with a comprehensive, detailed inventory or survey of the organization's existing and planned information resources. Next, an assessment is made of the actual costs of supporting inputs—personnel, equipment, and so forth. In contrast to the Incremental Modes of budgeting, which assume that such resources can be costed if only one could add additional categories to the object classification scheme, the Value/Use approach assumes that the primary problem is the identification of actual data use. Only after a conscious, careful, and deliberate search for and analysis of such resources is complete, can one then attempt to assess the costs of such resources.

A third step in the Value/Use approach is to analyze the relationship between the cost and use of data resources in the organization and the value of the data resources to individuals and units in the organization of various types of decision-making and analysis. The aim is to begin reducing the divergence between data which is collected and used by the organization but is of limited or no value and to move to a situation where information that is collected and used is of value to everyone. This latter task is, perhaps, the most difficult one confronting the effective adoption of the Value/Use Mode since it demands an assessment of the complex and varied perceptions of data use and value in the information processes of the organization. Not only is this type of assessment likely to reveal the lack of consensus within the organization about what information is of value, and what is not, but the fact that such questions of value and use are asked explicitly is likely to raise previously submerged or latent sources of conflict or disagreement over the collection, maintenance, and dissemination of information resources.

Finally, a fourth aspect of the Value/Use Mode is to begin moving toward the development of a coordinated approach to data resource management. Unlike the Comprehensive Mode, which suggests centralization of control and elimination of redundancy and overlap, the Value/Use approach is based on the assumption that it is neither necessary nor desirable to eliminate all redundancy and overlap. The key is to coordinate efforts at data resource management within existing organizational and functional structures. Changing the latter to meet the demands of the former is like letting the tail wag the dog. Coordinated data resource management does not depend on redesigning the organization but aims rather at reducing those areas of data resource intensiveness which are unnecessary or inappropriate.

SUMMARY

In most organizations, whether in government or in industry, when it comes to data budgeting we are plowing new ground, and whatever course is taken will affect the organization in fundamental and permanent ways and probably most of the key decision-makers in the organization. Therefore, the approach should be gradual, step-by-step, based on consensus-building within the organization over what should be done, and how it can be done. In the end, the specific approach selected must depend on a higher order of considerations, policies, organizational values, and the like. What we have done here is outline some avenues that might be taken.

It must be clear that to budget information successfully, we must have first costed information resources. So let us see how, under the heading "accounting," what some of the approaches to costing are.

QUESTIONS FOR DISCUSSION

1. Is it possible to budget for information without first identifying, measuring and costing out underlying information resources (i.e. products like computers and reprographic equipment; services like abstracting and indexing)? Is it practical? In short, what is the relationship between "information budgeting" and "information accounting?"

2. Short of being in a position to assign some kind of monetary value to the qualitative use of information products and services, what might the organization's budget officer do to furnish top management officials with some kind of budgetary estimates?

3. The phrase "line item in the budget" has led to some controversy and confusion when applied to the information resource. On the one hand, some believe that every information product and service should be explicitly identified in the organization's detailed budget schedules, down to the punched card, inch of paper or magnetic tape level. Others prefer to use the phrase more descriptively than literally; they believe information should not be made a line item in the budget. Debate the pros and cons of the two views.

4. Do we budget for information inputs, or outputs, or both? If we take the view, for example, that data is transformed into useful information much the same as pig iron is transformed into bar stock and rolling stock of steel, then how would the "Value Added" concept used by economists apply to the budgeting of information in an information firm that transformed "raw data" into saleable information products and services?

5. How do the notions of Transfer Pricing and Chargeback apply to the preceding question?

6. The Administration of President Jimmy Carter made much of the introduction of Zero-base Budgeting into the Federal Government in 1977 and 1978. How might the principles of zero-base budgeting be applied to information firms, such as market survey companies that undertake studies of potential markets for new products and services for a fee?

FOOTNOTES

[1]Kerker, Robert P., *"Justify Your Budget,"* (Remarks delivered at the Seventh Annual Meeting of the National Association for State Information Systems (NASIS), published in Government Data Quarterly, Nov./Dec., 1976) pp. 21–23. In the last few years two important national state organizations, the foregoing National Association of State Information Systems (NASIS) and another, the National Association of State Budget Officers (NASBO) have both become increasingly concerned over mushrooming information, computer and communication costs. Their 1975, 1976 and 1977 meetings all involved important addresses by leading public and professional figures; readers may wish to obtain the proceedings of the forums if they desire to pursue the information management question in the State context.

[2]Horton, Forest. W., Jr., *"Recycling Information and Zero-Base Budgeting,"* (Journal of Systems Management, May, 1977) pp. 36–67, Vol. 28.

[3]Marchand, Donald A., and Stucker, John J., *"Information Management in the State University,"* A report of the Information Management Study Group, Commission on Federal Paperwork, Washington, DC June 15, 1977. This landmark study probes deeply the facets of information management in the state university context. It is the first comprehensive treatment of the subject matter and is highly recommended to the student of political science and public administration, concerned with the problems of university-state legislature relationships, freedom of information in the academic setting, power relationships within the university structure, and similar concerns.

8 INFORMATION ACCOUNTING

We saw in the preceding chapter that information budgets must proceed from sound cost and expense data. We cannot budget for information unless we build the budget up from historical cost data, plus future projections. There are two major components of "information accounting." One is an information cost accounting *structure* and the other is the use of accounting *analytical techniques* to illuminate trends, interrelationships and possible problem areas. We will examine here the principles and concepts involved in both these areas. It needs to be stressed at the outset that no tested and verified empirical approaches exist in this area.

Some work has begun. But it is very preliminary and needs to be further tested, refined, and evaluated. Our discussion, therefore, will of necessity be more exploratory and experimental than doctrinal or dogmatic.

An *information cost accounting structure* is an essential prerequisite to effective management of the information resource. This is not to say that the organization's conventional chart of accounts is necessarily incomplete or inadequate to satisfy this objective. Rather, it is to emphasize that the use of cost information *on information* places a positive emphasis on the receipt of value for resources used. This emphasis gives greater prominence to cost aspects in the planning and operations instead of placing the primary emphasis on such factors as staying within budgetary allocations. But first let us review some general cost accounting principles.

In both government and private industry, every expense is conceived of as a cost of some essential, planned activity. Because costs furnish important measures of performance, the construction of the organization's chart of accounts and the design and development of its accounting system require the involvement and participation of both accountants and management officials.

For example, in the Federal Government, individual agencies are admonished that their accounting practices for allocating indirect overhead costs be devised with care to avoid producing cost data that obscures the total cost for which responsible managers should be held accountable.

Another precept which agencies must follow is the maxim that cost accounts and the cost accounting system be designed to reveal the significant expenses of the organization. However, because of the complexities of some Government operations, it is sometimes just as satisfactory, as well as more economical, to use cost finding techniques, rather than restructuring cost accounts to produce cost data needed for special purposes. In short, we may not need to radically overhaul our cost accounting structure, but rather to use approaches such as cost finding, cost estimation, sampling, post audit and other techniques.

INTERNAL COSTS

We introduced in preceding chapters the notion of an "information line item" in the budget and said its development should proceed step by step. Recall that the first step was to identify and extract both "internal" and "external" information items and cost figures. Let us review how the internal activities are dealt with first. In this regard, the three steps appear to be:

1. Determining primary central service organizational components which are essentially "data service" in character;
2. Identifying those activities which are essentially "data handling" in character; and
3. Identifying specific objects of expense for steps 1 and 2.

There are typically a dozen or so units within large organizations which can be classified as "central service" units and which deal in data services. Similarly, there are perhaps an equal number of activities in any large organization which are essentially "data handling" in character regardless of their organizational location. The reader may wish to refer back to Figure 7-1.

After isolating both the organizations and the activities, what remains to be done is to identify that portion of both overhead (administrative) and direct program costs borne by the specified organizations in carrying out the specified activities. This can most conveniently be done in government by using the "object class" approach. For example, for all of the organizations identified in Figure 7-1 and for all of the activities identified in Figure 7-1 we would add up the expenses which fall into the following object classes:

- personnel compensation and benefits;
- equipment acquisition and lease;
- materials and supplies;
- office space acquisition and rental;
- related contractual service; and
- related guarantees, grants, loans, and investments.

This data is then developed on the principle, that, in addition to salary, everything an employer requires to do the job of creating and processing information and paperwork should be counted as a cost, regardless of physical format or handling medium or location within the organization.

Clearly the particular mix of information units and information activities will vary from organization to organization. Nor do we suggest that our lists in Figure 7-1 are definitive. To compound the problem, nomenclatures differ between sectors, industries, professions and regions. But the idea must be clear. We have two dimensions—one a central service and support dimension; the other an "organic activities" dimension. Before we can make sense out of the situations, we must, for our own organization, prepare lists to correspond to Figure 7-1; remember those lists are illustrative, not definitive. Yours will differ somewhat.

EXTERNAL COSTS

Next, we should precede to external costs. In the public sector, external costs would appear to be divided into two major classes: First, those borne directly by the respondent from whom the Government collects information; and second, those borne by some other element in the public sector—for example, another agency from which the information is collected. So we see that the terms "internal" and "external" refer to the organization's boundaries; anything outside of the organization, or more accurately, any costs borne by an outside organization, are considered "external" for our purposes. In private industry "external" would refer to information purchases from outside the company, "internal" to those from inside.

It is at this point, however, that a major divergence occurs in the manner in which the cost computation would proceed. On the one hand, we can pursue what might be called a "bottom-up" approach;

and on the other hand, we could take a "top-down" approach. We briefly discussed and contrasted these approaches in the last chapter. Under the bottom-up approach, which is essentially an input oriented approach, we are not at all concerned with the output side of the equation, that is, the *uses* to which the information resource is to be put. The bottom-up approach to information cost accounting depends heavily on the so-called "object classification" scheme, a major scheme used to record financial transactions in the Federal Government. Under the object classification scheme, the *nature* of the service or article for which an obligation is incurred is financially recorded *regardless of the purpose or program served.* Thus, obligations for purchasing an automobile are classified under object class 31, equipment, whether the automobile is used for national defense, law enforcement, or construction activities. Object class data present the total amount required to purchase the needed article or service. The price of an automobile, for example, may include charges by the supplier for transportation, and the entire amount would then be classified under object class 31.

To understand the bottom-up approach, we need to look more carefully at the Object Classification scheme. While I am here referring to the scheme used by the Federal Government, the schemes used in the private sector are very similar. We'll come back to the top-down approach.

THE OBJECT OF EXPENDITURE CLASSIFICATION SCHEME

In the Federal Government, the five major object classifications are:

- personal services and benefits;
- contractual services and supplies;
- acquisition of capital assets (which includes equipment, lands and structures, and investments and loans);
- grants and fixed charges (which includes subsidies, insurance claims, interest, dividends, and refunds); and
- miscellaneous (which includes administrative expenses, changes in the book value of selected resources, and a few others).

The number of sub-object categories differs from one kind of revenue source to another. By and large, however, the sub-object categories for the first three major object classes are fairly standard. For example, the three primary sub-object classes for the personal services and benefits object are: personnel compensation, personnel benefits, and benefits for former personnel. Similarly, the principal sub-object categories for the second major object class, contractual services and supplies, are also fairly standard: travel and transportation of persons, transportation of things, rent and communications and utilities, printing and reproduction, other services, and supplies and materials.

Let us take an example to see how the bottom-up approach would work. Suppose we had an organization with a simplified structure with only five divisions. Divisions A and B are our two product line sales groupings; division C is marketing, division D is manufacturing and division E is administration.

Under division E we have six departments which are primarily data handling in character, including the central printing and reproduction department, the central computer center, the central library, the central document clearinghouse, the central records center and the central statistics office. Based on a survey, we've identified some 24 different activities throughout the remainder of the organization (including the other departments in division E).

We then, using accounting information and the approach described above, go through each organization and each activity and aggregate costs for all objects of expenditure, including salaries, supplies, and so on. We can then array the aggregated costs in a variety of formats, as shown in Figure 8-1.

By contrast, under the top-down approach we are concerned with the overall purposes of the organization. For example, take a law enforcement program in government. We begin by asking the following kinds of questions:

- what is the underlying basic purpose of this program?
- what is it really intended to accomplish?
- what approach is to be taken in the program? For example, will it be capital-intensive, labor-intensive, or information-intensive?
- what role will each of the resources play in helping managers to achieve the program purposes?
- specifically, what role will the information resource play? Is new knowledge required, thereby requiring a large scientific and research effort? Or, by contrast, will data and information play a secondary role and existing information and knowledge be adequate to support decisionmaking and problem-solving needs?
- in what form will the data and information be needed?

	Direct Funds	% of Total	Overhead Funds	% of Total	Total Funds	% Info of Total
FORMAT A—*INFORMATION INTENSITY BY COST CENTER*						
Cost Center 1						
Cost Center 2						
Cost Center 3						
Org. Sub-total						
Total All Cost Centers						
FORMAT B—*INFORMATION INTENSITY BY PROGRAM/ PRODUCT/ACTIVITY*						
Program/Product Activity 1						
Program/Product Activity 2						
Program/Product Activity 3						
Product Line Sub-total						
Total all Programs/Products Activities						
FORMAT C—*INFORMATION COSTS BY OBJECT OF EXPENSE*						
Cost Center 1						
Program/Product Activity 1						
Information Object of Expense 1						
IOE 2						
IOE 3						

(*or reverse major/minor sequence, making program major, cost center minor*)

Figure 8-1. **Information intensity by cost center**

Will substantial technical reports be needed? Will operating reports be required on whether the program is being managed efficiently or inefficiently?
- How frequently will the information be needed, and so on.

Of course at some point, eventually, we must get down to the object of expenditure level in order to do the costing. But the route we've taken under the top-down approach is radically different than the one we took under the bottom-up approach. Here we've made no *a priori* judgments at all on whether a particular organization or activity should be considered "data handling." Rather, we've examined the basic goals and objectives of what it is the organization is trying to do and then proceeded down the costing pathway.

COST INFORMATION REPORT FORMATS

Whether a top-down or bottom-up approach is used, information costs assist in the identification of information-intensive and high cost information programs and activities. We saw in the last chapter that a simple "paperwork/information-intensity" ratio could be developed as a useful tool. But what other tools and formats might we consider?

For one, simple information cost reports can be prepared for operating units (by cost center) to provide a test of applying the IRM concept. Reports may be based on a general definition and identification of information costs, using existing classifications for objects of expenditure. Based on favorable results from these reports, the basic concept can then be refined and items of information costs more specifically defined. This should improve the quality and utility of information cost reporting. See Figure 8-1.

The preliminary cost reports would be intended to focus on several questions regarding information costs. Here are a few typical questions:

- What programs and activities have a higher ratio of information cost than others (our intensity ratio)?
- Do labor-intensive programs have relatively higher ratios of information costs than capital-intensive ones?
- Are information costs higher for joint venture projects than those undertaken alone?
- What are the information ratios of pure research programs versus applied research programs?
- Do certain classes of programs or activities, such as advertis-

ing and promotional ones, tend to have the same information cost relationships between different subsidiaries or departments?

- Do the same types of sales programs in different geographic locations have similar information cost ratios?
- Are information costs considered in company return-on-investment and capital budgeting calculations?
- Do higher dollar value programs have a higher ratio of information costs?
- What objects of information expense appear to be consistently higher than others?

Answers to these questions can focus subsequent analysis to determine the basic causes of high information and paperwork costs. This can lead to the application of appropriate solutions in managing information to support program objectives and reduce unnecessary costs and burdens. On a program-by-program basis, probes can be initiated to determine what programs of similar dollar value have differing ratios of information costs.

Simple information cost reports will not provide automatic solutions, but they should provide answers to questions that aid the identification of problem areas that do require solutions. They should identify what is presently unidentified, provide the basis for management evaluation, and allow the application of sound management principles for improvement by, for example, highlighting those areas where information planning and management techniques might be focused.

Other formats for illuminating breakouts are feasible beyond cost centers, for example, breakouts by product and by expense categories. These formats, depicted in Figure 8-1, show information costs related to overall costs. In addition, Format B shows the percentage of different sources of funds allocated to each program / product. Format C furnishes a third possibility based on specific objects of information expenditure. All three formats can be used to analyze the myriad interrelationships between information expenses.

Of course there probably will be some disagreement within the company or government agency as to the precise identity of the cost elements that should go into the "information column." Depending on the nature of the business of the organization, how complex its products, how diverse its product lines, how large its organizational size, how dispersed its plants and sales offices geographically, and so on, the task of identifying the specific cost elements will be more or less difficult. Certainly it will take time for line and staff officials to become familiar with the new structure as a normal way of viewing budget and costing information. We are all more comfortable with conventional portrayals.

INFORMATION STANDARDS AND VARIANCE ANALYSIS

Collecting and portraying cost data is only the beginning of the process. Measures of performance and productivity must be developed, and standard information costs must be established to give us a baseline against which to measure whether changes instituted have had any effect. Standard information costs, and the use of variance analysis techniques to measure deviation of actual costs from planned costs, are almost virgin territory now in the information resource area. Technocrats blame the everchanging and accelerating pace of technological innovation for failure to pause and take a breath to develop standards. The accounting profession at times seems bemused, bewildered or just plain overwhelmed by the complexities of the problem, and the various professional financial groups, such as the Cost Accounting Standards Board, the Federal Government Accountants Association, and others, have not moved as aggressively in this area as they might.

A study undertaken for the Commission on Federal Paperwork by the Academy for Contemporary Problems which tried to assess the magnitude and character of the "paperwork burden" imposed by the Federal Government of State and local levels of government found that a distinction between "core" and "noncore" costs was essential.[1] The study defined core costs as those necessary to actual delivery of a government service to its recipient and noncore costs as "everything else." The study affirmed the idea that certain "minimal or threshhold" administrative costs must be incurred simply to operate any program, and that core costs must include not only the cost of the actual service provided, but also minimal administrative costs necessary to safeguard the fiscal and managerial integrity of programs being administered, such as fiscal, personnel, and equipment and supply utilization records to verify that funds were actually expended according to plan, employees used their time for assigned, legitimate tasks, and supplies and equipment were used for the purposes for which purchased.

This study points out, however, that reliance on budgeting and accounting data alone would inhibit useful measures of information handling costs because, for example, fund data per se does not indicate what portion is spent on delivery or nondelivery aspects of money expended. Consequently, the study undertook a "line-by-line" analysis of the budgets it examined (the State of California's, for example). For approximately 200 of the State's departments and programs, budget costs were broken into three categories: (1) administrative costs; (2) core costs; and (3) payments to local governments and individuals, not including purchased services such as highway construction contracts and Medicaid payments to providers. Significantly, the study found that the largest portion of California's expenditure consists of subsidies to state subdivisions or to individuals (63%). Only 32 percent related to core service costs, and the remaining percentage (between 5 and 6%) to administrative, non-core costs.

The Academy Study emphasized that, in the end, what constitutes "core cost," and what non-core is, is subject to judgmental determination. It points out that, though the basic concept may be readily accepted, substantial negotiation among public administrators, officials, and members of the public will be required to develop core cost standards. "The development of such standards is absolutely vital, and their use in measuring information and paperwork burden on the American public" is, in the words of the study, a "critical concept."

In short, developing standard information costs is really the beginning of the process, yet it is a road which must be embarked upon by any organization if the important accounting tool of variance analysis is to be effectively employed.

HISTORICAL TRENDS—PPBS

It is perhaps instructive to point out at this juncture that, when the Federal Government moved to the program-planning-budgeting system (PPBS) in the middle Sixties there was some expectation at the beginning that input-oriented classification schemes and management systems might eventually be discarded since PPBS, be definition, was an output or results-oriented management approach. More specifically, there was a body of opinion that believed that the input-oriented object classification scheme could be dispensed with at some point after Congress and the Executive Branch gained sufficient familiarity with the concept, procedures and other details. However, it became rather evident after the first year of operation that the Congress was not about to discard the object classification scheme nor, for that matter, were senior budget officials within Executive agencies. In short, it became evident that *both* an input and an output scheme would be required. So we are drawn to ask: In the accounting for information resources, do we need both an input and an output oriented scheme?

It does not seem practical to this author to add another classification scheme on the input side of the equation to capture "information resources" as a sixth major class of object of expense. Indeed, not one authority interviewed contends that we should radically restructure our fundamental accounting systems to set up a new major category entitled "information." Rather, the consensus at this point seems to be that information costs should not be captured in the abstract sense, but rather as derivative costs of the existing resource categorization. The costs of the conventional resource categories—human resources, physical resources, material resources, and financial resources—should be costed for information purposes to the extent that those resources are consumed in the production, handling, and assimilation of information or the generation of intelligence, or knowledge, from that information. If, then, we don't radically alter the input side, what do we do with the output side?

A "USE" TYPOLOGY

On the output side of the equation, a number of groups have explored the utilization of a "use typology" to account for information values and information costs. One such use typology which has already been briefly alluded to in preceeding chapters, in the context of management of Government programs, has been called a "use" typology and would classify and aggregate information costs into one of five breakouts:

- information needed to plan programs;
- information needed to operate programs;
- information needed to administer and manage programs;
- information needed to evaluate programs; and
- information which is of a general purpose character, such as general purpose statistical information.

Crucial to the employment of this approach are judgments as to precisely what information is needed to operate programs versus all of the other categories. In one study this distinction was referred to as T-1 and T-2: T-1 information was information needed to operate programs; T-2 information was all other data including the other four categories indicated above (planning, administering, evaluating and general-purpose). There is a certain intuitive appeal to this approach insofar as it does seem to acknowledge that much of the information explosion can be traced to the growth in both government and in private industry of large organizational units, primarily staff units, which deal with traditional staff functions rather than line functions.

However, it must be quickly pointed out that the conventional line / staff distinctions do not necessarily hold. The problem becomes the usual hierarchical one; that is, within a manufacturing division of a large corporation, if one looks at the organizational chart carefully, clearly there may be staff units advising the head of the manufacturing unit. The question then becomes: Should these staff units at the organizational level be subsumed under the T-1 or T-2 category? One might simply take the position that information accounting, like information planning or information budgeting, depends upon the perspective one takes. That is, the approach the top manager takes in terms of aggregating costs may be quite different when looking at the organization as a whole than when looking at each successively lower echelon.

METAINFORMATION IS MISSING

One very serious problem confronting us in accounting for information resources is that we do not have a well established body of doctrine of descriptive information *on information.* Recall earlier we used the term *meta data* to substitute for the more awkward phrase "information on information." Unlike the other resource categories where over the years we have developed data descriptions and data categories that help us conceptualize, visualize, and make more tangible to our understanding the employment of the other resources—human resources, material resources etc.—such is not true in the case of information. Indeed, except for the computer equipment area and the records management programs which have been with us for a long time, we are just now, apparently, at the threshhold of developing cost accounting meta data on information resources. For example, what is the accounting entity for costing information resources? In the Federal Government, an accounting entity may be an entire agency, a subdivision thereof (such as an organizational unit), or one or more legally established funds. Taken together, the collection of all accounting entities constitutes the account structure, which in general accounting is referred to as the system of general ledgers. The basic structure of accounts for a typical agency operations, for example, might be:

- accounts for assets;
- accounts for liabilities;
- accounts for investment of the U.S. Government;
- accounts for investment of others; and
- accounts for revenues and costs.

ACCOUNTING FOR ADP COSTS

Carl Palmer has explored some accounting entity definitions for computer-based information systems and related activities. In a paper dated May, 1974, Palmer offered four possible definitions of the appropriate entity for costing the "information systems activity":

- the organizational information system or total information processing activity;
- the formal management information system, or all formal information processing activities;
- the computer-based, electronic or automatic, data processing activity or simply
- the data processing facilities or department, however organizationally defined.

In this discussion, Palmer points out that perhaps the most succinct definitional work regarding the first of these approaches, the organizational information system, comes from the work of Anton, Emery, and Linn, with significant contributions by McFarlan, Nolan and Zani.[2]

The second approach, the formal management information system, follows somewhat the approach of John Dearden. Other authors who have explored this conceptual definition include Anthony, Blumenthal, Forrester, Hartman, Matthes, Proeme, Sackman and Teichroew, among others. The entity definition for the formal management system, according to Palmer, might read something like: "All resources accumulated and expended for the purposes of recordation, storage, retrieval, process, transmission, presentation, modeling, and decision through formally defined processes relative to the organization."

Under Palmer's third approach, the costing of computer-based information processing or data processing systems, implicitly data processing is viewed as a subordinate category to information systems supported by the data processing activity. The virtues of this approach from an accounting standpoint are rather obvious. This approach avoids the difficult problem of dealing with higher order uses of information, such as for intelligence and knowledge generation purposes. Instead, this approach falls back on the conventional data processing function which is fairly circumscribable.

Perhaps the greatest conceptual weakness in any one of the four approaches set forth by Palmer comes in what the author himself describes as "the principal deficiency." He says this deficiency "comes from the lack of ability to clearly attribute and match the costs of computer-based information processing and its aggregate the computer-based information processing function, or its subset the computer-based data processing, through the decision to the yielding of value to the outcomes of these systems of functions. One could argue, however, that this is just another missing link in the matching process along with the entire decision execution process." I would concur with the author that one *could* argue that. However, it seems to me that any accounting approach to the management of a resource must take into account both the output side of the equation as well as the input side.

THE VALUE-ADDED APPROACH

Another methodological alternative to handling the information costing problem is the value-added approach. This approach flows from the assumption that at each stage of its life cycle, information acquires new value, and a new net worth computation can be affected at each stage. Such an approach has both opportunities and pitfalls. From a purely conceptual standpoint, it does follow closely the approach which is used in the materials resources area. Indeed, cost accounting and cost structures in the materials area have long employed this approach to track the transformation of raw materials through a variety of intermediate, semi-finished stages until finally, at the end of the pipeline, finished products are produced. The analogy to the information resources area is obvious, if not compelling. Data enters the pipeline in "raw, unevaluated form." Its cost at that entry point is essentially the acquisition cost. As analytical skills are brought to bear on the data, through the processes of summarizing, interpreting, correlating, and so forth, the data takes on increased intrinsic value. For example, it may add to the value of a basic record, a report, a statistical computation, and so on. These products can then be priced on a value-added basis.

THE PERFORMANCE EVALUATION APPROACH

From time to time the objection of costing information is heard which runs along the lines of "the quality and utility of information is too diverse, too abstract, too amorphous to cost and value it." Nonsense. Is the use of the information resource any more complex than the use of the human resource? Hardly. Human beings are just as diverse as elements of information—more so, some might argue—and yet Government agencies and private corporations are obliged to cost and value their human resources. The "worth" of a human being is the subject of a major sector of social science research, namely human resource accounting; this is yet another avenue worth exploring in the information costing area. Personnel management specialists and budget officials have long since concluded that there are no precise formulas that can tell the company head or an agency chief exactly how much a secretary, or a middle level management official or a technician of some kind is worth. Although there is a marketplace in which individuals are "bought" and "sold," in the end the range of values that we might be tempted to assign to individuals is extremely broad, so broad, in fact, that we must use a qualitative judgmental scheme to make such valuations. Commonly the term performance evaluation, or performance rating evaluation, is used.

Why not a similar approach in the information area? The typical employee performance rating form evaluates employee effectiveness and efficiency or anywhere from ten to perhaps a hundred or more factors, depending on how complex the system is. One sees this kind of list for the factors:

- quantity of work;
- quality of work;
- cooperativeness;
- dependability;
- communicating ability;
- creativity;
- leadership; and so on.

Then a simple rating scheme of, usually, three to five or six rankings is offered: inadequate, marginal, fully meets requirements, exceeds requirements, and exceptional. A composite ranking of all factor ratings is often computed for the purpose of giving an overall rating to the employee, such as "unsatisfactory," "satisfactory," or "outstanding."

Why couldn't we do this for information products and services as well? Bearing in mind our above context, this line of approach would be more in the nature of the "item accounting" type, rather than the "financial accounting" type, since we are not dealing with dollars but with a qualitative evaluation. It certainly does meet our criterion of a broad "accountability" type of definition for accounting, not just financial accounting.

We have until now dealt with information accounting in a micro-sense. Much of our attention has been on the cost accounting side.

But of course there is more to accounting than cost accounting. At higher levels of management, there are macro considerations which we need to look at too.

Another way of saying this is that despite the fact that our accounting structures and accounting systems may be deficient in one or more ways, and to greater or lesser degrees in capturing, recording, identifying, measuring and portraying the full and complete costs of information handling, nevertheless we can and should make some attempt to look at *aggregate* information costs. When the Federal Paperwork Commission and other government bodies have tried to do this, they found quickly that they couldn't easily find the boundaries between three major categories: *paperwork, information and communications.*

PAPERWORK, INFORMATION AND COMMUNICATIONS

In the course of its work in 1976, when the Commission on Federal Paperwork undertook a study to determine the total cost of government paperwork, it immediately ran into definitional and measurement problems. Everywhere this Commission turned to for a figure lay more questions than answers—"it all depends on who you ask"; "do you mean equipment, or people or both"; are you talking about direct or indirect costs"; and "hard copy paper and printing costs are one thing, related processing and handling costs are quite another."

A number of efforts in both the public and private sectors have dealt with fractions of the total cost, but all of these efforts appear to understate the full magnitude and true character of the costs.

The term "paperwork" obviously has negative connotations. On the other hand, the terms "information" and "communication" are usually positive concepts. However, the Commission found that one man's "information" was another man's "paperwork," that the distinction between "good" paperwork and "bad" paperwork was often blurred. Therefore, it was found that both "good" and "bad" paperwork must be costed in the government's accounting system. Insofar as possible, the total cost of the communication process between citizens and their government must be captured.

A second definitional problem comes in distinguishing between "paperwork" as a narrow term taken to mean reports, records and other physical documents, versus the use of the word in a much broader sense to mean "information." The latter term connotes a broad array of government activities, involving far more than the collection, processing, use and storage of physical documents. Information, in short, is more than documents. It involves the myriad *products and services involved in the communication process* between government and people; among and between governmental levels and agencies; and among and between units within the same agency.

The Commission decided that it must adopt the broader definition of paperwork, to include *information products, services and processes,* not just physical pieces of paper, their printing, and their replication. In adopting the broader definition, additional complications then present themselves.

For one, if we carry the definition of information cost in its broader, communication context, to the extreme, should we include, for example, the cost of the time of government officials spent on the telephone, or in meetings, talking with one another and with citizen-constituents? How about the time spent reading the morning mail, or technical reports, or newspapers? Or writing letters, dictating and giving oral instructions to subordinates? Or training, travel and conference costs? It was decided not to include some of these costs because the figures would be so high as to be virtually meaningless.

THE COSTS WE MUST PAY

This study estimates the total *Federal Government* paperwork, information and communication costs imposed directly on the American taxpayer to be in excess of $43 billion a year. However, this tentative figure does not take into account the cost burden imposed directly on the public by State and local governments, estimated at an additional $17 billion (see Figure 8-2). Even that resultant total still underestimates the full burden in a number of important ways.

For one, beyond the "direct" costs imposed by the Federal Government on you and me as taxpayers, there are five other major classes of cost burdens which we must bear 8-2. First, there are the "indirect costs" incurred by the Federal Government. We certainly must pay for them in the form of taxes on us as citizens, but they are not discretely identifiable in government's accounting systems as expenses, for example, for postage or the salaries of government employees in tabulating statistics. Rather, they are "hidden" and "buried" in both overhead and program accounts, including some with labels like "Other Services."

Next, we must pay corresponding direct and indirect costs for paperwork, information and communication requirements imposed by State and local levels of government. Sometimes these levels of government are simply acting as intermediaries. For example, when

TOTAL PAPERWORK, INFORMATION AND COMMUNICATION COSTS IMPOSED BY GOVERNMENTS ON THE AMERICAN TAXPAYER[1]
(in billions)

1. Direct Federal Government Costs (e.g. salaries, printing, postage, etc.)	$43
2. Direct State/Local Government Costs (paid from Federal funds)	11
3. Direct State/Local Government Costs (e.g. salaries, printing, postage, etc.)	17[2]
4. Indirect Federal ("Shadow Government") Costs (contractor documentation, "other services"; paid from Federal funds)	13[3]
5. Indirect State/Local Costs (corresponds to item 4 above; paid from State/Local revenues)	8[4]
6. Private Sector Costs directly incurred by Citizens and Businesses to pay for government paperwork	41[5]
7. State/Local Government as a respondent to Federal Information Requirements	9[6]
TOTAL	$142

NOTES

[1]Many cost estimates directly ascertainable from Federal income and expense accounts; many estimated by statistical sampling and statistical extrapolation;

[2]This estimate takes into account differences in the makeup of the State/Local government workforce and the Federal Workforce (e.g. higher percentage of occupations and budget in education and law enforcement; see Figure 14)

[3]Excludes subcontractor costs incurred responding to paperwork requirements imposed by prime government contractors

[4]Figure based in part on a ratio of the sum of items one and four to the sum of items three and five ($5 billion), supplemented by an additional amount, with supporting data, in the test.

[5]Includes $32 billion private industry, $8.7 billion for individuals, .350 billion farmers and .075 billion for labor organizations; see separate CFP Study on Paperwork Impact on Small and Large Business.

[6]Also see joint CFP-Academy for Contemporary Problems Study, separately available.

Source: Commission on Federal Paperwork technical paper "Our Shadow Government: The Hidden Cost of Government Paperwork, Information and Communication Costs to the Taxpayer." (available from the author) (1977)

Figure 8-2.

they administer Federal grants, the revenues used to defray the costs of these activities are Federal revenues. In other cases State and local revenues are collected to pay for the programs.

Moreover, we must also pay taxes so that our own State and local levels of government can themselves respond to the Federal Government's information demands; we, as citizens, are not directly involved in these transactions, but we are taxed to pay for them of course.

And finally, we must directly bear the costs of filling out government forms and reports whenever, for example, the Census Bureau sends out a questionnaire, or a regulatory commission of government wants certain business and financial information, or we apply for a welfare, educational, veteran, or some other benefit to which we're entitled.

In short, the costs which we may pay are essentially of two types: (1) direct costs imposed on us as citizens, businesses and other members of the "private sector," and (2) taxes which are levied on us to defray the cost of governments' collecting, handling, disseminating and communicating paperwork and information. In the case of the direct costs, we may or may not be able to shift them to someone else. For example, a businessman may shift the cost to a consumer in the form of higher prices.

In the case of taxes, our leverage must be in helping government wage its war on paperwork and joining in a partnership to seek less costly ways of administering government programs.

INPUTS VERSUS OUTPUTS

A third major definitional and measurement problem that crops up when one tries to compute a total government paperwork and red tape cost imposed on the American taxpayer comes about in trying to segregate and cost out paperwork and information "inputs." In his Ph.D. thesis "The Information Economy," and in the nine volume report he authored for the Department of Commerce, "The Information Economy: Definition and Measurement," dated May, 1977 (OT Spec. Pub. 77-12), Marc Porat says "Part of the Federal Government's bureaucracy necessarily communicates with 'outside' entities—private firms and State and local governments. The bureaucracies 'talk' to each other in managing the economy. And that volume of bureaucratic chatter has grown to stupendous heights in the past 50 years." Porat characterized government as essentially an "information producing, distributing, and consuming organism. Bureaucracies plan, coordinate, command, evaluate, and communicate. They process information. They survey, gather intelligence, write reports."

Our difficulty arises in trying to distinguish which, and how much of this activity should properly be accounted for as "information input" (information resources) and how much under the program output.

Porat himself tallied the "information inputs" of the Federal Government and said the total cost of information resources in 1967 was $50.5 billion, of which only $11.8 billion was in the form of direct purchases of goods and services from the primary information sector. One big item in the $50.5 billion figure is the cost of R&D to develop new weapons and space systems for the Department of Defense and NASA. Porat estimated that cost at $13.1 billion. Another big component was "employee compensation to information workers" which he said accounted for $16.6 billion in 1967. The latter figure he obtained from data produced by the Civil Service Commission on the occupational and compensation structure of Federal employees. This study followed a similar track pursued by the Paperwork Commission and gave it a basis with which to compare independently-derived Commission figures.

GOVERNMENT ADVERTISING?

Dr. Porat estimated that in 1967 the Federal Government spent $111 million advertising itself, placing the amount somewhere between the amounts spent by Colgate-Palmolive Company and R. J. Reynolds Industries. This is in addition, he said, to the $260 million worth of advertising offered free as public service advertising. "The Government knows quite well that it is selling its output, even though no explicit market transaction occurs other than mandatory taxation. Our study here estimates $147 million for DOD "recruiting advertising" alone."[2]

George Beveridge, *Washington Star* ombudsman, went further than Porat in discussing the legitimacy and justification for government spending in the area of public relations and advertising. In an article he authored April 19, 1976, published in the *Washington Star,* he alluded to a four-part series which appeared in the newspaper in preceding weeks, "Selling the Government" by John Fialka. Beveridge said (of the Fialka series):

> (he, Fialka) described a Federal public relations colossus so uncontrolled and so dispersed in the bureaucracy that no one can accurately assess its true size or worth. The articles (in the series) questioned the degree to which some of the myriad 'informational' activities of the government serve political self-interests rather than the public interest and how much

> of the taxpayer's money may be wasted in the process . . . But the article's main thrust was something quite different: That the current organizational morass of information activities is so diffused and so uncontrolled that it is difficult, if not impossible, to separate those vital, valid functions from the pure puffery and self-serving political material that pours out. What the issue boils down to, it seems to me, is that a clearer definition of what the government's public relations functions should—and should not—be is long overdue.[3]

Reference to the Beveridge commentary is included here because attention needs to be drawn to two problems. First, should advertising, promotion and public relations costs of government be considered "information and communication expenses?" Second, one of the serious problems in trying to get a handle on paperwork and information costs is that much of the "information activity" of government is hidden and buried. It is diffused and dispersed throughout many overhead and direct expense accounts at all government levels. In particular, government agencies do not always give complete visibility to their "public relations and advertising costs." These expenses are oftentimes carried under some other heading. See Figure 8-3 for some categories and figures.

In summary, the Treasury Department, the General Accounting Office, OMB and other central government management authorities which "oversee" agency financial and information management systems have not prescribed adequate guidelines and standards for determining what kind of component expenses should be carried under the heading "paperwork, information and communication expenses." Of course they cannot and should not be indicted on this score; no one may have asked them to. Agencies have tended to resist attempts to standardize such accounting definitions as "overhead" and "other services." But we know, certainly, that many paperwork, information and communication expenses must be *somewhere* in agency accounts; instead of trying to estimate their magnitude and character by indirect, deductive methods, why don't we tackle the problem head on and redefine the component expenses by direct methods?

FEDERAL INFORMATION COSTS

In a brief study "Federal Information Increases 11.8 percent in 1976," Washington Researchers created a composite index of some 7 key indicators which they felt were "representative of the amount of data and information available by the Federal Government." The 7 indicators

INFORMATION, COMMUNICATION AND RECORDS COSTS**

1. Salaries of White Collar Workers doing I&R Work	$19,442,270,141
2. Salaries of Blue Collar Workers doing I&R Work	860,744,844
3. Salaries of Military Personnel—Officers doing I&R work	1,326,935,608
4. Salaries of Military Personnel—Enlisted doing I&R work	2,552,291,772
5. Salaries of Foreign Nationals—Indirect Hires	414,500,000
6. Printing	951,000,000
7. Postage	549,673,000
8. Office Space (GSA controlled—SLUC only)	817,228,000
9. ADP Space (GSA controlled—SLUC only)	18,940,392
10. Communications Civilian Agencies (voice, data—GSA/ADTS control) (Excludes personnel)	357,000,000
11. Communication DOD (voice, data satellite) (excludes personnel)	3,836,000,000
12. ADP Operations (excludes personnel) FY-76	6,120,966,000

13. Advertising (Recruiting—DOD) FY-76 (excludes personnel)	147,330,000
14. DOD publication of newspapers and periodicals (excludes personnel)	25,847,347
15. New Construction—"Information and Records" Buildings: *Library of Congress-James A. Madison Building *Social Security Computer Center, Woodlawn, Md. *Lester Hill Center for Biomedical Communications DOD Admin. Bldgs. (Costs prorated over 4 year average construction period)	81,000,000
16. Office Supplies and Equipment	1,100,000,000
17. Rents and Communications	1,337,000,000
18. Intelligence Information and Record Costs (includes personnel)	3,300,000,000
TOTAL	$43,238,727,104

**This does *not* include an additional $24 billion of paperwork costs paid from Federal funds ($11 Direct, $13 Indirect—See Table I-1) in carrying out Federal programs at the State and local level, contractor paperwork burdens in major procurement, reimbursements to carriers for medicare, and a variety of information and record functions contracted out (consultants, graphics, composition, procedural manuals, etc.). A separate listing of these appears later in this report.

SOURCE: Same as Figure 8-2

Figure 8-3. **Information, communication and records costs****

include: GPO spending; spending on Congressional printing; spending on statistical programs; research and development; the number of computers; the number of *Federal Register* pages; and the number of NTIS publications. Figure I-1 showed during the six year time span (1971–1976) when the Federal budget expenditures rose 19.1 percent, the "information index" rose 68.8 percent, or over three times as great.[4]

Another measure of the growth of Federal information can be obtained from the Special Analysis of the Federal Budget which deals with statistical programs of government. During this same six year period, 1971 to 1976, figures show that obligations for the principal major statistical programs rose from $161.2 million to $492.5 million.

A third estimate of the cost of Federal information comes from an analysis completed for the Commission's Value/Burden Study by Donald W. King. In his study "An Estimate of the Value of Scientific and Technical Information Derived from Federal Funds," King derived cost estimates based on what users are willing to pay for scientific and technical information published by such government organizations as the National Technical Information Service (NTIS) and the Government Printing Office (GPO). The information product studies were disseminated in 1976, based on R&D completed in 1975. The costs were estimates of the average price and number of subscriptions of scientific and technical journals as well as price and distribution of technical reports disseminated from NTIS and GPO. The costs determined by use were also estimated. Although King was more interested in getting at the "value" of information, his research is valuable from a cost standpoint as well. The total costs of technical reports sponsored by the Federal Government came to an estimated $406.5 million. A rough estimate of value of scientific and technical information produced through Federal funding was estimated to be $4.7 billion.

A fourth insight into government's increasing paperwork and information costs can be seen from Figure 8-4 which is a chart published by the Federal Highway Administration, Department of Transportation, in connection with the current wave of government requirements for public participation in governmental processes. In the stub column are listed "techniques," which means those governmental activities in which the public is requested to participate. Nearly all of these activities require paperwork.

The central point we're making here is that concomitantly with increasing public participation in the governmental process comes paperwork as an implicit requirement. And of course, someone must bear the cost. But increasingly the citizen, business or private sector entity is absorbing the cost of public participation in government

Key: Planning Stage
S: Systems
C: Corridor
D: Design
O: Occasional use

Technique	Action Plans: Alabama	Alaska	Arizona	Arkansas	California	Colorado
1. Public Hearings	S C D	C D	S C D	S C D	S C D	S C D
2. Information Meetings	S	S C D	S C	S C D	S C D	C D
3. Legal Notices	C D	C D	C D	S C D	S C D	S C D
4. Mass Media Advertisements	C D	C D	S	S	S	S C D
5. Mailing Lists	C D	C D	S C	S C D	S C D	C D
6. Citizens Committees	S	S		S	S	S C
7. Speaking Engagements with Interested Parties	S C D				C D	C
8. Circulate Project Reports	S C D	O				C
9. News Releases			S C D		C D	
10. Pre-hearing/ Post-hearing Meetings		C D				
11. Conduct Surveys		O			O	
12. Public Workshops		O	S C D		O	
13. Direct Contact with Affected Property Owners	C D					

Figure 8-4. **Public highway agency actions plans**

directly, thereby shifting the burden from public sponsorship to private sponsorship.

The latest available annual figures on the volume and maintenance costs of Federal records are for September 30, 1976. Figure 8-5 shows total agency, Federal Record Center, and National Archive holdings were in excess of 34 million cubic feet. Of course not all records are in the form of physical, hard copy paperwork—a point often made in other studies. As Figure 8-5 shows, many agencies have very

VOLUME AND COST* OF FEDERAL RECORDS (9/30/76)

Total Agency Holdings	—20,110,330 cu. ft. @6.79 per cu. ft. equals—$136,548,937
Total Federal Record Centers Holdings	—12,824,959 cu. ft. @.54¢ per cu. ft. equals—$6,925,447
Total National Archives Holdings	— 1,287,349 cu. ft.
Total Federal Records	—34,222,608 cu. ft.

"TOP TEN" AGENCIES

Total Volume (cu. ft.) (In Agencies & Record Centers)		**Reels of Magnetic Tape** (Agency Holdings)	
DOD	7,401,352	DOD	4,786,900
Postal Service	1,684,433	NASA	948,325
HEW	1,470,038	HEW	532,923
VA	1,381,900	ERDA	385,892
Justice	1,104,047	Commerce	312,645
Agriculture	982,155	GSA	208,573
Treasury	943,269	DOT	203,573
ERDA	688,635	Postal Service	95,100
Interior	566,764	Labor	90,756
DOT	438,027	Interior	79,521

*Space and Equipment Only
SOURCE: Same as Figure 8-2.

Figure 8-5.

extensive computer magnetic tape libraries. The total number of magnetic tapes maintained by agencies amounts to 8,202,862 reels. So computerized records, not only "manual" paper records, must be included in any cost computations.

THE NATIONAL ARCHIVES AND RECORDS SERVICE

Responding to requests to help identify past efforts to estimate information and paperwork costs, the National Archives and Records Service (NARS) submitted an informal study it had completed in July, 1974, to the Commission on Federal Paperwork. "Information and Records Costs—Interim Report," had been undertaken by the Office of Records Management in NARS with the idea of coming up with some overall estimate of government's information and paperwork costs. The 1974 estimate was $32.1 billion, which the study said "was a minimum figure, since many costs are not yet collected." Based on the 1974 figure, the Commission extrapolated the increase on the basis of the increase in the Federal budget between 1974 and 1977. The extrapolated figure was in excess of $40 billion. Figure 8-3 reflects figures based on this "Information and Records" costing approach.

Whether one agrees or not with all of these preliminary figures, methodologies, inferences, conclusions and recommendations made in these studies, I would contend that one inescapable conclusion is that our society has moved into the Information Age. Physical paperwork, per se, is being replaced by electronic, microform and other media. When the costs of all the resources needed for information processing are summed, the total figures are truly astronomical.

As a first step in the study and analysis of the effectiveness and efficiency of information resources in accomplishing government's program goals, or industry's objectives, the definitional and measurement problems discussed above must be given immediate and direct attention if they are to be resolved.

Government sometimes takes the lead in these matters. Here, the Director of the Office of Management and Budget and the General Accounting Office could develop an Information Object Classification scheme. Such a scheme should bring together, identify and classify in useful ways, the information-related expenses now diffused among many different accounts and object categories. Both internal costs to government, as well as "external" costs to public respondents should be considered. A radical overhaul of the existing object structure is not recommended; rather, a "modified special analysis approach" should be explored.

The Director of the Office of Management and Budget, the Comptroller General of the United States, and the Secretary of the Department of Commerce could also examine the conclusions and recommendations reached in the Department of Commerce's report "The Information Economy: Definition of Measurement," dated May, 1977 (OT spec. Pub. 77-12), and those reached in other study reports which touch upon "paperwork and information-related expenses" questions of identification, measurement and definition, with a view to developing standard definitions, measurement approaches, nomenclature, terms and abbreviations that could be used government-wide ("in the emerging Information Economy,") and in both the public and private sector. For example, productivity and workload indicators of the type used by Washington Researchers could be very useful. The assistance of recognized private and public sector authorities should be solicited in this regard, including the Cost Accounting Standards Board, the Information Industry Association, the Joint Financial Management Improvement Program, the American Institute of Certified Public Accountants, the American National Standards Institute, the National Association of Accountants, the American Statistical Association, and others.

ARE PERSONNEL COSTS THE KEY?

Study after study, including the foregoing, seem to indicate that the real culprit in the information resources cost picture is not the hardware, nor the software, but "people costs." Another way this is expressed is to say that the cost of collecting, storing, and processing information and data, while significant, are relatively small compared to the costs of analyzing and using the information. Of course, only human beings can do that, with the minor exception of closed loop, process control machines which govern an operation. If these studies are correct (and intuition alone would seem to bear them out), we should spend some time examining the "personnel costs line item."

In the seminal Federal study completed in 1974 that served as the "model" for the Paperwork Commission's report discussed above, an attempt to find the costs of creating, handling, and storing Federal records, the significance of the personnel line item did indeed stand out. That study estimated that the annual cost of creating and processing information and records relating to Federal programs was $32.1 billion. The authors believed that figure substantially understated the complete costs since many occupational categories were not included on the grounds that their primary function was not information processing. Like the Paperwork Commission study, the data was developed on the principle that, in addition to his salary, everything an employee requires to do the job of creating and processing information and records should be counted as a cost (space, office equipment and supplies, office machines, office furniture, printing, computers, communications, and so on). Also, the study included and costed everything defined as records regardless of physical format, including audio-visual reports and records, scientific and technical reports and records, and publications other than normal agency administrative directives and publications.[4]

One important conclusion reached by the study was that many costs related to information processing and records handling are not obvious because they are placed under a budget category of "Other Services." No Civil Service employees are included in that object classification of expense, but in FY 1973, the total cost of "Other Services" in the Federal Government was $49 billion! There is no question but that a large portion of these costs must be related to information processing. For example, seven agencies examined showed a total of nearly $2 million for stenographic and court reporting alone!

Some have called these hidden overhead costs the cost of the "Shadow Government" or the "Invisible Bureaucracy." Many career bureaucrats within government have tried to grapple with this problem for years, but overhead costs seem to continue their rise, unabated.

SUMMARY

Accounting for data and information costs is a crucial link in the information resources management chain. Like the other links in the chain, budgeting, planning and so forth, it cannot be separated easily from the processes which go on before it, and those which follow it. Inevitably, accounting affects budgeting, and vice-versa; and planning affects accounting, and the reverse is true. What is important at this point, it seems to me, is a reiteration of the obvious: Accounting principles and practices have an important *role to play* in information resources management. Information managers, therefore, would do well to study these principles and practices to ascertain where and under what conditions they can be applied to help improve the management of their data resources.

I believe the so-called "top-down" and "bottom-up" approaches described in this chapter, and the "Use Typology," as well as other approaches, all offer promise; further experimentation and testing should proceed along a broad front in both government and private industry, and in the accounting and other professional groups. It is to be hoped that officials in these institutions will recognize the urgency of the need, and see their way clear to foster intensive research and development, in both leadership and financing roles.

QUESTIONS FOR DISCUSSION

1. If we follow conventional accounting practice, we would capture, record and accumulate "information resource" expenditures according to the existing chart of account entries for the company, agency or other organization. Suppose we purchase some dataphones, electronic instruments that can be used to transmit data over the telephone. Suppose further than the dataphones are expected to replace a substantial portion of our mail handling, postage and related costs. Would we classify the purchase of this equipment under "mail and postage" or "data processing?" What information accounting principles does this "dilemma" pose to us?

2. An entire array of computer-controlled typesetting hardware and software technology is now being marketed. Are the costs associated with the acquistion and use of such equipment, following the preceding question, properly classifiable as "printing and reprographic" costs or "data processing?" In addition to this example, and the preceding one, can you think of other examples of how conventional accounting categorizations are being affected by our transformation from an industrial society to an information society?

3. *From a management accounting standpoint* would you record all, or a fraction of the time of company employees spent in meetings, reading the morning mail, reading technical reports, writing letters, dictating and giving oral instructions to others, or receiving instructions from others, as an "information and communications-related expense" or an "overhead item" that should not be disaggregated and charged back to cost centers? Discuss the pros and cons of this line of agrument.

4. Within your own company, if another department asked you to set up a special set of files and records solely for the purpose of being in a position to respond to their information needs (e.g. a periodic report they may require, but for which you have no use), would you insist that the cost of establishing and maintaining that duplicative record set be charged to the other department in the company's internal

accounting machinery? Discuss the pros and cons of this contention. If you were the organization's chief executive, with responsibility for both your own, as well as the other department, what position would you take?

5. If you as a citizen were asked by a government agency to fill out a form for a service or benefit to which you were legally entitled, do you believe you should receive some kind of reimbursement for the cost you incur in filling out the form (e.g. an application), such as a tax credit or rebate, direct reimbursement, free mailing of the application form, or a similar benefit?

FOOTNOTES

[1]Palmer, Carl R., "*Computer-Based Information Systems and Related Activities—Accounting Entity Definitions,*" (Paper prepared for the U.S. General Accounting Office, May, 1974). This is an excellent review of some of both the theoretical and practical dimensions of accounting for, budgeting for, and managing computer and add resources. It is to be hoped that GAO will build upon and expand this initial study to include all facets of information resources management, of which ADP resources are only one (albeit extremely important) part.

[2]"*Impact of Federal Paperwork on State and Local Governments: An Assessment,*" Volume I of the Report of the Commission on Federal Paperwork, Academy for Contemporary Problems, Washington, D.C., (undated, but report submitted in May, 1977).

[3]"*Our Shadow Government: The Hidden Cost of Government Paperwork, Information and Communication-Related Costs to the American Taxpayer,*" Technical study prepared as a background staff paper to support other Commission on Federal Paperwork Studies. January, 1978. This important paper examines in detail some deficiencies in classification and presentation of expenses under the Federal Government's Object Classification System, as set forth in OMB Circular A-44. It uses the "Information and Records" approach as the premise upon which to estimate fractions of the various Government occupational series spent in "paperwork and administrative" tasks versus "substantive decisionmaking and problem-solving." May be obtained by contacting the author.

[4]"*Information and Records Costs—Interim Report,*" Special Report prepared by E. J. Basgall for the National Archives and Records Service, July 29, 1974, Washington, D.C. This is the predecessor study of the foregoing CFP study. This important study lays the groundwork for the "Information and Records" Approach described in the text.

9 THE INFORMATION ORGANIZATION

What kind of an overall organizational structure is needed to manage information as a crucial company resource? Where should it be located? How should the information unit be structured internally to manage information? How should the unit be staffed? To whom should it report? Should a centralized or decentralized approach be followed? Is a company-wide data base administrator needed? An information administrator? What kind of skills are needed?

These are all important questions. It is my contention that the information unit can be effective at various levels within the parent company, providing: information resources management policies are strong; top management becomes directly interested and involved in spelling out the company's information programs; and necessary financial and human resources are budgeted to support the information unit. In the end, the exact level and precise structural location at which the information unit is placed within the parent organization is a function of the kind of business the organization is in and several other considerations we'll examine. However, in no case should the information unit be placed at a level lower than that of conventional resource management functions with which it competes and must closely interrelate, viz · the personnel, materials, financial and others. But first, let us examine some alternative structures and locations for the information unit.

A FUNCTIONALIZED APPROACH

Figure 9-1 shows how information and data services might be organized along "purely" functional lines in a Federal Government agency. This approach, which is in contrast with more traditional and conventional approaches, hinges on the nature of the end services

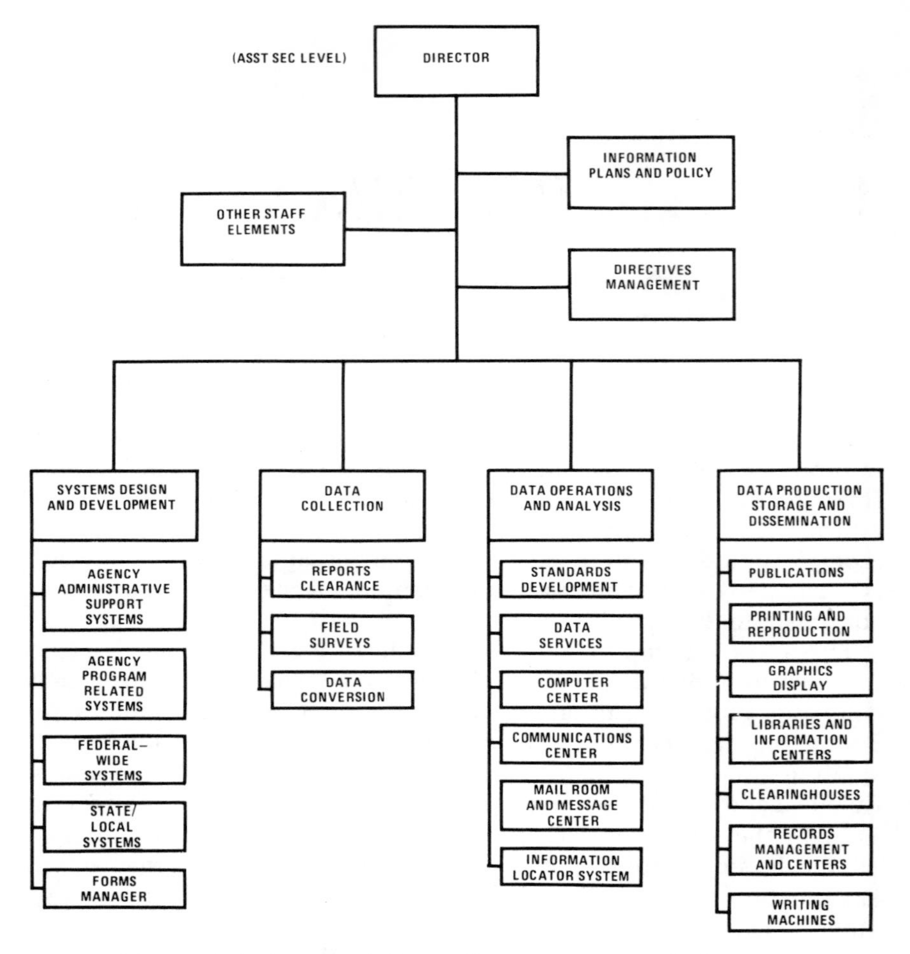

Figure 9-1. **Agency information management structure**

to be performed. But the functionalized structure illustrated in Figure 9-1, it should be pointed out at the outset, is not necessarily the best structure for every organizational context. Note that related information and data services are grouped together, irrespective of information handling physical media or modes of collection, storage and transmission. Rather, the structure is based on various common information functions which need to be performed in almost any organization.

Implicitly there is more emphasis given here to the role of "data" as opposed to the other two major classes of information—documents and literature. For example, librarians may well take umbrage at being "lumped together" with clearinghouses, records centers and publications people under a heading "data production, storage and dissemination." Certainly a great deal of data collection is involved in any library operation, and the design and operation of a bibliographic system for the library, for example, might well be circumscribed under the "system design and development" functional heading. Parallel arguments might also be made by the heads of the clearinghouses and records center activities to justify higher and different locations for their functions.

This leaves us, it seems to me, with the inescapable conclusion that the so-called "functional approach" is neither "pure" nor "preferred." On the contrary, to a large degree it may be misleading since it presupposes some clear and unequivocal standards and precepts that could be followed in defining just what the various specific information functions are and where they should be located. We can see several stumbling blocks to such a simplistic approach. First, organizations which deal more heavily in automated data forms, such as the process control industries like petroleum refineries, may well have a completely different approach to information functionalization than, say, a scholarly institution where information is in the form of scientific and technical document and literature holdings. The information unit structure of the latter kinds of organizations may come closer to Figure 9-1 than would organizations where data is primarily in process control modes. Where the library is a crucial information resource, for example to scholarly pursuits, then we might well see the primary organizational breaks for the information unit oriented to documents and literature, and not simply data.

Another stumbling block we should consider is the role of the information resource itself. In some businesses, such as the brokerage industry and in airline reservations, up-to-the-second, accurate and highly reliable data is a critical resource. In such instances the computer and communications networks come to center stage. The library and information center in these organizational contexts may have a secondary or even tertiary role.

In short, the "pure functional approach" is but one model, not applicable in all organizational contexts. Instead, whether it is selected over alternative approaches depends on a number of variables, including the distinctive business of the organization, the role of the information resource, the organizational level with which we are concerned, and other considerations. This makes it necessary to examine other structural forms for the information unit.

A MORE CONVENTIONAL APPROACH

By contrast, Figure 9-2, depicts a more conventional information organization structure: we have a library, a computer center, the printing and reproduction plant, a communications, a mail room and so on. In contrast with the functionalized information organization shown in Figure 9-1, the central focus here is around conventional information handling media and modes of collection, storage and transmission.

Here, organization of the data and information resource is structured along conventional activities which have traditionally been assigned management and control responsibility for every stage of the information life cycle falling within their purview. Thus, the library has traditionally been the information unit accountable to top management for the acquisition, storage, retrieval and dissemination of literature holdings; the information center and the clearinghouse for document holdings; and the computer center for data holdings. Within each of these three major information classes, information management sub-sets have become specialized organizationally under a variety of labels and functions. For example, the mail room has been responsible for the correspondence subset of the document holdings class; the records center for the records subset of the document holdings class; and the publications department for the publications subset. Specialized units also exist for other data, document, and literature subsets as well.

As we pointed out earlier, however, these organizational boundaries and labels have become blurred with the ascendancy of the computer, communications and other modern information handling technologies such as micrographics and word processing. Indeed, the tendency of some parent organizations to try to hold on to outmoded and obsolete organizational definitions of information activities, in the light of radical transformations of modern information handling media and modes, has caused many management, accounting, budgeting and control problems. We mentioned, for example, the metamorphosis of media for handling correspondence from document (hard copy) to automated media. In many accounting systems much of the cost of "mail handling" still is hidden in computer, communication and reprographic cost centers, as well as elsewhere.

A MIXED, TRANSITIONAL STRUCTURE

A third alternative between the fully functionalized approach in Figure 9-1 and the more conventional approach depicted in Figure

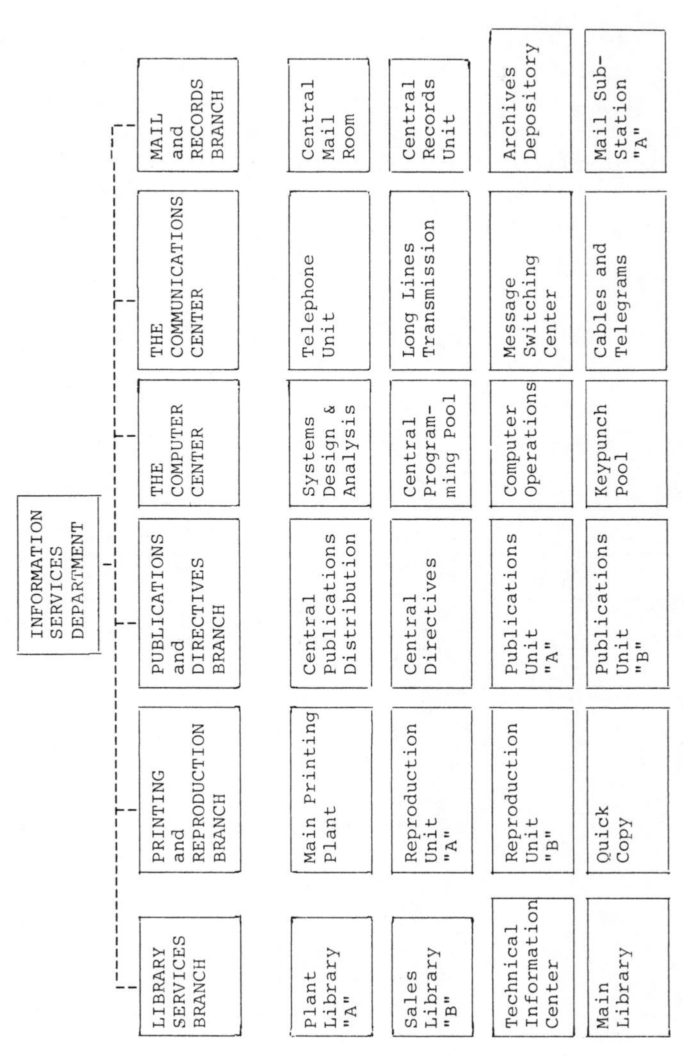

***Figure 9-2.* Traditional information structure**

9-2 is a "mixed" transitional structure shown in Figure 9-3. Here, the information storage and processing functions are partly consolidated across media and mode lines, but the information collection and dissemination functions still approximate traditional labels and functions.

Implicit in this "transitional" structure is the idea that, on the one hand, a great deal of common-purpose data can and should be managed so as to maximize its utility and value to a wide variety of organizational user while, on the other hand, the information analysis and information systems development functions are considered "higher order" activities, which demand a totally different kind of approach, skill base and management system. Here we see that the organization recognized

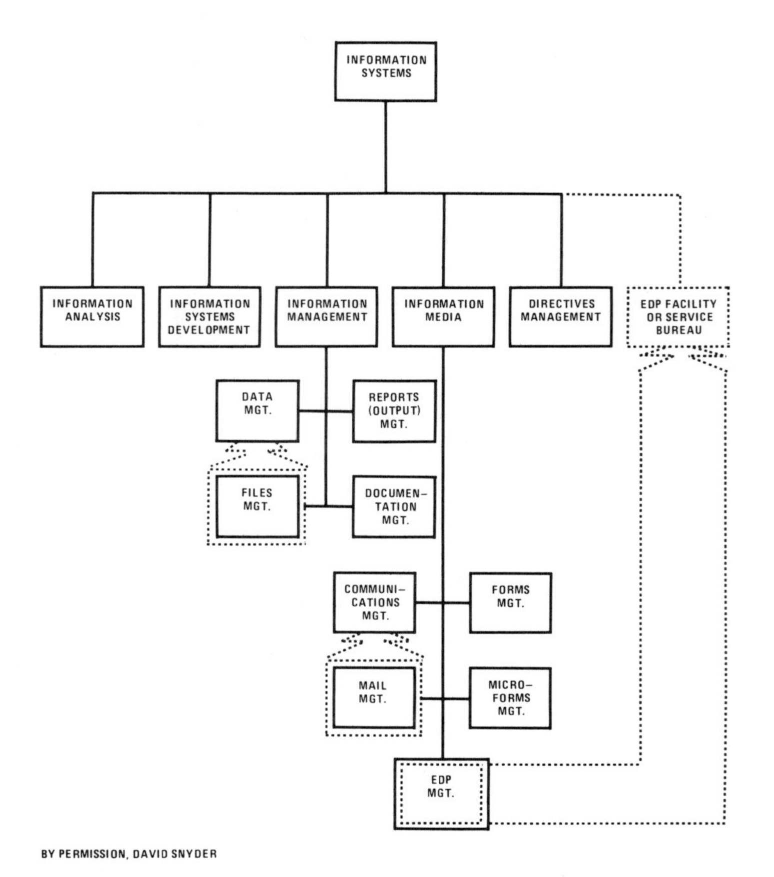

***Figure 9-3.* A mixed, traditional structure**

that its files (that is, physical files and records) should not be separated from the more generic "data management" function; nor mail handling separated from communications. Other functional bridges are constructed organizationally between the more traditional "hard copy" view of information and the post-industrial "information resource" view.

SOME GENERAL PRINCIPLES

The organizational theorist tells us that we should take a number of important considerations into account in planning the information organization. We've already briefly alluded to a few of them, but let's review the list more systematically. First, the distinctive nature of the business. This question is important because the *role* of the information resource vis-a-vis the role of other resources (capital and labor) differs from one enterprise, trade, industry, and profession to another. Moreover, the form and substance of data needed differs substantially from one to another. For example in the commodities futures market in Chicago, up-to-the-second information in the hands of buyers and sellers is absolutely vital to transacting hundreds of millions of dollars of business in the timespan of a few minutes. Incomplete, inaccurate, unreliable or garbled data can be disastrous. To a lesser extent, the same is true of other financial markets such as Wall Street, the brokerage industry, and in international government trade negotiations such as the Kennedy Round of Trade Negotiations conducted in Geneva in the 1960's, and similar negotiations more recently in Tokyo.

The form and structure of the information organization, then, is absolutely crucial to the organization's goal achievement. In many organizations neither capital nor labor, nor creative entrepreneurship in almost any amounts and for almost any value, can be traded-off or substituted for failure to provide that most precious commodity—timely data. In these organizations the information unit will be at relatively higher levels, reporting to more senior officials.

At the other extreme, some kinds of professionals, organizations and businesses barely need data resources. The painter or composer, for example, may be virtually oblivious to the need for external data stimuli. His or her creative inspiration may spring exclusively from internal resources already available. Restaurants, theaters, cleaning establishments, grocery stores and many other kinds of retail establishments fall into this category.

MAKE VS. BUY CONSIDERATIONS

Another important consideration which the information theorist admonishes us to take into account in planning the structure of the information unit is the extent to which the parent organization is in a position to produce most of the information it needs from in-house resources or, conversely, whether it must buy the information products and services it needs from outside resources. To some extent this determination is a function of the first considerations we reviewed—the nature of the business and the exact role of the information resource in that business. If we are in the business of producing information as our primary product—for example, if we are a publisher, an abstracting service, a research organization of some kind, a market research organization, or if we're the Census Bureau in the Federal Government—then clearly the kind of information unit we'll have is quite different than if we're an automobile manufacturer or a processor of scrap metal or a drug manufacturer. If information processing is our business, then we would already have on-hand many kinds of information specialists. Chances are we may have a sizeable computer center, an excellent library, and a battery of research analysts skilled in the arcane arts of searching out "hidden" bits of data in dusty archives, back rooms of newspaper publishers, or out-of-print titles. We can, in short, produce many if not most of the needed information products and services in-house.

On the other hand, if our business is fabrication, or assembly, or manufacturing, we may be fortunate to have a number of information specialists that we can count on one hand. Therefore, instead of a sophisticated, highly structured, specialized information organization which is tiered at several levels vertically and spread horizontally, we may cluster our limited information specialists together or locate them as satellites on a strong staff group with related interests—such as long range planning, or economic and market analysis—and we may have to buy most of our data products and services commercially.

PROFESSIONAL INFORMATION RESOURCES

Still another important factor is the quality and strength of available professional information human resources. In the next chapter we will deal more specifically with human resources, but it should be obvious that there is more to the organizational chart than blocks, templates and theories. More often than not the key to an effective organizational structure lies in the strength, drive, foresight, and initiative of a few strategically placed individuals who have the stamina and power of their convictions.

This is one of the problems many organizations have with their librarians. Traditionally we've conceived of the librarian as a meek, shy individual with the large "Silence" sign on his or her desk. Too many librarians, schooled and disciplined in this model, are poorly equipped by temperament and training to enter the ring with the computer center chief to do battle for today's tight budget dollar. And yet the librarian, and the needs of the library may, in fact, be more critical. My advice to these librarians is take one of those assertiveness/intimidation courses!

In short, where a strong individual does exist, the organization can be built around the individual, rather than the other way around. Rather a strong computer center chief, or data base administrator, with some understanding and sensitivity for the role of the information resource in the organization, playing an effective leadership role than an inexperienced manager "off the street" with little or no appreciation for what this area is all about but with the nominal label of "information manager" on the office door. Organizational placement and functional authority do indeed go a long way to helping establish new programs, but in the end people run programs.

INFORMATION AS A DETERMINANT

We've talked rather vaguely until now of the "role of the information resource" as a determinant of the level and configuration of the information unit in the parent organization. Let us try and be more specific. Two "opposite" Federal examples can be illustrative, one in the foreign affairs community, the other in the intelligence community. As Figure 9-4 shows, the positioning of the information function depends on its organic function and purpose or "role," as we've said. In the Department of State, for example (or another foreign affairs agency), traditionally the foreign policy objectives fall into two major clusters, political and economic. Depending on the ebbs and flows of domestic politics and the exigencies of international conflicts, crises, and other factors, socially-oriented foreign affairs programs may or may not be co-located with the other two; if they are "on the charts," nearly always they have been traditionally placed on a level a half-notch below the other two. Because data and information are the lifeblood of foreign affairs, I would contend that information

1. A Structure in Foreign Affairs

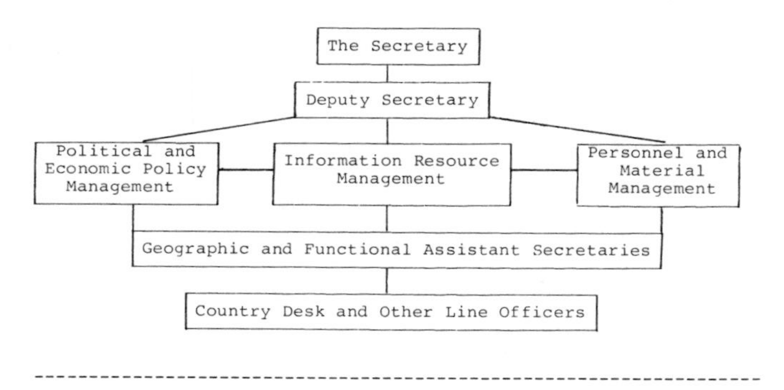

2. A Structure in Intelligence

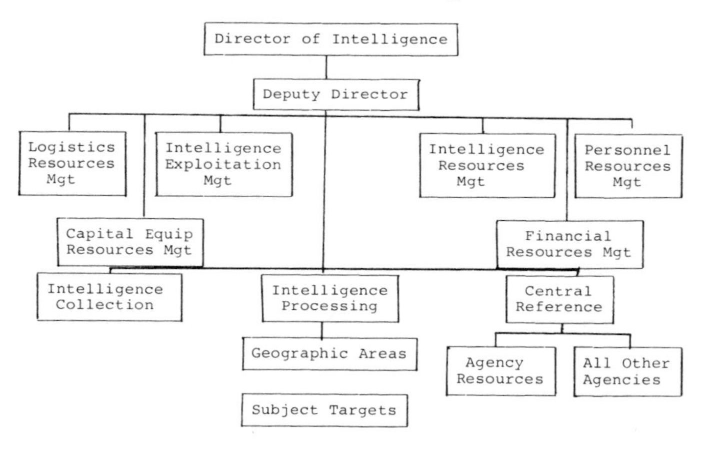

Figure 9-4.

resources should be placed on a level with "sustantive" programs. In the intelligence community, information, once evaluated, is called intelligence. Two major functions are traditionally involved at the highest organizational level—intelligence exploitation and intelligence resources management. The latter involves housekeeping functions now, but there is some indication that moves are being made to upgrade the definition of intelligence resources to a higher order (e.g., knowledge) definition—not just data processing. What we are trying to illustrate with both of these examples is that:

- the placement of the information resources management

function is first, and foremost, a function of the kind of business we're in;
- and next, the role the information resource is expected to play;
- and then the kinds of specific information products and services the organization requires to do its work, which in turn governs the kinds of skills, equipment, materials, office and plant and laboratory space, and other resource requirements.

Certainly there are no magic formulas in the organizational area, any more than elsewhere, but guideposts are available, and we should use them where we have them. Optimally, the knowledgeable top manager will call together his organizational specialists and establish a task force, or project team, to consider alternative information unit structures and make recommendations. There may be no "pure" or "optimal" structure; for example, a transitional structure may be needed to bridge the gap between the existing structure and an idealized structure to which the organization would eventually want to move. Clearly, budgetary, human, technical, and policy constraints may mitigate moves to some idealized information unit structure.

In any event, I think it fair to say that few if any organizational charts in either government, private industry, or elsewhere reflect the importance of the information resource in modern society. As we move from lower order, elementary and basic definitions and uses of data processing to higher order, more sophisticated and complex definitions of information processing, our organizational structures must certainly keep abreast of doctrinal evolution.

FUNCTIONS OF THE INFORMATION ORGANIZATION

Moving from some of the theoretical aspects of the information organization to more practical ones, let us consider what a hypothetical list of functions for the information organization might look like.

1. *Top level advice.* The Information Organization should be prepared to offer advice and counsel to senior organizational officials, particularly the chief official, on fundamental questions of how to use "the information and data resource" effectively in accomplishing the organization's overall mission. We are not talking here about how many computer terminals the organization needs or how big the library should be but, rather, questions of the *role* of the information resource

in the broader scheme of things in the organization.

2. *Coordination.* Clearly the Information Organization must be prepared to play the central coordinating role to insure that all of the various specific information activities and programs of the organization are pulling together, not pulling apart. The Information Organization must work closely with all of the line and staff departments and divisions to insure that their information programs are mutually reinforcing and complementary and that there is a minimum of overlap and duplication between and among them.

3. *Information Applications.* The computer analyst is accustomed to thinking in terms of "computer applications," that is, in what areas and operations the use of the computer can assist manual processes to make them more efficient, or more effective, or both. The head of the Information Organization has a responsibility, however, to insure that this "applications thinking" is an organic part of not the automatic data processing area alone, but every facet of the overall information program. Broadly speaking, where is new, or different, or more, or less, information likely to offer payoffs? The Information Organization, then, like the organization and methods department, must be prepared to work with the line and staff departments in examining their operations and activities to see how the application of information and data resources might be useful.

4. *Technical Assistance.* Much of modern information-handling technology is extremely complex, specialized, and esoteric in concept and application. This implies a role which the Information Organization will be expected to play, and must play, carefully and with advanced planning. For example, what training courses will people need? To what extent will/should line departments have their own technical expertise? The Information Organization must help identify, apply, and evaluate the usefulness of the whole array of advanced information-handling technologies to each departmental unit.

5. *Feasibility Studies.* The Information Organization should be prepared to take the lead role in planning, organizing, and getting underway feasibility studies exploring the expected benefits and costs of major applications of information technologies to the organization. Again, we are talking about computers and automation methods, microform, reprography, telecommunications, COM, word processing and all the rest.

6. *Development of Information Systems.* The Information Organization must take the lead in planning, organizing, and getting underway design and developmental efforts involving the creation of organization-wide, multi-purpose information systems, in order to insure that such systems are truly in support of approved organizational goals.

Priority should be given to the multi-purpose systems and the avoidance of the proliferation of narrow, single-purpose systems that serve only a small band of users.

7. *Standards.* The Information Organization must be prepared to establish an information standards program, and a set of policies, and practical operating guides for the development, use, and evaluation of information standards in each of the technology areas. Standard areas include data element terms and definitions, codes, interchange standards in communication systems, microfiche, ultrafiche, and many others.

8. *Directory of Organization-wide Information Resources.* Elsewhere in this work emphasis was given to the need to develop a baseline of where the organization currently "stands" in terms of existing and planned information resources. The Information Organization is the logical choice to initiate a comprehensive, systematic, inventory of existing and planned information sources, systems, products, and services. Of course, such an inventory must cover all three major classes of information—data, documents, and literature.

9. *Dictionary of Data Elements.* A companion tool to the directory is the dictionary of data elements which are in common use throughout the organization, with the objective of developing a consensus (or at least cross-reference) of standard meanings for terms and the codes and symbols.

10. *Information Resources Management System.* An entire chapter was devoted to the concept and operation of an information resources management system. It is obvious that the Information Organization must undertake the responsibility for the design, development, and operation of this system. It is the framework, the "glue," that holds the individual information systems together and determines whether the total information system and process of the organization is viewed in an integrative context or a disjointed, fragmented context.

11. *Information Networking.* In addition to an information directory of resources, and a data element dictionary, a third of the organization's information tools is the networking, or linking together, of its geographically and physically dispersed information capabilities. This is particularly important in the case of multi-national organizations with offices, plants, sales, and marketing outlets around the globe. Again, capability must extend not only to the document clearinghouse type of interchange or the high speed data transmission interchange, but to the orderly transfer and interchange of entire collections.

12. *Training, Education, and Career Programs.* In the next chapter on the Information Manager we will touch upon the importance of addressing each of these three areas. Again, the Information Organiza-

tion will be expected to take the lead in planning for, developing and evaluating the effectiveness of such programs and activities. Cross-training in the application, use, and evaluation of each of the information technologies is essential if personnel at all levels are to gain the necessary hands-on experience with the different technologies.

13. *Information Accounting Structure.* Our chapter on information costing and the one dealing with information budgeting make it clear that the Information Organization must develop some kind of accounting structure for managing the information resource. Staff should work closely with the organization's financial management staffs—accounting, programming, budgeting, planning, and so forth.

14. *Safeguards.* In a chapter to follow, we will stress the importance of effective organization safeguards to ensure that data is not advertently or inadvertently disclosed to unauthorized parties. These safeguards must be part of an integrated program dealing with the facets of physical security (i.e., building security, computer locks, and so on), technical security (i.e., the software keys governing access to automated data banks); the human security (i.e., security clearances for personnel in sensitive positions). Moreover, the safeguards program must address both automated and manual systems and practices, not just the computerized ones. There are close, working relationships and interfaces between manual and automated systems throughout most modern organizations which extensively use modern information handling techniques, tools, and equipment.

FOUR KEY OBJECTIVES

In summarizing the role of the Information Organization it is useful to review four key objectives of the function:

1. *To Define the Role of the Information Resource.* How critical is data and information to the mission and goals of the organization as a whole? What kinds of data and information streams and flows should be established? What information products and services will be produced in house? Which procured on the market?

2. *To Relate Information Requirements to Decision-making and Problem-solving.* The substance, form, and shape of information requirements must flow from a thorough and careful study of the organization's decision-making and problemsolving processes. This is no abstract exercise. It is absolutely vital if the information is to define itself, so to speak, in terms of decision problems, not just "nice to have" shapes and sizes.

3. *To Establish the necessary controls to insure that all of the*

information which is of value is used, and all of the data which is collected is used, and only that data which is of value is collected and used. As the chapter on planning information requirements demonstrated, there are many leverage points in the information flow process and in the management process in general at which control can and must be exercised to insure that the wrong information isn't collected, information isn't lost or misused, data isn't hidden in filing cabinets and isn't used, and wrong decisions aren't made because information is misinterpreted or misapplied in the development of solutions to problems.

4. *To insure that information resources are acquired, enhanced, exploited, and disposed of in cost-effective ways, to achieve stated organizational goals.* This objective, in essence, pays attention to the information life cycle and its meaning in the context of information resources management, that is, information should be viewed "from birth to death," not in a disjointed fashion.

The information manager-designate might do well to develop an organization planning checklist, to insure that he or she doesn't overlook all of the dimensions of the problem. The checklist should contain headings for structure, staffing, training, key officials, relationships of the information organization to other departments and the front office, priorities, timing, strategy, and last, but not least, goals and objectives.

THE LOUDEST VOICES ARE THE ONES HEARD

Getz's research into the reasons why companies raised the level of the information unit to higher organizational levels, with broader responsibilities and authority, is revealing and gives us some clues as to possible strategies for the organization now struggling with this problem. Here is his list:[2]

1. Recognition of the importance of data as a resource to the company, and that it requires professional management.
2. Personal involvement of the top officers.
3. The level and performance of the people involved.
4. Volume and rapid growth of the industry.
5. Development of systems to meet operational and planning needs (as contrasted to accounting or data processing needs).
6. Advance of technology permitting consolidation of many separate computer systems into one.

7. Importance of company-wide functions.
8. Proliferation of computers through rival organizations (engineering and finance).
9. Excessive costs of equipment and data.
10. Combination of related operations (computer systems, mathematics, etc.), thus maximizing use of the company's resources.
11. High payout ratios demonstrated.
12. Increasing recognition of the importance of computers to company operations.
13. Technical staff in the computer department did not want to report to the Controller.
14. The increasing costs and difficulties of obtaining information essential to the changing management needs of the organization.
15. Increasing pressure to reduce overhead in field operations while gaining more central control.
16. The functions began at its present high organizational level because management recognized it was vital to the company's entire operations and existence.

Four other findings of Getz's research are also illuminating for our purposes. He analyzed the impact of data upon the centralization/decentralization issue, an issue which he found to be "the most controversial subject found during the research."

1. There is a growing trend to move data processing oriented organizations to higher levels. It is suggested this is due to the higher dependence upon the computer for business operations and the increasing size and cost of computer operations. It is not caused by any sudden recognition of data as a resource, although the results are similar.

2. There is a trend to consolidate data-related services under the new, emerging information systems executive. Communications, teleprocessing, reproduction services, operational analysis, computer operations, systems design, programming, data presentations, etc. can often be found under a single executive. It is suggested that this trend will also continue.

3. Regional data processing utilities are gaining favor over single, large centers or highly decentralized operations. This is causing organizational changes. The situation is somewhat confused as new hardware and communication capabilities force frequent reevaluation of operations. The advent of the very small computer has made it economically attractive to decentralize some routine matters and interface with larger central computers for larger jobs. The consolidation

(or centralization) of data processing facilities does not, in itself, cause a centralization of management control. However, the potential of control exists and may be expected.

4. Without specific reference to the term, management of the data resource has become a reality in some organizations in recent years. It would appear this trend will also continue. The data resource, it is suggested, can be managed by a specialized organization created for that purpose.

Precisely as this book has contended, some organizations have brought about this situation not necessarily because of theoretical conviction, with names like the "information resources management department," but because of the practical realities of the role of the computer and automatic data processing, increasingly tight budgets, and the need for closer top management attention. The names, labels and titles are not what really counts; what counts is what is behind the label. In some organization it may make sense to retain traditional titles and labels for this new function if the organization is more comfortable with them or if suppliers and customers are more at ease because of familiarity with them and so on. To risk calumny over the metaphor, "a rose is a rose is . . ."

"THE ENTERPRISE ADMINISTRATOR"

Berry and Cook advanced a theoretical and organizational structure to carry out the functions of their knowledge resource enterprise. See Figure 9-5. They concur in the thesis advanced here that it is not necessary to physically consolidate all of the appropriate functions in one, large, central, and monolithic organization. Their key executive, the "enterprise administrator for the knowledge resource," would direct and control a series of line and staff functions, including the operations of a knowledge resource center, the resource policy staff, a security and privacy group, a standards group, a technology assessment group, a unit which would interface with external information resources, the data base administration shop, and an applications management group. Most of the functions are straightforward and do not diverge too much from alternatives presented in this chapter. However their suggestion that the so-called applications administrators have a dotted line relationship to the various user organizations rather than be under the direct control of the enterprise administrator is noteworthy. They appear ambivalent about this. I suggest that perhaps the source of ambivalence may lie in Nolan's theory of organizational growth; that is, in those advanced organizational forms which have reached the

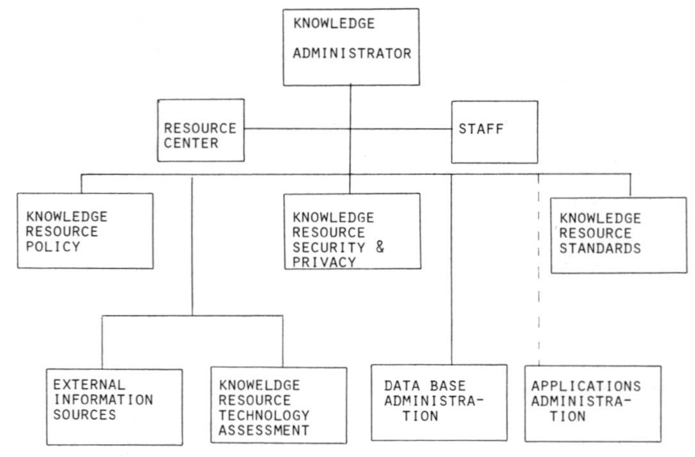

By permission, Berry, James F. and Cook, Craig M.

Figure 9-5. **Knowledge resource organization**

final stages of evolution with respect to their internalization of the principles of information resources management, an unequivocal decision can be made as to whether supporting technical functions, such as systems analysis and design, should be positioned within major user groups or left centrally. The decision usually hinges on how critical the information resource is to the unit(s) in question, how frequently changes to existing systems and data flows take place, how large the organization is, the extent to which it can affort to hire mini-staffs, and similar factors.

I suggest also that the kinds of skills needed to staff the organization also depends in part, on the stage of organizational growth. Clearly we should be careful not to overburden a fledgling organization moving from Stage III to Stage IV (see Chapter 2) with a high-powered group of information generalists which might be counterproductive to the organization's growth stage.

AN ECLECTIC PERSPECTIVE

There is one other important consideration for the emerging information resources management organization, the need for a generalist, eclectic perspective in exercising each of its many important roles—planning, technical assistance, systems design and development and so on. There is a certain divisiveness among the several information worlds now. They have each long been accustomed to doing things in their own way, without regard to the methods and approaches of their sister and brother disciplines. The appearance of the information organization on the organizational chart may or may not augur well for their customs, traditions, mores and ways of doing business. As in all changes, some adjustments, inevitably, must be made and, as in all professions and disciplines, there may be resistance to change because the information organization will require a certain degree of compromise and integration among the different support disciplines if it is to work. The statistician, for example, may or may not be comfortable working in close quarters with the computer systems analyst. The abstract/index expert may be suspicious of the programmer. The communications expert may not be completely at ease with the publications people. Yet all of these skills and perspectives are needed if the information organization is to fulfill expectations and exercise its role satisfactorily.

Support for the multi-disciplinary approach to information management is coming from all quarters. One important study recently completed by the Mitre Corporation for the National Science Foundation, for example, has this to say about scientific and technical information: "It appears certain that issues relating to scientific and technical information policy will become more intertwined with general information policy concerns. It will be increasingly difficult to draw a line of distinction between scientific and technical information and allied areas such as health, medical, or consumer information."[2] One could say the same of the boundaries between information in general and:

- management information systems;
- information storage and retrieval systems;
- statistical data systems;
- recordkeeping systems;
- reporting systems;
- other "systems."

Each of the underlying disciplines has some distinctive, unique and valuable contribution to make to information management. It cannot, and should not, be a case of one or the other dominating the organization's policy-formulation, decision-making, and operating modes. Inevitably there will be some coloration and some flavoring contributed by each. Nor am I suggesting we end up with some lowest common denominator consensus of conflicting perspectives and interests; rather, I'm suggesting a truly eclectic approach that blends the viewpoints of all and builds on the strength of each.

THE FEDERAL GOVERNMENT—AN INFORMATION ORGANIZATION

An examination of the structure of the Federal Government as a massive "information organization" offers, in my view, some unique insights and perspectives. Many, if not most of the "principles, concerns and considerations" we've put forward up to this point can be found on the organizational charts of the United States Government.

Marc Porat, in his doctoral dissertation, "The Information Economy," looked at the Federal Government as a whole and attempted to identify what he considered to be the primary information organizations.[3] He arranged them into eight major groups:

- printing and publishing;
- telephone and telegraph communication;
- advertising agencies;
- news syndicates and broadcasting;
- data processing services;
- education;
- library services; and
- statistical and planning information.

Within the first category—printing and publishing—he places the Government Printing Office, the National Technical Information Service, portions of the National Bureau of Standards, and the printing and reproduction activities of the various Executive Branch departments and agencies. In the second category—telephone and telegraph communication—he places the General Services Administration's Automated Data and Telecommunication Service and the Federal Telecommunications System. He also places in this category the major communication and telecommunication components of the various departments and agencies. In the third category—advertising agencies—he places the various agency public affairs and information offices. In the fourth category—news syndicates and broadcasting—are placed the media programs of the agencies.

In the data processing services category are the various agency computer centers; in the education category, the various educational and training programs of the agencies; and in the library services category, the Library of Congress, the various national libraries, and the Smithsonian's museum programs. Finally, in the last category—statistical and planning information—are the programs of the major statistical agencies.

Mr. Porat's approach presents several problems. First of all, I would argue with the inclusion of some of the components of his "advertising agency" category. Public affairs offices, for example, do not deal with information as a "value-neutral" commodity. Quite the contrary. Their business is often to slant information to serve various ends—for example, "selling" the agency, building up its image, and screening or filtering out certain adverse data. Libraries, printing and reproduction centers, and computer centers do not normally engage in this kind of activity. That is not to say that on occasion an individual in charge of or assigned to one of these activities may distort or misuse information entrusted to his or her custody, but such is the exception and not the rule. It is in this sense that the term "value-neutral" is used.

Classification problems also exist in the statistical area. Again, once we lay aside such aphorisms as "figures don't lie, but liars figure" or "there are lies, damn lies, and statistics," we must still, I believe, conclude that statistical organizations *should* be dealing with information as a "value-neutral" commodity. Company executives and Government officials may choose to "play games" with statistics, by arranging to release them at propitious times, for instance. But statisticians can hardly be blamed for that!

The "education" category presents the next problem. Much "training" is directly concerned with the imparting of skills and knowledge at the technical level, rather than being "informational" in character. It is hard to see how the training of a pilot to operate an aircraft can be included under the heading of an "information organization."

Another problem with this thesis is that a number of important categories of information organizations are entirely omitted. For example, in every large agency of the Federal Government there are central reports control offices that may be manned from anywhere from one or two to twenty-five or more people. There is no category for this. Next, there are records officers and records offices in virtually every Government agency, and yet there is no category for this. Also, there are various management information systems (MIS) support groups which may be entirely separate from the data processing component or a statistical component. Where, for example, is the MIS group? And where are the records centers and records depositories? Moreover, there is no evidence that data and documentation centers and an entire array of information analysis and information referral centers are included. Perhaps they are under Porat's category of library services, but this is not clear.

WHO "OWNS" INFORMATION?

We have talked so far about structure, but let us consider some other considerations. For example, to what extent is information and data within the organization viewed as a resource which is "owned" by the central information organization, or entrusted to it, in which case the central organization becomes a data custodian? Many organizations in both Government and private industry are experimenting with the data base administrator concept. Under this approach, a senior official—who heads the central information organization—is responsible for the development, maintenance, and management of the company's central data base(s) resource.

A wide variety of alternatives which have been followed in the definition of the central data base resource. Typically, a central data base is defined as containing only the organization's most commonly used data elements. In a nontechnical organization, this typically includes the central data concerned with the company's housekeeping and administrative chores, for example, personnel, supplies, equipment, and so on. The company's financial resources are supported by a central accounting system, would also be embraced by the central data base. As we move away from central housekeeping and administrative functions to operating functions, however, significantly different approaches begin to show up with respect to the ownership/custody question. The more sensitive the information, the more difficult to collect and maintain, the more critical the information is to the well-being of the organization, the *less* likely the data would be included under the jurisdiction of the data base administrator in the company's central data base. In short, ownership becomes a real not a theoretical issue. In the technical organization, business and financial data, to be sure, may be retained in the central data base, but scientific and technical data usually is retained in a scientific information retrieval system, where management and control is exercised more on technical reports and documents than on data elements.

The problems of data ownership have become more critical as issues of privacy and safeguarding sensitive information continue to get headline treatment. The problem of "who shall have access" is still a critical one, and so long as the political, administrative, and technical problems and barriers to guaranteeing the confidentiality of data remain so formidable, the notion of the "information czar" will remain with us. (We will deal more with this issue in the next two chapters.) Notwithstanding these problems, there have been some innovative approaches to dealing with it. For example, one rather interesting approach is the notion of the information confederation using a kind of data roundtable or turntable (like the locomotive roundhouse).

The information confederation idea is, in essence, a loose federation of information resources which are networked together. Under this approach, data ownership (autonomy) is still retained by the "sovereign" functional owners of data, even though the data itself may be loaned to (shared with) a central bank and replicated in many geographically dispersed locations and in many technically disparate forms. The data base administrator under this approach is, indeed, a custodian of the data, but functional managers retain legal, policy, and security keys governing access to the information. Appropriate administrative and technical safeguards ensure that the data cannot be assessed by unauthorized parties. The data roundtable would act as a central switching device, to assure that common use data elements needed by one department within the company are obtainable by another department quickly and easily, so long as the second department is authorized access. The data roundtable concept assures that the *integrity* of the data is maintained regardless of when it is used, who uses it, for what purposes it is used, and so on. In short, it enjoys the advantages of assuring that a single set of master data is maintained and updated in lieu of multiple sets of potentially redundant, inconsistent, and incompatible data maintained in compartmentalized locations.

SUMMARY

We've examined alternative organizational structures and concluded that the state-of-the-art of information resources management is still too primitive to postulate "preferred" arrangements. Instead, there is a set of guideposts which can be followed to help the parent organization determine where in its overall set-up the information unit should be positioned, how high on the ladder, with what powers and authorities, and with what "straight line and dotted line" relationships to other functional units. None of these guideposts are guarantees, however, that the ultimate position of the unit will necessarily be the "right" one. Instead, the parent organization should reevaluate its initial decisions in the light of actual operating experience, to see if results are being achieved.

QUESTIONS FOR DISCUSSION

1. How would you expect the authorities, roles and functional responsibilities of a (1) Knowledge Administrator; (2) Information Manager; and (3) Data Base Administrator to differ? In what kinds of organizations might you expect to see a Knowledge Administrator flourish? Conversely, what organizations might see such a role as a threat, or counterproductive force? Are the three roles simply stages in the growth and evolution of Information Management in the same organization, or might all three roles be viable in the same organization?

2. Some organizations insist that the senior information official, whatever his title, be given full ownership and control over all of the information resources of the organization; others prefer the role been viewed as a custodial or fiduciary one. What kinds of organizations might you expect to reflect the former attitude? Which the latter? Think across the spectrum of business and industry, public institutions, not-for-profit organizations, and so on.

3. One school of thought uses the "value-neutral/value-laden" criterion for differentiating between those functions within the organization which should come within the purview of the information manager, and those which fall outside of it. According to this school, an organizational unit which deals with information in "value-neutral" contexts would make no political judgments whatsoever with regard to its substantive content. A unit which looks upon the information commodity as a medium for effecting value judgments, by contrast, would fall into the other category. Following this train, how would you classify a university from "an information management" standpoint? An advertising office? The intelligence service of a government agency? A management consulting firm?

4. Following the preceding question, it may be fairly said that even libraries and statistical offices may not always move along "the straight and narrow" with regard to dealing with their data, document and literature holdings in a "neutral" sense. Apart from obvious questions of ethics and "office politics" what kind of statement might you prepare for inclusion in a comprehensive position description for your organization's Information Manager job, with an eye to maximizing "information neutrality" and minimizing "information politicizing?"

5. Compare and contrast a fully centralized information management approach in an organization, to a fully decentralized one. In what kinds of organizations might you anticipate seeing the former model; which the latter? What factors might be paramount in determining

which of the two, or what combination of the two, would be most appropriate?

FOOTNOTES

[1] *"Scientific and Technical Information: Options for National Action,"* prepared for the National Science Foundation, Division of Science Information, by the Mitre Corporation, METREK Division, McLean, Virginia, November, 1976. This report is a very good update of the issues involved in the "STINFO" (Scientific and Technical Information) area, including questions of organizational roles and authorities nationally (both the public and private sectors).

[2] *"An Analysis of Management of the Data Resources,"* Dissertation for the Degree of Doctor of Business Administration, The George Washington University, October, 1969, (Library call Nr. AS 36 .G3), Getz.

[3] *"The Public Bureaucracies,"* (Chapter Eight of Ph.D. Thesis, Marc Uri Porat, *"The Information Economy,"* Stanford University, August 1976). The substance of Dr. Porat's thesis has been incorporated into a nine volume report, with the same title as the Ph.D. Thesis, published by the office of telecommunications Policy of the Department of Commerce.

10 THE INFORMATION MANAGER

Who is the information manager? Where does he sit in the organization? What role does he play? How does his role differ from the modern data base administrator (DBA) or the more traditional paperwork manager? What are his duties, his experience qualifications, his academic credentials, his training requisites? How high can he expect to rise?

These are all important questions. Surely the modern executive who knows how to manage information and data will be a key person in today's modern organization. For example, the task of managing a multinational corporation's far flung resources and assets is indeed a formidable and information-intensive task. It will demand the most imaginative and creative talents of energetic and enterprising individuals. There is every likelihood that many computer center managers will not, for example, rise to the challenge without additional perspectives, skills, and experiences. Similarly, it is doubtful that the librarian, the information center chief, the reports control officer, the records manager, the chief statistician, the chief of the printing branch, or even the trained information scientist, will be able to rise to the challenge without additional experience and training. In short, today's modern information manager must be a multidimensional, multi-faceted executive. He brings to his job a set of unique, generalist perspectives, and he will be entrusted with the organization's valuable information assets only if he demonstrates a keen appreciation and sensitivity to the demands of his new role.

PRESENT MANAGERS OUTMODED

Records managers, forms managers, and paperwork managers in general will need a transformation if they are to rise to the challenge of the information manager's responsibilities. The job of the paperwork manager has too long been regarded as an abomination! The terms "paperwork management" and "records department" cause many to snicker. Perhaps our troubles started when Webster defined paperwork as an "incidental but necessary part of a job." Who wants to deal with "incidentals," anyhow? For much too long our records and paperwork managers have been thrown "administrative leftovers" by their line-manager bretheren.

The convergence of at least four facts seems to argue the revitalization of the "lost profession" of paperwork manager in the context of our discussion:

1. Managing documents and records is indeed important, but the real culprit behind the paperwork profession's fall into management oblivion in recent years has been the ascendancy of the computer and related automated information-handling equipment and technologies.
2. As the primary medium for collecting, handling, storing, and disseminating information, the "document" is losing ground. More and more information is being handled in computerized, microform and other advanced media at the sub-document level because it is generally cheaper and faster to handle it in these media. The implications of this transition for the paperwork profession are far-reaching.
3. The current population explosion of the planet, coupled with the depletion of non-replenishable resources, places a premium on reusing available resources, including information resources, instead of discarding them. The notion of "recycling," discussed elsewhere in this work, has brought into play a whole new set of arts and crafts with respect to handling information. Paper and documents are not the most efficient and effective media for recycling.
4. The information explosion itself caught the paperwork profession with its file drawers out. The proliferation of data and documents was so rapid, so diverse, and so pervasive that the paperwork community was simply unprepared to deal adequately with it. An image of the records depository as being simply another archival form quickly materialized and has stuck.

In the months and years ahead the information manager will find himself, increasingly, being called into thickly carpeted front offices (threshholds which the paperwork manager hardly ever dared cross before) to provide counsel of a highly technical nature to top officials. A few of our paperwork and records managers have already found their way out of the filing closet and have begun to update their credentials in the new fields of information science and telecommunications science. For the paperwork manager to be transformed into the information manager, not only must the skills, techniques and tools of the traditional time and motion study analyst be acquired, but the information manager must know something, too, of the design and development of computerized information storage and retrieval systems, automatic indexing and bibliographic search procedures, and the arcane theory of classification systems being jointly developed by multidisciplinary teams of semanticists, etymologists, and taxonomists.

Another important dimension of the "new" theory of information management as we enter the era of zero-base budgeting will be the use of the systems approach to improve program administration and management. For a long time many practitioners of systems analysis and the systems approach have looked upon paperwork systems as something of a stepchild. If they weren't working on more exciting and exotic organizational systems, planning systems, evaluation systems, and whatever else, they might condescend to do some kind of paperwork systems study. One might have thought that, long before now, the evolution from traditional paperwork systems management to information systems management would have progressed in a logical and orderly fashion, both in concept and in practice.

I do not mean to suggest that every paperwork supervisor should suddenly roll down his or her sleeves, put on a new set of clothes, and buy a new lapel button proudly proclaiming status as the "information manager of the 1980's." Nor am I suggesting that there is some magic formula, or turn-key approach, that will provide the alchemy to turn paperwork lead into information gold. All of the traditional, functional components of paperwork management which have been carefully developed and refined over the years—records, files, mailroom operations, and so on—will continue to play a vital role in the arsenal of the information manager. Before we talk "transformation" we must first understand the nature of the information manager's job.

COMPLEXITY AND SPECIALIZATION

One simple and direct way of reviewing the nature and extent of specialization and complexity of the information manager's job is to review the list which the American Society for Information Science periodically publishes for job vacancies.[1] See Figure 10-1. Here are a few position descriptions:

- Library Systems Analyst—Using modern technology to improve access to the large store of library information;
- Abstractor-Indexer—Processing the intellectual content of documents for ready retrieval;
- Microform Technologist—Using a wide range of sophisticated equipment to miniaturize or reproduce documents, tapes, and other records;
- Technical Writer or Editor—Conveying technical information intelligently to other technical audiences or to the layman;
- Technical Information Specialist—Using one's subject background to assist colleagues in satisfying their information requirements;
- Information Broker—Performing specialized information-retrieval services on a fee basis;
- Bibliographic Searcher—Using modern information systems, in batch or on-line mode, to identify or retrieve pertinent publications;
- Information Scientist—Conducting basic research on the phenomena of information, or teaching the fundamentals underlying the science of information;
- Professor of Information Studies—Educating others in the planning, design, management, and evaluation of the total information process;
- Computational Linguist—Analyzing word and language structure to determine how the computer can manipulate text for indexing classification, abstracting, search, and retrieval;
- Applications Programmer—Modifying existing software to implement specific information tasks;

The Society says:

> Thousands of people are making a good living because they know something special about the nature of information. They have learned how to handle information as a valuable commodity and have learned how to contribute their skills to information-related problems that arise in academic institutions, government agencies, industrial business organizations, and many other places of employment.

CAREER OBJECTIVES	SALARY RANGE	YEARS EXPERIENCE
Asst. Dir. of Libraries	15–17,000	7
Bibliographic Searcher	13,000+	2
Bibliographic Searcher/Librn.	14,000+	6
Dir. MIS or data services	35–40,000	15+
Editor-In-Chief/President	60,000	26
Energy/Enviro. Mgmt/ Consultant	—	10+
Exhibits Manager	20,000	11+
Health Science Librarian	—	—
Indexing/Abstracting	part-time	—
Information Administration	20–25,000	14
Information Broker Support	12,000	3
Information Management	13–16,000	1
Information Management	18,500	7
Information Manager	open	8+
Information Manager	18–22,000	10
Information Manager	25,000	10
Info. Mgr. Sys. Des. Mgmt.	20,000	6
Information Scientist	15–1800	11
Information Service & Research	10,000	3
Information Specialist	open	1
Information Specialist	18–20,000	5
Info. Specialist/Research	12,000+	1
Info. Specialist/Trainee	10,000	1+
Info. Systems Management	40,000	25+
Info. Systems Management	16–22,000	8
Law-related/Library	13,000+	2
Librarian	14,000+	2
Librarian	14,500	16
Librarian/Indexer	open	1
Library Director	19,000	8
Management	open	25
Management	25–30,000	—
Management	30–40,000	20
Manager	17,000	3
Manager	35–40,000	15
Manager/Info. Systems	27,500–32,000	25
Mgmt/Research	open	7
Market Research	17,000	3

Figure 10-1. **Typical information management positions**

Planning & Managing Info.	open	10
Product Manager	18–20,000	3
Project Staff	20–25,000	10
Research Analyst	13,000+	2+
Research Lib/Info Specialist	15,000+	10
Searcher/Ref. Mgmt	15–20,000	3
Sr. Level Prog. Analyst	24–28,000	12
Specialist/Program Adm.	20–25,000	20
Supervisory Lib. Info. Mgr.	17,300–18,000	3+
Systems Analyst	14,500	2
Systems Analyst	open	—
Systems Development	open	4
Technical Information	20,000	10
Tech Info. Specialist	15,000	2+
Translating	part-time open	10

Source: The American Society for Information Science

Figure 10-1. (Continued)

These people in the Information Science community have backgrounds, work experiences, education, and skills as varied and diverse as any other profession or occupation. Although anyone with a basic educational background can become an information professional, the field requires a unique combination of skills, interests, and specialists.

Information Science activities appeal to those who like to try new ideas, enjoy working with novel equipment, and face exciting intellectual challenges. Information professionals are enthusiastic in their efforts to satisfy the information requirements of others. Most are articulate and possess good writing skills, have orderly and retentive minds, can think clearly and logically, and understand qualitative and analytical methods.

Since Information Science is a fast-moving field, the people in it must be flexible, adaptable, able to tolerate ambiguity, and capable of exercising sound judgment. An information professional must have better than average organizational and communication skills to work with a variety of persons, organizations, subject interests, and techniques. He or she must be able to integrate and use various perspectives in understanding information needs and then applying the appropriate technique to satisfy these needs.

Most information professionals have specialized knowledge in a subject outside the Information Science field. Many are equipped with competencies in foreign languages and in related fields such as computer science and librarianship.[1]

TRAINING AND EDUCATIONAL NEEDS

Another way of getting a handle on the job of the information manager is to take a look at the educational and training offerings of selected government and academic training institutions.

A recent cursory examination of the workshops, seminars, and other training formats offered to government employees by the U.S. Civil Service Commission (CSC) is revealing in terms of the breadth, scope, and degree of specialization now offered the information professional.[2] The following sample of descriptive course abstracts was picked at random from 1976 catalogs, brochures and pamphlets which are published, literally, by the hundreds.

Computer Design Forms—In a combination of lecture, demonstration and workshop sessions, the participants will gain knowledge and experience in forms analysis and design. The topics to be covered include the following:

- The Need for Forms;
- The Role of Forms Analysis and Design in the Systems Development Process;
- Forms Analysis: Input/Output
- Forms Design: Input/Output
- Cost Effectiveness of Information Collection Alternatives; and
- Agency Standards.

Advanced Computer Systems Technology—The course is designed to update the technical knowledge of the computer specialist as a professional by acquainting him with the latest developments in computer hardware and software technology. Among the topics to be discussed are:

- Computer Technology in the Future;
- Nature of Telecommunications;
- Distributed Data Entry Systems; and
- Management Sciences.

Indexing and Abstracting—After attending the INDEXING AND ABSTRACTING FOR ADP INFORMATION SYSTEMS workshop, the student should be able to:

- Define the basic indexing and abstracting concepts;

- Evaluate the different approaches to indexing;
- Develop an abstract of a technical document; and
- Identify the applications of computerized techniques to the indexing and abstracting processes.

Computer Programming—Upon completion of this course, the student will have a basic understanding of ADP fundamentals and be able to explain the use of the basic flowcharting symbols. The student should be able to develop a flow chart from simple problem specifications under the supervision of an experienced programmer.

Computer/Microfilm Information Systems—Upon completion of this three-day seminar, the student should be able to:

- identify the components and characteristics of a computer/microfilm information systems;
- develop the criteria for determining the suitability of such a system for their information processing needs; and
- evaluate the different COM systems available to computer users.

Advanced Scientific Computing Techniques—This five-day course (lecture and workshop) will teach scientists, engineers, and mathematicians to use a digital computer to solve advanced problems from their professional areas. Emphasis will be on methods for solving ordinary and partial differential equations. Computer terminals will be available for student use throughout the course.

Systems Design Considerations in an On-Line Environment—The course presentations describe techniques for designing on-line systems and explore the implications of available hardware and software in systems design. Techniques for predicting and measuring performance of the system, definition of design constraints, and problems and solutions associated with the design and operation of on-line systems will be discussed. The topics to be covered include:

- Types of on-line Systems
- Differences Between On-line and Batch Processing
- On-line Software
- Designing an On-line System
- On-line Files and Data Bases
- Error Recovery and Fallback.

Systems Workshop for Computer Specialists—The objective of this course is to provide a forum for an exchange of information and ideas in the area of minicomputer technology have impacted the management approach to data processing. User-managers need to learn more about the whole concept of minicomputer-based distributed processing in order to make more intelligent decisions concerning their computing requirements.

Automated Personnel Systems—The participant upon completing the course will be able to use this tool in work simplification to:

- Analyze work distribution of individuals, processes, systems and paperwork flow;
- Identify and eliminate weaknesses in agency operations and procedures;
- Understand and apply management flow charting techniques;
- Collect data, communicate ideas, and document operations through the use of standard management flow charting symbols; and
- Enhance oral and written proposal presentations.

Creativity in Systems Design—All levels of government are spending billions of dollars annually developing on-line applications and converting batch systems to on-line systems. However, these systems are frequently not controlled as well as they might be, nor do they allow for effective management evaluations and audits using traditional tools and techniques. This course is designed to present appropriate new tools and techniques to be used for on-line systems.

Systems Analysis for Computer Programmers—The objective of this program is to provide information about the fundamental concepts and techniques of ADP Systems analysis and design. This course is not intended to make ADP systems analysts out of trainees; it is intended to increase the efficiency of functional area employees in the performance of their day-to-day responsibilities in the area of ADP applications. The course will provide the necessary conceptual foundation in the ADP systems development process to permit effective on-the-job working relationships with representatives of the data processing organization (systems analysts and programmers).

ADP Systems Analysis Seminar—This course is specifically designed for computer programmers who are preparing for assignments in ADP systems analysis or who, because of expanding responsibilities, must deal directly with either systems analysts or user personnel. A thorough knowledge of computers and computer programming concepts will be assumed so that the program may move immediately into the application of this knowledge to the functions of systems analysis and design.

Auditing On-Line Systems—The course outline is as follows:

- Introduction and Motivation;
- Solution Sequence and Rules of Heuristics Workshop Exercise: Algorithmic Solutions;
- Strategy for Solution;
- Heuristic Reasoning Workshop Exercises: Developing Analogies, Identifying Parameters, and Problem of Rates
- Presentation of Solutions.

Process Flow Charting for Analysts—The following topics are among those to be presented during the seminar—Automated Personnel Systems:

The Computer as a tool in:

- Recruitment and Selection
- Records Maintenance
- Training
- Labor Relations
- Statistical Reports
- Other Personnel Function.

Case studies in automated personnel systems. Government-wide activities related to centralized ADP systems.

Introduction to Minicomputers for User-Managers—This two-week session will permit the new systems analyst to become more proficient with systems analysis techniques. In the first week, through lectures and practical exercises, the learning is closely tied to the application of each technique. The second week is then devoted to a single case study problem. In small groups, the class develops a systems project step by step from problem definition to conversion planning. Each group works independently and at key points in the system development process, presentations are made to the class and the team of instructors to insure that each team is progressing toward a workable solution.

- Analyzing Data: Nonparametric Statistical approaches;
- Managerial Effectiveness Seminar;
- Advanced Management Seminar;
- Management Use of Financial Information.

The lists and offering go on and on. And they duplicate and overlap one an other to a considerable extent; for example, those of the Graduate School of the United States Department of Agriculture, the Federal Executive Institute at Charlottesville, Virginia, and others. The point is the administrative, technical, and behavioral skills needed by the information manager are more extensive, detailed, specialized and complex than ever before. (Figure 10-2 is another "random list," without descriptive abstracts.) To some extent, the formal and on-the-job education, training and practical experience he acquires will equip the information-manager to anticipate and deal with many issues he will inevitably confront effectively. But there are many pitfalls—more accurately minefields—in front of him. That is why we added "behavioral skills" above as a category of training and experience. Though we may exaggerate to claim the wisdom of a Solomon will be needed, certainly the nature of many of these issues is more political and social than technical and economic. Some of these are dealt with in the next paragraphs.

ATTITUDE AND POSTURE

If the information manager zealously overguards his precious information assets, he will be accused of being an information czar. On the other hand, if he is too permissive and does not aggressively pursue companywide programs of standardizing common data element terms and their corresponding codes, he runs the risk of presiding over the splintering and fragmentation of his resource. The struggles and conflicts will be many. The battle lines are already drawn. On the one side we have strong line and staff managers who, like all of their predecessors, can be expected to protect their self-interests. That is, many feel that so long as they are making a profit for the company, it makes little difference how demanding and uncompromising an attitude they take in extending the complete control over, not only information resources, but all resources. How many times have we heard them say, "As long as I'm making a profit, the boss will give anything I need" or "I never go to work for a company unless it is clear that I can get anything I want so long as I achieve its goals and objectives."

- Management Introduction to Minicomputers
- Operating Computer Peripheral Equipment
- Survey of Data Entry/Computer Output Devices
- Management of Data Communications
- Fundamental Telecommunications Concepts
- Automated Financial Systems
- ADP for Administrative, Clerical and Secretarial Personnel
- Introduction to Parallel Processors
- Library Automation
- Storage and Retrieval Techniques
- Design of a Computerized Management Information System
- Management Introduction to Automated Data Bases
- Management Introduction to ADP
- Introduction to ADP Systems Analysis
- An Introduction to ADP
- Government Property and Recordkeeping Procedures
- Computer File Structures and Data Base Design
- Scientific Computing with Digital Computers
- Introduction to State Variables
- Analyzing Data: Nonparametric Statistical Approaches
- Successful Implementation of the Freedom of Information Act and the Privacy Act
- Workshop in Performance Analysis
- Reviewing Other People's Writing
- Effective Briefing Techniques
- Writing Effective Letters
- Report Writing Workshop
- Fundamentals of Writing
- Basic Communications Skills
- Effective English Workshop
- Word Processing—A Clerical Orientation
- Essentials of English
- Word Processing—An Overview for Management
- Creative Problem-Solving
- The Management of Information
- Middle Management Institute
- Management Analysis and Review
- Advanced Management Analysis
- Statistics for Paraprofessionals
- Statistics for Paraprofessionals II

***Figure 10-2.* Random selection of course titles from training catalogs of the civil service commission, U.S. government, 1977**

- Administrative Systems and Procedures Analysis
- Graphs, Charts, and Tables
- Paperwork Management—Analysis and Improvement
- Data Collection and Analysis
- Statistical Sampling in Government Operations
- Managerial Statistics
- Federal Financial Management Information Systems

Figure 10-2. (Continued)

In the case of the information resource, the problem has been aided and abetted by a benign top management posture. At least with capital resources, the controller was able to insert some limits and controls over the ambitions of zealous plant and product managers, and the accountable property officer was able to enforce some rules with respect to how many chairs and tables, how thick the rug, and how big an office our hotshot middle managers should have. But hapless records and report chiefs have little chance against strong line managers. Whenever the product manager runs the boss and threatens to shut down his production lines, or lay off his people because he can't get the information he needs to do his job, our information staff people are intimidated. In short, our vice-president for information has his job clearly cut out for him. The opportunity and challenge is there. But so are the risks!

RESPONSIBILITIES OF THE INFORMATION MANAGER

Let us look more closely at some specific tasks. In an earlier work, I listed eight functions of the corporate information manager:

1. Provide overall coordination of company-wide efforts to improve the planning, development, and operation of corporate and department information systems.
2. Develop specific policies and technical guidance to assist individuals operating departments and corporate headquarters in the continuing management of their information systems activities and in implementing responsibilities outlined in the overall company information management program.
3. Identify and initiate improved ways of achieving compatibility between information systems and different departments, through such programs as standard definitions and terms for

commonly used data elements and codes.

4. Provide for the establishment and operation of one or more company information centers. As a first step, develop and maintain a comprehensive inventory of departmental and corporate information systems. This inventory will service all authorized users by providing them, upon request, with information on the existence, name, location, purpose, content, and other data concerning both departmental and corporate information systems, as well as the substantive data content of such systems.
5. Provide for the establishment of training programs to encourage and enable departments to accomplish more effectively the goals and objectives of their programs and acquire the necessary technical and managerial know-how and skills.
6. Provide technical advice and assistance to departments in evaluating, modifying, and improving existing systems and information management practices and in developing new systems.
7. Prepare periodic, company-wide information systems improvement reports on both the short and long term information needs of the company as a whole, as well as the needs of the individual departments, in the management and coordination of information systems.
8. Make lead departmental assignments for the development of additional company-wide information systems and for the continued operation of existing corporate and departmental information systems.

Interfaces between the company's central information manager and the heads of individual departments and divisions is also important. The central information manager will be expected to:

1. Assist the heads of individual departments and divisions establish departmental information policies consistent with the general information policies of the corporation as a whole. For example, these might include the interchange of substantive data and information systems knowledge and technology and the development and utilization of company-wide information systems that are multi-purpose in character and use, in lieu of developing a myriad number of single-purpose information systems.
2. Assist departmental heads in establishing a comprehensive department-wide information management program to provide

for the orderly acquisition, enhancement, retention, and delivery of information resources within the department—an example of this activity might be the establishment of two to five-year plans for the development of departmental information systems.
3. To assist departmental heads in the development of procedures and controls to ensure adequate justification, documentation, review and approval of proposed new information systems or the modification of existing systems. A part of this process would be to ensure that alternate approaches were fully explored to satisfy the achievement of expected goals and objectives to be satisfied by the information systems.

DATA BASE ADMINISTRATOR

It may be instructive to look now at the differences between the role of the data base administrator (DBA) as it evolved in the middle or the late 1960's and the role of the information manager as it is now evolving. Some authors claim the data base administrator is the precursor of today's modern information manager, and as we have implied elsewhere, today's information manager may be the precusor of tomorrow's knowledge manager. The role of the data base administrator is still subject to debate. Figure 10-3 compares differences in data administration philosophies, different roles of the data base administrator, various alternative placements of the data base administrator on the organization chart, and various approaches to the kinds of staff required to support the data base administrator, for four different organizations: The Diebold Corporation, IBM, and two Federal agencies.

It is clear from an examination of these contrasting viewpoints that the role of the data base administrator, while much older than the role of the modern information manager, is still evolving. Data administration philosophies range from a relatively perfunctory concept of data control to a much broader and deeper systems approach concept, one that gets into questions of data integrity. Similarly, the role of the data base administrator, at one extreme, includes extensive, "hands-on" assistance to operating managers in the definition of their data requirements to a fairly mechanical approach to information restricted to questions of data base design, development, and operations. Conceptions of the placement of the data base function within the organization vary substantially. Some organizations consider the function to be a relatively low level service one; others place it at a very high level; but some intimate it should report to a computer center official.

	DIEBOLD	IBM	U.S. AIR FORCE	NAT'L. BUR. STNDS.
1. Data Administration Philosophy	Centralized control of the data base	A data base management system to manage and control data	Multi-user data base and all files within that data base	Flexible design and structure to meet different needs
2. Data Base Administrator's function	Data definition, standardization, liaison	Definition and organization of data base; protection; operation; documentation	Coordinates information uses and user needs	Data base design; administration; operations; monitoring; auditing; and systems development
3. Organization	Service function in EDP dept.; custodial; high level; group, not a czar	Removed from direct control of users, application areas; reports to highest level EDP executive	No optimum location;	New organizational element; location depends of purpose and objectives of organization

4. Administrator's staff	Multifaceted: legislator, diplomat, policeman, consultant, technician	Top man; dynamic supervisory skill knowledge of EDP technology, global diplomacy, college degree	Strength in technical areas; interpersonal relationship skills; familiarity with user operations	Extensive managerial, technical and human relations skills
5. Tools	Good computer capability; good software	Directory, descriptive language utilities, mapping facility, audit, monitoring	Data Element directory, dictionary, standards; software; hardware	Data Element Dictionary/directory systems; good software capability; good documentation standards

Figure 10-3. **Comparative study of four concepts of the DBA**

It is possible to develop a kind of idealized profile of the DBA's role, by comparing and contrasting the various functions involved in the DBA's role, based upon the composite views of the organizations researched in the above comparative study. Analysis of this idealized profile seems to reveal four important common denominators:

1. data base control does not mean that the data base administrator is the owner of the data; rather, he is the custodian of the data which is entrusted to him for safekeeping;
2. the data files within the data base should not be disclosed to unauthorized users; controls, therefore, must be developed in such a way as to conceal the substantive contents of the files and records in the data base where personal or proprietary data is involved;
3. the design and development of the data base management system should involve the participation and involvement of both top management and users, not exclusively systems analysts and programers; and
4. standard terms for commonly used elements of data and codes used to represent them, are absolutely essential if the data is to be captured, maintained, and disseminated with a high degree of cross-consistency and compatibility. Whether a standard programming language is used to develop the various components of the data base is of secondary rather than primary importance.

THE GOVERNMENT INFORMATION MANAGER

The emergence of the information manager in Government is traced by Richard Brown, who describes a relatively limited number of key milestones:

1. During the 1950's, there was an aggressive movement to increase data processing equipment utilization. Much routine workload was placed on equipment that should never have been placed there in the first place. During this period, automation was very popular and large staffs were established at all levels in the organization to accomplish this objective;
2. During the late 1950's and early 1960's, there was an increasing tendency to move to centralized decision making. This required

large volumes of detailed data to be collected and transmitted;
3. In the mid and late 1960's, the management information system (MIS) was being promoted in many quarters as a concept, almost a magical panacea, for solving management's problems.

Brown is careful to point out that, whatever steps we take to manage information resources more economically, we must be careful not to impede the management process; that is, management should always have the option of obtaining urgently needed information at almost any cost. In short, the role of the information manager, like the role of all other resource managers is to help line operating managers to do their job better. The information manager is able to do this because he brings to his job a certain technical expertise and skill to help the line manager articulate his information requirements more carefully, accurately, completely, and realistically, and his awareness of available information sources allows him to steer the line manager in the right direction. Another important facet of the government management picture that has direct bearing on the evolution of the role of the information manager is the trend in the last decade for three or four key management-related functions to become organizationally melded. Those functions are (1) computers and automatic data processing; (2) the organizational and methods (O&M) staffs; (3) traditional paperwork management (files, records, reports, and so on); and (4) administrative support functions (supplies, personnel, finance, and so on).

If one examines the organizational charts and telephone directories of major Federal agencies, it is apparent that the management support cluster of functions is gradually gaining some ascendancy. Traditionally these functions have been stifled by the fourth category—administrative support. Among the "classic" organizational battles which have taken place are:

1. The change in titles at the top organizational level from "administration" to "management."
2. The shredding out of the ADP function from under the control of financial managers, to separate status, either co-equal to, or under, or reporting directly to a generalist manager, such as a deputy administrator or under secretary.
3. The growth of specialized information centers and their organizational placement at higher organizational levels.
4. The rise of telecommunications management and its corresponding high location on the charts, as a result of the need

to manage high speed data transmission and keep abreast of skyrocketing communication costs and new communications technologies.
5. The gradual erosion of organizational boundaries between statistical functions and information functions. In lieu of calling major statistical capabilities in Government "statistical centers," we are seeing names like "data" or "information and statistics" center.
6. The ascendancy of the planning and evaluation staffs and their heavy reliance on data as the raw material which "feeds" their activities.
7. The emergence of public policy management as a field of study.
8. The emergence of resources management as a field of study (which we discussed in Chapter 2).

We can see from the above list that there is one important common denominator involved, that data and information are the critical resource which each of the organizational functions requires. The new management specialized functions all depend on information as the critical resource. Indeed, it is in part the demand from these new organizational functions that is forcing the definition of the role of the information manager because each of the new groups, left alone, would undoubtedly end by proliferating new data flows that were overlapping and redundant. The top management level can ill-affors to let that happen.

THE INFORMATION MANAGER AS COUNSELOR

Anthony Debons of the University of Pittsburgh highlights the helping role of the information manager by using the term "information counselor." He envisages the information counselor as a kind of extension of the librarian.[4] He says, "It is the business (of the information counselor) to help individuals form information from data, and apply this capacity to day-to-day problems that the information counselor's role finds expression." The central task of the information counselor then, is to improve the interface between the information user and the vast reservior of available data. Debons characterizes the information user as at the mercy of several highly complex situations:

- First, there is the ever-increasing growth of the data base;
- Second, the state of the art of data processing technology

is such that there are infinite ways to process and package data; and
- Third, the job of applying data to day-to-day tasks is growing ever more complex.

Debons refers to the work of Heastfield who outlines some nine competences that would characterize the training of the information counselor. He proposes that these competences be subsumed under three basic functions:

- First, the ability to diagnose the underlying motivational and personality factors which characterize the information need related to this specific task based by the user;
- Second, the ability to prescribe ways that the assessed needs can be satisfied through available data, resources, and technology; and
- Third, the ability to test the counseling function through continuous surveillance and evaluation.

John B. Dykeman, in an editorial in *Modern Office Procedures,* had this to say about the information executive:[5]

> After looking at and learning about the recent wave of new hardware and related software that engulfed the marketplace in the past six months, the office executive should ponder his or her future role in the future office function. The traditional definition and concept of the office is archaic. Webster has defined the office as 'the building, room or series of rooms in which the affairs of a business, professional person, . . . etc., are carried on.' The office has become an umbrella that covers all administrative functions in an organization, regardless of where they're performed.
>
> For today's office executive, the name of the game is managing a system of business information so that it achieves two main objectives; (1) to provide the necessary knowledge for all authorized levels of management to make possible accurate and profitable decisions in planning, controlling, and carrying out business activities; (2) to employ the most cost-effective system of hardware, software, and personnel available to gather, enter, store, retrieve, analyze, and report that information.
>
> The keystone in future organization structures is information, and the executive who knows how to manage information will be the key person. His or her responsibilities may well cut across the traditional areas of middle management responsibilities, in both line and staff. This future is already here. A veteran data processing manager, and a long-time reader, recently told us of his new position with another firm, a job that offered

> a greater opportunity and challenge. The new position: vice president, of information systems.
>
> Traditional individual office functions are becoming vital subsets of the total information picture. An overnight swing to information executives won't happen much faster than companies will adopt office-of-the-future systems. But forewarned is forearmed.

THE ENTREPRENEUR INFORMATION BROKER

One of the most exciting opportunities for the modern information manager has come in an area which some have come to call the "information broker." In story after story in the news media and in the professional literature have come tales in the last decade of one entrepreneur after another who has sold innovative information products and services for a handy profit—from information sources which he or she obtained free from public or private resources. These stories have lent tangible credibility to the allegation of many writers that we have so much data we have no information. These information brokers have ingeniously sorted the information wheat from the data chaff.

One of the commonest products and services offered is a subscription service to "Where to Find" selective bibliographies of sources of information of interest to a given profession, industry, trade or other group. Such services typically buy a newsletter which is bimonthly or monthly and costs from $25.00 to $250.00 per issue. Special data reports are compiled and made available for various fees.

Interestingly, the service doesn't give advice and counsel—just information! Broker after broker wryly observes: we're continually astounded at how little large companies and government organizations know about where to go to get data they need, or even if the data they need exists at all!

The key is sifting, sorting, reaggregating, and rearranging existing data into arrays, data sets, formats and presentations which are simple, straightforward, easy to use and useful. The information brokers readily acknowledge that they have been able to carve out a market niche precisely because the gigantic data producers have traditionally produced, published and disseminated too much information in forms and formats which are arcane and useful only to narrow bands of highly technical, specialized users.

There is a lesson here for the information manager: being able to communicate quickly and effectively is the key.

SUMMARY

The Information Manager's role is by no means an homogenous list of tasks, functions and responsibilities. Rather, it varies from organization to organization, from business setting to business setting, from region to region, and from circumstance to circumstance. Nor is his role an easy one. Just as the other resource managers had to fight their way into closed-door board and meeting rooms, so the information manager will have to prove worth and value by dint of a combination of outstanding behavioral, administrative and technical skills. It will not be enough to "proclaim" knighthood by virtue of royal lineage, or loudly calling attention to information resources cost overruns. Like all professions, like all trades, and like all crafts, the data practicioner must demonstrate practical utility, and a sensitivity to the political, economic and social nuances which permeate all organizational forms, and at all levels.

Nevertheless, the opportunities were never brighter than they are now. For the technician who would become generalist; for the employee who would become supervisor; for the worker who would become entrepreneur. In an extraordinary number of instances in both government and in private industry, only the will to seize the initiative is what is required.

QUESTIONS FOR DISCUSSION

1. The notion of the *information manager* can be viewed in a generic context if we think of the role of a particular kind of manager. Thus, in an organization, an information manager may be the head of the Information Management Department, a digital computer systems analyst or programmer, a statistician, a reports analyst, the corporate librarian, the head of the mail room, or many other jobs. In the context of the organization as a whole, how would you define the Information Manager?

2. What can you say about the "ideal qualifications" of an information manager? Take, in turn, considerations of academic qualifications, on-the-job training, past job experience, professional and technical training off-the-job, and so on. Is there a single "profile" of the ideal information manager? Should there be one?

3. What kind of formal and informal relationships should the information manager have with "sister" resource managers, such as the

personnel chief, the vice president for finance, the property master, and so on? How about the company's staff offices at corporate headquarters level, such as long range planning and the legal staff? How about the company's line departments and divisions, such as manufacturing, marketing and product line heads?

4. In the vernacular of the times, do you believe the information manager will be "grown or born?"

FOOTNOTES

[1]Brochure, "*Looking for an Exciting Career in a Wide-Open Field? How about Considering Information Science?*" (American Society for Information Science, Washington, D.C., (undated)).

[2]Various brochures, U.S. Civil Service Commission, Bureau of Training, Washington, D.C. Both the Department of Agriculture and the Civil Service Commission produce annual catalogs of courses offered to Government personnel. Catalogs may be obtained by writing directly to these Government organizations.

[3]Research Paper by Richard Brown, Consultant to the Commission on Federal Paperwork, Information Management Study, Washington, D.C., 1976. The material referenced here may be obtained by communication with the author. Mr. Brown was a key architect of the Information Directorate in the Office of the Assistant Secretary of Defense (Comptroller), which has overall, DOD-wide responsibility for managing the information requirements of the Department of Defense.

[4]Debons, Anthony, "*An Educational Program for the Information Counselor,*" (Proceedings of the 38th ASIS Annual Meeting, Volume 12, American Society for Information Science, Washington, D.C., Oct. 26–30, 1975) pp. 63–64.

[5]Dykeman, John B., "*Here Now: The Information Executive,*" (editorial, Modern Office Procedures, August, 1976) Vol. 21, No. 8.

11 SAFEGUARDING INFORMATION

The American Civil Liberties Union Foundation puts the problem of safeguarding information into dramatic terms when it says, "The principal commodity of power in our society is information. Power may come out of the barrel of a gun, but far more power comes out of a computer or a data bank, particularly if the information in it relates to people who do not know that it has been collected or cannot challenge its accuracy or use. It is no accident that many of the great governmental power abuses that have come to light in the last few years—wire tapping, enemies lists, political surveillience, counter intelligence, secrecy and deception—have revolved around information practices." ACLU then goes on to endorse Alan Westin's definition of privacy as the "right to control information about one's self."[1]

Perhaps no other issues are more emotionally charged today than the right of privacy and the closely related issue of confidentiality. Certainly the information manager faces no more critical challenge than the achievement of a delicate balance between the needs for efficient information management and the need to safeguard information held in confidence. In this chapter, we will examine a series of issues related to the safeguarding of information, including:

- the Social Security Number and other universal identifiers;
- the personnel dossier;
- the National Data Bank;
- issues and problems of computer security;
- issues of access;
- constitutional issues relating to safeguarding information;
- the Freedom of Information Act and the Privacy Act; and,
- disclosure policies and issues.

THE UNIVERSAL IDENTIFIER

Expanded use of the Social Security Number for administrative and recordkeeping purposes by all levels of government—Federal, State, and local—is probably the most important single factor precipitating debate of the privacy issue in modern society. Spread of the Social Security Number made feasible an idea which had been only a dream of social scientists, computer analysts, and information specialists. Social Security Numbers and other "universal identifiers" have been used for a long time, but beginning in the 1950's such numbers began to assume a very conspicious role in the processing of very large quantities of data in both government and industry. Some people are not bothered by the notion of carrying around an identification card with a nine, ten, eleven, or even longer digit number. However, there are many people to whom such a number symbolizes all that they see that is dehumanizing in our increasingly cybernetic and technocratic society. With the spread of the Social Security Number came the obsession of many that the year 1984 was, after all, not far away.

Congress itself in 1974 came to the conclusion that, whether "justified" or not, such concerns of citizens had reached the point where it was necessary to take action. Thus, the Privacy Act put teeth into relatively benign provisions on the statute books which prevented Government agencies from disclosing specific categories of information relating to individual citizens. As many citizens, and citizen action groups celebrated the passage of the Act, equal numbers of computer specialists, information specialists, and Government officials at all levels bemoaned its enactment. It meant the creation of untold problems for tax collectors, law enforcement officials, doctors, lawyers, welfare workers, and many other officials who had come to depend upon the use of the Social Security Number as a fairly efficient and routine way to verify the identity of individuals in a host of different kinds of case files, dossiers, records, and reports. Whereas before the passage of the Act it was commonplace for agencies at all levels of Government to exchange information using the Social Security Number, this practice was substantially curtailed. The consequences of the passage of the Privacy Act, from the standpoint of data and information management, have not yet been fully assessed. Indeed, the machinery of information processing has slowed to a virtual halt in many areas.

TWO RIGHTS IN CONFLICT

Edmund Dwyer was among the first of those who called attention to the coming confrontation between the right of privacy and the technological needs of our post-industrial society. He makes the point that computers and communications in Government do indeed benefit the public, and without them we could not administer our vast health, education, and welfare programs, not could we fight crime on a national scale, manage resources needed for recovery from natural disasters, or deal efficiently with the massive data collection programs required by Federal agencies for statistical compilation and analysis. Dwyer foresees a gloomy future if the public and the Congress are led to believe that modern information handling technologies must cease to progress until fool-proof technological means are developed which would safeguard the rights of individuals.[2] See Figure 11-1.

Many believe Senator Sam Ervin rather concisely described the privacy issue during the course of the Senate Judiciary Committee's hearings which ultimately led to the Privacy Act of 1974. At one point in the hearings he said:

> Once collected . . . personal data about an individual is virtually out of that individual's control. The data takes on a life of its own as a part of a file, a dossier, a data bank, or an information system. It is valuable, can be bought and sold, stolen, altered, exchanged for other data, and used as the basis for decision-making both about the individual subject and about the categories in which the individual is thought to belong. It can be compared and interrelated with other data, and aggregated into a 'data profile' of the individual subject. Through advanced telecom-

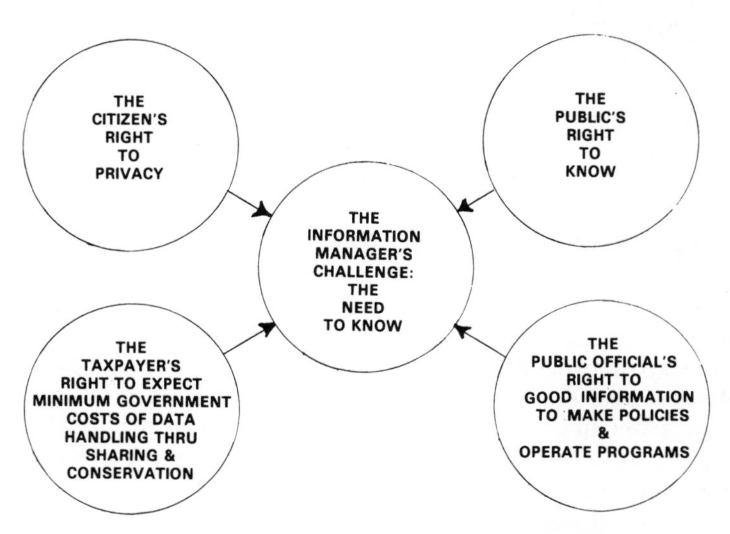

Figure 11-1. **Information rights and needs in conflict: The information manager's challenge**

munications networks, it can be instantly broadcasted to the farthest corners of the earth.[3]

A USEFUL PERSPECTIVE

A number of commentators have found it useful to deal with the privacy problem at three stages in the information life cycle: collection, processing, and dissemination. Looking first at collection, the problem can be rather concisely reduced to the question: "Who needs to know what about whom?" Alternatively, as one author put it: "Who is entitled to keep what secret from whom?" Investigatory studies conducted by the Commission on Federal Paperwork and the staff of the Senate Small Business Committee, which dealt extensively with the problem of the Federal paperwork burden on the public, both documented many examples, as did the Ervin Committee before them, wherein the Federal Government has appeared to ask for a great deal of information which proved eventually to be of limited actual use.

In report after report, record after record, questionnaire after questionnaire, witnesses testified before these various committees and commissions in detail and documented their testimony with specific examples: there are personal questions whose use appears to be very doubtful. On the other hand, when the requesting Government officials were taken to task, in many cases they argued eloquently for the need for facts and figures on which to base far-reaching decisions affecting matters of health, safety, and security of citizens, the regulation of business, the development of general purpose statistics for making major economic, fiscal, and monetary decisions, and so forth. Perhaps one of the most difficult dilemmas facing our national government, then, is how to plan for, mount, implement, and operate our vast citizen benefit apparatus without making significant intrusions into privacy.

Congressman Barry Goldwater, Jr., introduced the Privacy Act legislation in the House. His premise was a simple one: That any information system of a personal nature that is secret is automatically either unlawful or morally wrong. The Act establishes certain personal rights and administrative procedures to safeguard those rights. The rights are simply that every individual should know what information is being collected from him/her and the mere fact that it is being collected. Another right is that every individual on whom information is being collected should be able to examine that information and challenge its accuracy, relevancy, and timeliness. Congress created the Privacy

Protection Study Commission in 1975 to study the issues in greater depth and make its final report to the Congress in January, 1977. Carol Parsons, the Executive Director of that Commission has said:

> Although it is easy to dismiss the specter of the 'data bank society' as so much wild imagining, just as it is easy to exaggerate the speed and efficiency with which such a state of affairs might come to pass, I do think it is not unreasonable to predict that the major breakthroughs in the way of information about people is handled will be in the area of *use* rather than collection. That is, the new information management technologies in which we will inevitably come to depend will lead us to cut down on the number of items to which we attend in any given decision-making situation about an individual while at the same time, permitting us to marshall those items with unparalleled speed and efficiency, and with a growing confidence in their utility as descriptors, and predictors of human behavior.[4]

Clearly the Congress cannot legislate in a vacuum, nor can the President carry out Congress' will in an information vacuum. But it would appear that much closer attention should be paid to a workable set of "need to know" principles under which agencies would be required to justify in greater depth, and more carefully, the relevancy of the information they desire to collect to satisfy their various missions, goals, and objectives. No longer will they be authorized carte blanche authority to go out and collect whatever information they allege they need, from whomever they need it, without carefully following guidelines, standards, and criteria which touch upon the issue of relevancy, how the information will be used, and specifically what safeguards will be imposed to protect the confidentiality of the data.

Information processing presents an array of problems associated with the protection of data once it gets into massive computer systems and data banks. Robert McBride, in his important work "The Automated State,"[5] points out that until 1965, while many departments and agencies within Government were using computers and modern information handling techniques, there was no concerted effort to link together into some central computer system the individual data files and records that had been fragmented all over Government. But in April of 1965, the Director of the Bureau of the Budget (now the Office of Management and Budget, OMB) was asked by the Social Science Research Council to consider the feasibility of establishing a National Data Center. Edgar Dunn, at the time a consultant to the Bureau, stressed that he did not envision a central analytical capability directed toward policy and management, but rather a simple repository of data which then could be drawn upon by the various departments and agencies and the President as they so desire. Dunn foresaw the National Data Center as a central storage for the computer files of the agencies that comprised the so called "Federal Statistical System." The Center would serve as a central referral and reference service for all users of the data contained in the files. But it was too late. Strong forces had already been mobilized to move against the proposal. It was not long before the National Data Center proposal was under close examination by the House Government Operations Committee's Special Subcommittee on Invasion of Privacy. In one of the more memorable exchanges of the Subcommittee's hearings in which Executive Branch officials were being interrogated by the Congressmen, the following was said:

> "We do not want to impede progress," said Representative Cornelius Gallagher of New Jersey. "The computer is here to stay, and it can be a source for good. We would hope that you are not underestimating the computer. I think you are. I think in centralizing all this information in one giant computer, you have not realized the potentialities of the computer, because if you feel that you can control this kind of information you are not being realistic. You are placing tremendous power in the hands of an elite. . . ." Congressman Frank Horton of New York then added, "You can find out what happened to Frank Horton from the time he was born until right today by pushing the button—'EVERYTHING.' "[6]

Once information is collected and becomes stored in the various data files and records in Government data banks, the issue of access becomes paramount. Measures taken to safeguard data which has already been collected are based on a whole range of factors, not the least important of which is how sensitive the data is in terms of the rights of those parties who may access that data. The Freedom of Information Act of 1966, and the Amendments that were passed in 1975 to the basic Act, rather grandly state, "If Government is to be truly of, by, and for the people, the people must know in detail the activities of the Government." As it was originally passed, the Act contained no deadlines for compliance and no penalties for violations. For the first eight years of its existence, it clearly was a boondoggle. In 1974, Congress tried to close the largest of the loopholes in this key legislation. Former President Gerald Ford vetoed the attempt, claiming that it would be unworkable and even "unconstitutional" because it would be too much of an encroachment on Executive authority, but the amended Act was passed over his veto and became law effective February 19, 1975.

FREEDOM OF INFORMATION ACT EXEMPTIONS

This law now contains nine specific exemptions to disclosure. Any information in the nine categories which is specifically exempted may not be made public in response to a request. Because a document is exempt, however, doesn't necessarily mean that it must be kept secret; that is to say, Government agencies are free to disclose non-exempt documents. It is interesting to note that, though it is not listed among the nine specific categories, Congress itself is exempted. Here are the nine categories of information exempted from the amended Act.

- national defense or foreign policy information that is properly classified;
- information that is related solely to internal personnel rules and practices of an agency or department;
- data specifically exempted from disclosure by another Federal statute;
- trade secrets and commercial or financial information the Government has obtained that is privileged or confidential;
- personnel, medical, or other files that, if disclosed, would be considered an unwarranted invasion of personal privacy;
- investigatory files; but only to the extent that one or more of six specified forms of harm would result;
- certain bank records; and
- data on oil wells.

Since the passage of the amended law, there has been a deluge of criticism by Federal agencies that it is burdensome, costly, ineffective, inefficient, and, indeed, has unleashed counterproductive tendencies toward secrecy in Government that may not have even existed before the passage of the Act. In the summer of 1975 there were over 500 law suits pending in the Justice Department concerning the application and meaning of the Freedom of Information Act. Although no accurate record is being kept, it is probably safe to say that the number of inquiries that have come into Federal agencies for information has been in the tens of thousands. The House Committee on Government Operations estimated that an agency should be able to comply with new law for "modest sums," but the Defense Department said that its expenses in 1975 for complying with the law approached $6 million.

Some interesting side-effects have come to pass as a result of the passage of the Freedom of Information Act and its Amendments. Government investigators who conduct background investigations for the purpose of granting security clearances to persons who will have access to sensitive and classified information say that informants are reluctant to be candid and frank in their interviews because they fear that unauthorized persons will have access to their testimony. The Archivist of the United States, James B. Rhoads, says he's worried that historians of the future may wind up with less information available to them. He says, "I don't have any hard evidence that this is true, but from things I've heard people say, I get the impression that they may be putting less on paper than they otherwise would, that they may be handling matters on the phone instead. My concern is that it (the information law) might create a less full, informative, rich record of what the Government has done. Society as a whole is the loser if that results."[7]

HOW SAFE IS THE COMPUTER?

Evidence to date seems to indicate that computer security is a sub-set of a much larger problem—that of safeguarding personal information falling within the purview of the Privacy Act and related legislation and the confidentiality of sensitive information relating to, for example, the trade and proprietary secrets of a business or, in the case of government, State secrets. This more general problem of safeguards pervades all forms and media used for the collection, storage, and handling of information, whether hardcopy, microform, computer data banks, or some other medium. Solution of the computer security problem is dependent, therefore, to a greater extent on solutions to the unauthorized disclosure problem than to ironclad technological guarantees of tamperproof hardware and software.

While measures taken to strengthen computer security safeguards must be tailored to the particular information, software and hardware forms and media, the more serious problem is the need to integrate and coordinate all safeguard measures across such media boundaries. The aim should be to insure that any strengthened safeguards program reflects an integrated, cohesive, and carefully thought through set of policies, procedures, guidelines, and criteria. These policies and procedures should be mutually reinforcing, consistent, and compatible. In short, the bigger part of the computer security problem has been, it would appear, the proliferation of piecemeal controls which address facets and stages of the overall problem in a disconnected, individual way, instead of developing a cohesive, integrated information safeguard program, of which computer security is an integral but by no means necessarily most important part.

To date, there are far more documented instances of unauthorized disclosure of data from manual records than from computerized record systems. In short, the human being, not the computer, would appear to be the weakest link in the computer security chain. There are no foolproof, guaranteed safeguards for protecting data in computers any more than such measures exist for the protection of manual files and records, but the possibility for a state-of-the-art breakthrough in this area is not promising. As in the case of manual systems, the steps taken to safeguard data in computerized data banks vary in effectiveness, cost, and technological complexity. The measures chosen should strike a balance between the degree of sensitivity of the data to be protected and the total cost of achieving the needed level of protection. See Figure 11-2.

Crime by computer is a popular subject nowadays. It has been discussed, studied, and examined in academic, government, company, and news media channels extensively and intensively in the last decade. The use of automated data handling techniques, especially the computer, has brought a great many benefits and values to the simplification, mechanization, and streamlining of recordkeeping, reporting, and other administrative activities of both Government and private industry. But it has also introduced the very real concerns for the privacy and protection of confidential data submitted to organizations by both individuals and other organizations, either voluntarily or under some mandatory provision of the law. At the heart of the matter is a fundamental confrontation between two forces. On the one hand, efficient handling of information would seem to suggest maximum efforts to centralize, consolidate, and promote the sharing and interchange of data and information between suppliers or providers of information, and users. On the other hand, there is a need to insure that the data, once collected and stored, is properly safeguarded and protected from inadvertent or fraudulent disclosure.

The orientation of the current computer explosion in both the public and private sectors, is towards speeding the management decisionmaking and technical problem-solving processes. A particularly significant attraction of this technology is the promise of collecting, storing, and retrieving large repositories of information in such fashion that it can be conjured up and reviewed quickly from any number of perspectives in support of the activities of those who are authorized access. The question is: Who should have access?

CATEGORY OF SAFEGUARDS	EXAMPLES
1. Legislative Safeguards	Privacy Act of 1974; Freedom of Information Act and amendments; Laws constraining inter-agency sharing
2. Policy Safeguards	Statements of Privacy Principles at Corporate and agency top level ("all employees shall have a right to know what records are kept on them, and be able to challenge, inspect and correct those records")
3. Procedural Safeguards	Computer operating room controls: who shall have access and under what conditions; records of access identifier date, accessor and other data
4. Hardware Safeguards	Terminal identity keys, passwords and codes to control entry and access; crytographic approaches; circuit protection; "footprint detection"
5. Software Safeguards	Separate programs and routines for data entry, storage and retrieval of personal and proprietary records, apart from non-personal and non-sensitive data
6. Audit Safeguards	Unannounced, period checks and inspections of compliance with established controls
7. Human Safeguards	Background investigations of personnel in key, sensitive positions; bonding; training both on and off-the-job
8. Technological Safeguards	Advanced techniques for detecting fraud which go beyond the physical computer itself and attendant software and procedural safeguards; holography

Figure 11-2. **The computer and privacy**

THE ISSUE OF TRUST

Perhaps the single most significant impact of the technological enhancements to permit better collection of data is the fear of the citizen that the information government collects for what is reputed to be a legitimate, positive purpose, will be used indiscriminately for punitive purposes. What, in short, is government's guarantee that personal information, once collected, won't also be used against the provider? Testimony of IRS and Census Bureau officials before various committees of the Congress which have recently explored the problems of safeguarding such information heavily underscore the importance of the trust dimension. Even with assurances by the Congress that a National Data Bank will not be created, these suspicions are justifiably raised, given the increasing pervasiveness of computers in more and more aspects of our lives and the pall of Watergate still hanging over us.

It seems likely, given the climate of the privacy and secrecy-in-government issues at this time, that we will pass through a phase lasting into the early 1980's of continuing test, experimentation, and probing. Where should the lines be drawn? The law is trailing here now—another example of technology outstripping man's abilities to keep abreast.

THE WESTIN STUDY OF MEDICAL RECORDS

Under the sponsorship of the National Bureau of Standards, Dr. Alan F. Westin recently completed a landmark study of computer security problems related to medical records. His report of December, 1976, and his conclusions and recommendations deserve careful review and study. *Computers, Health Records, and Citizens Rights* was the result of a two-year research effort. Here are the most important recommendations:

1. There should be a procedure for issuing a public notice and privacy-impact statement whenever an automated data system is created in the health field, filed with an appropriate outside authority, and communicated to any continuing population of individuals whose records will be affected.
2. Socially-acceptable standards of relevance and propriety in the collection of personal data should be worked out for data

use, through public discussion on appropriate policy study mechanisms.

3. Individuals should be given a clearly written account of how their personal information will be used whenever they are asked to supply personal information to a health data system, along with the procedures to be followed before any uses are made of their data other than those originally specified.
4. Forms used to release personal information from the health data system should be authorized for a specific purpose; describe the information to be released; authority be limited in time; and the individual's consent to such releases should be informed as well as voluntary.
5. Managers of health-base data systems must take steps to see that personal records are as accurate, timely, and complete as the uses to which they are being put require them to be for protection of individual rights.
6. Data security measures must be taken to control access according to the policy set by law or by management, and the adequacy of those measures will be measured by the previous history of threats of data confidentiality in that type of organization.
7. Health data systems managers should conduct special orientation training programs to inculcate respect for citizen rights among their staffs and to deal with problems that may arise.
8. Each health data system should prepare and distribute a patient's rights handbook and install a readily-available and independent patient rights representative in the organization.
9. Because new issues are posed whenever health data systems adopt new file applications, there should be provisions for periodic independent review of these systems.
10. Special effort should be made for confidentiality rules not to interfere with the public's right to know what is being done by Government agencies or by private recipients of government funds and to carry out critical oversight functions in the public's interest.
11. For organizations operating health data systems, a fullscale "privacy audit" should be undertaken periodically.
12. Public interest groups play a particularly critical role in the area of safeguarding personal data contained in automated data systems and should be encouraged to continue to play such active roles.

Westin concludes that computerization of personal medical information has been marked so far by haphazard growth; it has not developed according to thoughtfully conceived plans for achieving integrated health information systems within individual facilities or throughout the health care field. At the same time, policy as to the citizen rights issues of privacy, confidentiality, and access are also developing on an individual, ad hoc basis, for the most part simply carrying over into computerized files the same practices—good or bad—pursued with manual records. The basic concern of health care professionals, civil liberties observers, and others with automated medical records is with the flawed procedures and policies currently employed with respect to manual records that promise to be seriously inadequate for the computer.

INDUSTRIAL ESPIONAGE

Belden Menkus points out that the management of information assets is a relatively new chore for the organization, one that will require fundamental changes in the ways in which business executives and government officials undertake their work.[8] It will alter the very goals of some organizations and certainly the means by which these goals are achieved. Of course we have always had the problem of industrial espionage and espionage involving the theft of state secrets, but that has historically been a fairly esoteric endeavor. Now, with movement toward the development of a doctrine of managing a much broader array of information assets, there will be a need to be far more specific and explicit with regard to the identification, classification, measurement of that data and information which is to be safeguarded versus that which does not require such safeguards. Menkus identifies nine basic business intelligence data categories:

1. *Assets.* Plant and equipment location, size, type, and performance capabilities;
2. *Stock.* Purchases of raw materials, subassemblies, and operating supplies, and sales or transfers of surplus stocks to others;
3. *Production.* Units produced or warehoused, volume scrapped or reworked, the number and nature of defects and the volume produced by private label;
4. *Sales.* Dollar volume by product, product line, industry type, customer size, geographic location, and discounts given;
5. *Sales planning.* Promotions, advertising, exhibits and relations with representatives and distributors;
6. *Financial.* Condition and status of accounts receivable and payable, as well as capitalization, both short and long term;

7. *Personnel.* Salary, bonus, benefit structure (including labor contract provisions), job assignment and duty locations, career development, records indicating probable future promotions and assignments; and
8. *Research and development.* Product, process and material substance qualities and performance.

Menkus points out that management's growing obligation to safeguard its information assets and the way in which they are used is changing the fundamental ways in which information systems are designed and developed and operated. He says that as the scope of these legal, social, and moral responsibilities continues to expand, management's obligation to the prudent user of information can be expected to intensify. The impact of these events on the organization can be eased by careful and expeditious development and installation of protective policies and procedures. In the end it is top management that will be held accountable for what happens to the organization's information assets. That is nothing new. Top management is now held responsible for what happens to all of the organization's assets, but by dealing with information as a resource, there will be a greater opportunity to devise effective safeguards and controls than would be the case if data and information were viewed by management as abstract and intangible assets.

GOVERNMENT PROLIFERATION

Lawrence Miller points out in a paper written in January, 1977, that managers and information specialists who fail to "consistently monitor and evaluate the effects of Federal laws and regulations on their information-handling and distribution activities may be putting themselves and their organizations into serious jeopardy." He points out that various information systems, including those relating to the management of human resources, are often the primary targets of compliance with record-keeping and reporting requirements of various Federal laws and regulations and that most of these laws and regulations carry various civil and/or criminal penalties for failure to comply with the necessary safeguarding and protection provisions. Miller points out that one of the problems which organizations increasingly have is the very heavy paperwork burden and information handling burden imposed on them by these various laws and regulations which forces them to add or reallocate human, machine and other resources, which are often considered nonproductive. These costs in many cases may be passed on to consumers, taxpayers and others in the form of increased prices for goods or higher taxes and so forth. He also aptly points out that, when taken in the aggregate, the total of laws, codes, rules and regulations at all levels of government—international, national, Federal, regional, subregional, state, local and sub-local—numbers in the thousands, and of course none of these are static; they are continually being changed, so that the sheer problem of trying to keep up with the dynamic changes in these laws, not to mention the various administrative systems and procedures that go along with them, is a gigantic task. He aptly calls this the "requirements explosion." Some organizations find it necessary to hire batteries of legal counsellors, lobbyists, and various other kinds of professionals just to keep management advised about the relevant developments on these various fronts. For example, one survey undertaken by the Commission on Federal Paperwork found that many corporations have a unit within their legal counsel, or perhaps public affairs office, which does nothing but read the *Federal Register* daily to learn of such changes. Indeed, the Office of the Federal Register, which is a unit of the National Archives and Records Service, periodically conducts classes in how to use the *Federal Register*![9]

SAFEGUARD STANDARDS—A NEW CODE NEEDED

In trying to arrive at the "delicate balance" between the needs and objectives of information managers to efficiently handle massive quantities of data which may in part contain personal records and the equally important need to safeguard the legitimate privacy concerns of individuals with respect to the information which is collected by government about them, one approach deals with a so-called "reusability" or "recycling" code which would come into play at the time information is first collected. For example, suppose the Census Bureau or some other statistical agency of government wanted to collect certain data from individuals that might be considered within the domain of being "private." At present, under existing procedures, government does not systematically and regularly solicit the views of the respondents with respect to whether such information, once collected, could be shared with another agency for purposes other than that for which the data was initially collected.

From the taxpayer's viewpoint, such an initial determination has the virtue of helping to preclude the re-collection of duplicative data by many agencies which may be unable to get their hands on such data from the agency which first collected it. On the negative side of the ledger, however, there is evidence that the quality and level of administrative, technical and human safeguards and controls developed and applied by different government agencies are far from being uniform and consistent, in part because at the time this is written there are no standard safeguard controls prescribed for the protection of such data for government agencies.

By instituting such a procedure, and coupling it with appropriate data handling safeguards (which of course would need to be legislated in the first instance) the sharing of data for research purposes would perhaps be encouraged, and the re-collection of duplicative data, which burdens the taxpayer twice—once when the data is first collected from the taxpayer-respondent and then again when the government handles duplicative data—would be ameliorated. Giving an individual taxpayer-respondent the option to deny "reusing" or "recycling" his/her data means, in part, that a few of the sets of respondents to a given survey, for example, can effectively require that the total set be recontacted to provide the information required for new use. Certainly the encouragement of recycling, or sharing, data would require a set of statutory data handling constraints, safeguards and penalties. The Commission on Federal Paperwork recommended that a single set of data handling procedures be developed for application across the entire Federal establishment and that its provisions should be at least as stringent and protective as those provided in Title 13 of the U.S. Code, which governs the conduct of the Bureau of the Census. Such a requirement is needed so that those Government employees handling safeguarded data on citizens, regardless of their agency affiliation, would realize that they would be subject to strong sanctions and penalties for the abuse and misuse of such individual data. Such legislation might also provide various remedies for redress for an individual to employ against specifically named individuals who have misused or abused the data.

Perhaps, in the end, what we need to achieve this "delicate balance" is what some have called an "information bill of rights." Richard C. Taeuber says that "a technological society is developing around us and its dynamic nature is challenging many traditional values and benefits. In particular, this technology may threaten the sovereignty of the individual, the very basis of our social structure. Our challenge is to make certain that the enormous benefits made possible by computer power are placed at the service of all individuals, and equally to insure that the same power is not allowed to circumscribe or suffocate our individuality, and therefore our dignity as independent human beings."[10] See Figure 11-3.

AN INFORMATION BILL OF RIGHTS

Article I

No government agency or private enterprise shall keep records or other information on an individual without that person's full knowledge and permission

Article II

Every individual shall have the right to inspect and access records kept with his or her permission, for the purpose of challenging its accuracy, timeliness, completeness and relevance to the purposes for which it was initially justified, and to make corrections

Article III

Every government agency or private enterprise which establishes and maintain a system of records on an individual shall establish a program for the purpose of periodically and systematically reviewing the continued relevance of information retained, and take action to purge those records and that information which is obsolete

Article IV

Information collected for one purpose by a government agency or private enterprise shall not be used by the same organization for another purpose, or shared with another organization for the same purpose, without the prior express permission of individual affected

Article V

Every government agency or private enterprise which establishes and maintains a system of records on an individual shall establish "need to know" criteria and standards for internal use, that embrace considerations of user identity, use conditions, access rules, and other information

Article VI

Every government agency or private enterprise which establishes and maintains a system of records on an individual shall establish a program of safeguards to insure that protected information is not inadvertently or fraudulently disclosed to unauthorized persons for unauthorized purposes; such safeguards shall include technical, procedural, policy, administrative, personnel security, hardware, software and other components, integrated in such a way as to constitute a comprehensive, interdependent and mutually reinforcing system of safeguards

Figure 11-3.

There seems little question but that personal information will soon become the subject of more intensive legislative and judicial treatment, beyond the initial thrusts of the Privacy Act and the Freedom of Information Act, in terms of a property right. Property, copyright, patent and other sectors of both civil and criminal law all have much to contribute. But new ground must be cultivated, and new seeds sown. Surely not all information can be regarded as sensitive personal data. Some judgments must be made based on the degree of sensitivity, "need to know" and quality of available safeguards. A comprehensive safeguards classification system, that takes into account all of these factors, and others, should go a long way toward helping our officials tread their way through this minefield.

CONFIDENTIALITY AND SHARING

The confidentiality of data reported by the private sector to government is critical because it is a direct cause of duplicative and overlapping reporting. The problem arises when Federal agencies pledge confidentiality to private respondents, in order to obtain the information they need for policy formulation and to operate their lawfully approved programs. But the confidentiality pledge hinders the sharing of data. The refusal of an agency to share information with another agency is not always a capricious decision, however. In many cases there are laws in place which specifically preclude such sharing, even when both the sharing agency and the receiving agency desire to share.

To give some examples—the Bureau of the Mines releases confidential data to agencies outside the Department of Interior on an aggregate basis (i.e. three or more companies). As mandated by law, they disclose individual company data to constituent agencies within the Department of Interior, to Federal defense agencies, and to the Congress, provided they pledge to maintain confidentiality. The U.S. Geological Survey obtains a pledge of confidentiality before releasing individual company data. The Bureau of Census, however, is prohibited from making disclosures of individual company data by Title 13, United States Code.

The Federal Power Commission follows an administratively determined policy of releasing sensitive information to other Federal agencies provided no protective order has been issued and the requesting agency pledges to maintain confidentiality. To obtain confidential data from the Federal Energy Administration (now subsumed in the new Department of Energy), an agency must:

1. Make the request in writing;
2. State with particularity the information sought;
3. State the need for and intended use of the information;
4. Cite the legal basis, if any, upon which the agency submitted the data to the Department of Energy;
5. Assure the Department that the confidential status of any information provided will be preserved; and
6. State the means that will be used to protect confidentiality.

The Commission on Federal Paperwork found that although much company data, such as figures on refining capacity and financial data (in the case of the energy industry) have been available to the public for years in reports to stockholders, industry still views certain data as highly sensitive.[11] For example, public disclosure of field-by-field reserve information is a matter of great concern to the petroleum industry, which claims that such disclosure could result in a competitive loss for a company that had undertaken the initial exploration and development risks. In responding to this concern, the Texas Railroad Commission, for example, seeks to protect companies from a competitive disadvantage by delaying publication of reserve data for a period of six months. Delay allows companies that have spent large amounts of money for exploration to complete critical lease agreements before data are released to the public.

What seems obvious is that much information, despite the need for confidentiality pledges, can still be made public. A small amount, to be sure, must be kept secret for legitimate commercial interests. What is needed, it seems to me, is agreement between government and private industry on the *classification* of data. In short, the issue here in the confidentiality area parallels closely the issue in the privacy area: Exactly what information should be kept confidential and private, under what conditions, to be accessed by whom, and for what purposes.

SUMMARY

Safeguarding information is a central and priority task of every information manager. This responsibility cannot be delegated to technical personnel, to security specialists or to lawyers charged with drafting legal and administrative guidelines. Instead, it is a daily, hour-by-hour job of every information manager at every level in the organization. There will be times when duplicative data collection, storage and dissemination is a small price to pay for the preservation of Constitutional freedoms. There will be other times when data handling costs may be so prohibitive so as to call into question arbitrary privacy and confidentiality guidelines, pledges and standards. The "solution" to this problem lies in further extensive research into the nature of data held in confidence, by both government and private industry, and perhaps the development of an Information Bill of Rights. Such research, new legislation and new administrative and technical information safeguards, will require intensive collaboration of privacy experts, computer experts, management and systems analysts, and a variety of other professions and disciplines. Short of a comphrensive approach, following the leadership of the Federal Government, and by State and local governments, each organization must address itself to this problem with care and priority.

QUESTIONS FOR DISCUSSION

1. In 1977 the final reports of two Federal Commissions were released within a few months of one another. One, the final report of the Privacy Protection Study Commission, recommended that all further expansions of the use of the Social Security Number, or any universal identifier, be withheld until the implications of such further extension and expansion could be studied. On the other hand, the final report of the Commission on Federal Paperwork disagreed, and stated that there was no particular reason why extension should be expressly stopped, so long as appropriate safeguards were applied. The Paperwork Commission attempted to justify its position partly on the grounds that the monetary investments in automated information systems employing such numbers was already so gigantic, that modifying them to expunge the SSN was "unthinkable." What do you think about the issues involved?

2. It is contended by many that "the very efficiency" of computerized information systems, by itself, poses a threat to personal privacy, and the safeguarding of other information furnished government by businesses and institutions such as trade secrets, inventions and the like. Do you agree or disagree? Support your position.

3. At what point should the reproduction of information held in a company or government file by xerographic, photographic or similar means be considered a misdemeanor? A tort? A crime? If you were writing an omnibus crime bill with regard to the unauthorized disclosure of confidential and proprietary information, including appropriate sanctions and penalties for such unauthorized disclosure, what factors

would you take into account in determining the magnitude of the offense, the degree of punishment, the type of punishment?

4. Current efforts in the Federal Government to establish a central index or locator of data, document and literature holdings go to great lengths to point out that no actual data would be contained in such a locator system; only meta data. Why is this distinction important?

5. Some observers of the current privacy/Freedom of information debate suggest the passage of a "Fair Information Practices Act" that would consolidate and codify the existing profusion of statutes which have varying and oftentimes conflicting provisions with regard to privacy safeguards. On the other hand, some argue that just as "we shouldn't use a universal identifier because it will make the extension of computers into our personal lives irresistible" so we shouldn't "rationalize and codify statutes on information safeguards and disclosure provisions, because the current hodgepodge and confusion serves the citizen better." How do you feel about the issue?

FOOTNOTES

[1]The Privacy Report, Issue No. 3, Volume II, Jan., 1975, and issue No. 8, Volume III, March, 1976, Project on Privacy and Data Collection, American Civil Liberties Union Foundation, New York, New York.

[2]Dwyer, Edmund, *"The Right of Privacy Versus Technological Advance,"* (The Bureaucrat, Vol. 4, No. 3, October, 1975) pp. 293–298.

[3] *"Privacy: The Collection, Use, And Computerization of Personal Data,"* (Joint Hearings before the Ad Hoc Subcommittee on Privacy and Information Systems of the Committee on Government Operations and the Subcommittee on Constitutional Rights of the Committee on the Judiciary, U.S. Senate, 93rd Congress, 2nd Session, June, 1974).

[4]Parsons, Carol, remarks before the Annual Conference of the National Association of State Information Systems, Hershey, PA, Aug. 16–18, 1976.

[5]MacBride, Robert, *"The Automated State-Computer Systems as a New Force in Society,"* (Clinton Book Company) pp. 110–121, 156–168, 180–187.

[6] *"The Computer and Invasions of Privacy,"* (Hearings before a subcommittee of the House Government Operations Committee, House of Representatives, 89th Congress, 2nd Session, July, 1966).

[7]In Conversations with officials of the Commission on Federal Paperwork, and the Public Documents Commission, 1976/1977.

[8]Menkus, Belden, *"Management Responsibilities for Safeguarding Information,"* (Journal of Systems Management, December, 1976) pp. 32–38.

[9]Miller, Dr. Lawrence R., *"Law and Information Systems,"* (Journal of Systems Management, January 1977).

[10]Taeuber, Richard C., *"The Right to Privacy,"* (Bulletin of the American Society for Information Science, Vol. 1, No. 10, May, 1975) pp. 17–18.

[11]See in particular the Paperwork Commission's *Energy Study*, and Position Paper "The Issue of Confidentiality and the Potential for Sharing Energy Data" by George Wakefield, 1977, available from the author, now at the Department of Energy.

12 EVALUATING INFORMATION

Now we come to the most difficult task in managing information resources. On the "input side of the equation," costing information requirements, our task was comparatively easier. Certainly as the information industry now begins to emerge as a separate industry, with suppliers, manufacturers, products and services, and increasing numbers of marketplaces to buy and sell information, we will have better data on product availability, price, quality, substitutes, and other information. As products and services become more and more differentiated and stratified, refinements in pricing strategies, policies and standards should eventually bring us to the point where "the value of information" is not the dilemma it is now. As this is written, however, the state-of-the-art of valuing information products and services is very primitive.

By "evaluating," as the term is used here, we do not mean to deal exclusively with questions of value. Rather, we are using the term in the "management process" sense; that is, after one passes through the earlier stages in the management cycle—planning, programming, budgeting, implementing (or operating), and so forth—one comes to evaluation, the whole range of activities which involves a thoroughgoing appraisal of the entire activity to be examined. Evaluation, then, deals as much with the substance of what is being appraised (i.e., whether goals and objectives are achieved) as the processes by which the activity moved forward. One of the major findings of the Commission on Federal Paperwork, for example, was that in Government a tendency to dismiss administrative processes as "superficial" or "secondary" was partly to explain for the enormous paperwork burden government has been imposing on the citizenry in recent years. That is to say, government officials, beginning with elected officials in the Congress, seem to be almost exclusively preoccupied with matters "of substance"—program benefits and goals. If administrative redtape becomes intolerable, then, and only then, does oversight come into play. Congress and the Executive Branch rarely consider the impact of the administrative costs of proposed programs, in any systematic say, prior to enacting new legislation.

So evaluation is a broad, in-depth appraisal of both effectiveness and efficiency, not only in achieving substantive results, but assessing whether the means by which those results were achieved were themselves cost-effective. Since information is a resource that is employed at every stage of the management process, it is clear that evaluation has a role to play at each stage of the process.

EVALUATION AIMED AT PLANNING

First, how is information used in the planning process, and how can evaluation play a role? We dealt with this subject initially in Chapter 6, Planning Information Requirements. There we traced the processes which lead to the articulation of information needs. A number of Figures in that Chapter schematically illustrated the steps in the process. Evaluation comes in at each step. For example, take personnel or manpower planning. A high-payoff evaluation area is the examination of procedures and processes used in planning and coordinating manpower planning activities. The Federal Government, for example, expends considerable funds in assisting the States in the development, coordination and evaluation of means for improving the planning and coordination of manpower programs at the State and local levels. What, then, should we "evaluate" here?

In the first place, *is* there a plan? Without one, at least in complex costly operations, it is very difficult, if not impossible, to review, improve, integrate, and develop information requirements and resources; assess whether the requirements and resources are reasonable and feasible; and specify what uses are going to be made of the information once collected. Indeed, when information specialists and managers complain that line and staff officials whom they support collect too much information, for the "wrong" purposes, often the problem can be traced to the absence of policies, procedures, and guidelines for developing an information requirements plan.

What should a "good" information requirements plan contain? As a minimum the following:

- an analysis of specific organizational goals and objectives, carried down to as low a cost center level as may be necessary to be meaningful;
- an information requirements analysis that details why in-

formation is needed, for what purposes, to be used by whom, when, and where;
- time-phased plans for meeting those information requirements on a priority basis;
- total costs over the expected lifetime of use of the information, including both capital acquisition costs (e.g., a new computer, new microfilming equipment, new plant and equipment for printing, and so forth), and annual operating costs; and
- a consideration of alternatives in satisfying the organizational unit's information needs.

The Alternatives Assessment is perhaps the key link in the planning chain. It is in the consideration of alternatives to satisfy information requirements, in the choice of options, that the costs involved can be significantly controlled and reduced. In the Chapter on Planning Information Requirements, six fundamental attributes of data itself were listed: subject, scope, measure, time, source, and quality and precision. Evaluation exercises should zero-in on whether or not these key six attributes are explicitly addressed in the context of information planning policies and guidelines. Checklists are useful tools for planners to use, and a well articulated list of "things to remember" is a simple, but effective means to assist managers plan more effectively.

Another important dimension of the planning process which should be evaluated is the notion of *shifting.* That is, costs incurred can be shifted from one element in the chain to another. In Government, for example, when an agency requires a businessman to fill out a form providing the agency with certain information it alleges is needed for Government policy-making or program operation, the businessman may absorb the costs himself or shift the costs onto his suppliers, his customers, stockholders, or some one else. Whether costs are shifted, to where, or by how much is an important facet of the information planning process. We constructed several cost curves for this purpose.

At some point a decision must be made to select the "preferred" alternative from among those considered. In the short-term, planners should try to select the option which is the least costly (or, if some other mix of variables and constraints is employed, the selection could be "maximized," "minimized," or "optimized" along some other line) to the organization from an overall standpoint. But of more interest here, in the longer term the evaluation effort should suggest ways that the organization could focus information research and development efforts and resources into three areas we've already touched on:

1. developing more effective methods and techniques for handling data at all option levels;

2. finding ways to extend the organization's ability to accept information in the low end of the option area; and
3. performing research on methods to reduce information handling costs in areas that lie in the "critical path" and therefore would be expected to impact the overall costs to the organization.

Now, going back to our main discussion, in addition to the Alternatives Assessment, there are other steps in the planning process for information needs which should be carefully evaluated. Have the needs from the various departments and divisions within the organization been coordinated? Overlap, duplication, and redundancy are serious and costly problems, both in government and in private industry. One doesn't necessarily have to go the route of centralized data base management approaches, either, to do something about those problems. Every effort should be made to develop information requirements which are multi-purpose in utility, capable of serving a variety of needs and uses throughout the organization, instead of relatively narrow, special purpose and parochial needs of a single unit or a single group of users.

Where it is apparent that requirements can serve a broad audience, the organizational head, or his information delegate, may wish to make "lead assignments" to a single department or division. That office then has the responsibility to develop requirements to meet the needs of all of the offices and users to be served. Of course, this process is much easier to describe in concept than to carry out in practice. Too often units at subordinate levels act as if they were sovereign states and take the position that only they are in a position to define their own needs. In the absence of strong top management postures, these units use all kinds of ploys to avoid joining with other units in a shared information requirements development mode.

Another facet of planning evaluation is the notion of zero-base reviews. With the advent of the Carter Administration and introduction of the zero-base budgeting concept on a government-wide basis, it was inevitable that Washington should extend the principles to other management processes in government. In the information area, the term "zero-base reporting" was coined in early 1977. In our context, zero-base information planning might be defined as the need for organizations to develop and install a schedule for the periodic review and validation of all operational data flows, including company-wide and departmental information systems and data bases, statistical data systems, reporting systems, and individual reports. As a general guideline, each major data flow could receive a baseline review every three or four years, or more often if the company or government agency had undergone substantial change in mission, function, resource authority, or some other dimension of equal significance.

Still another important aspect of information planning which should be the subject of evaluatory review is the need to "crosswalk" the organization's central budgeting and accounting structures with regard to information resources which have been costed. In Chapters 7 and 8 it was pointed out that budgeting for information and accounting for information need not involve the radical restructuring of the organization's conventional budgeting and accounting structures and systems. At the same time, it is necessary to insure that information resources are related to the organic accounting structure; otherwise the costs of information resources cannot be systematically juxtaposed and correlated with other resource costs.

EVALUATION AIMED AT PROGRAMMING

Passing now from the planning stage of the management process to the programming stage, perhaps the first activity that should be addressed is the need for a baseline. Bearing in mind what we said in Chapter 5 with regard to Information Resources Management Systems, it is absolutely essential to "know where we are before we determine where we are going," or as the adage says, "it won't make any difference which road we take if we don't know where we're going." To plan information requirements efficiently and judiciously, it is essential that organizations be aware of information resources already on hand and in planning stages, and we define "resources" as we did in Chapter 2 to include information systems, sources, products, and services.

Once an initial inventory is undertaken, a baseline is established and from that point additions, deletions, and other significant changes to resources "update" the baseline inventory. Should information resources be large in number, complex in design and utilization, subject to use by large numbers of users, in geographically dispersed locations, the organization may determine that it needs more tools than a simple inventory to cope with the situation. Locator systems, directories, data element dictionaries, controlled thesauri, data base management systems, management information systems (for information resources per se) and other tools may come into use. The evaluation exercise should address these possible needs after a careful consideration of the variables of size, complexity, and so forth. There is no "golden rule," in short, that would tell us precisely under what conditions a directory or a dictionary might be needed.

Let us summarize at this point the steps we've evaluated:

- identified and verified parent organizational goals and objectives (as a backdrop against which to intelligently appraise information requirements);
- identified key decisions to be made, program outputs to be produced, and information products to be generated (i.e., how information collected will actually be used);
- conducted an "alternatives assessment" of various options open to satisfy established and approved information requirements, and the presence and use of practical, working checklists and guidelines to assist planners in this regard;
- estimated and made explicit the total costs to be incurred for each alternative considered, broken by stages in the information life cycle: requirements design, collection, processing, use, and disposition;
- selected a preferred alternative, after weighing expected benefits and values against burdens and costs;
- the presence and use of an integrated, organization-wide plan for information requirements and resources, that carefully correlates information needs of all the operational units of the organization, at some appropriate cost center level, for the purpose of identifying overlaps and duplication, and conversely gaps in areas where information needs projected may not be going to be met by the plan.

Programming information requirements, then, move us into the design phase of special information collection instruments and modes. For example, do we need a consumer or market survey of opinions, buying habits, or buying attitudes? Should we send out questionnaires to a selected sample? Should we subscribe to a certain periodical, or journal, or abstracting service, or selective dissemination service?

EVALUATION AIMED AT BUDGETING AND USE

Budgeting, the next step, was discussed in Chapter 8. We should now examine to what extent information requirements and resources are considered in the organization's budgeting processes. The details need not be repeated here, they should follow directly from a review of the discussion in Chapter 7.

Eventually, information (at long last) begins to flow into the organization. It is there and then that we come to information *use* and the need to measure information *value.* For example, was the information actually used for the purposes for which it was collected? If so, did its use result in positive results for the organization; partial results; or marginal results? How much information that was collected was actually used? How much of what was used resulted in positive value?

To answer these questions we can effectively employ the use of schematic diagrams. By juxtaposing the three critical stages—information collection, information use, and information value—we can illuminate disharmonies, and as we shall see, lead to a theory of *information efficiency* and *information effectiveness.*

Conceptually, the overall effectiveness of an organization's information management program can be determined by comparing the amount of information the agency uses to the amount of information that is "of value." That is, information that contributes to a decision which has positive, beneficial results to helping the organization achieve its goals and objectives. The optimal situation is one where most, if not all, information used is of value, as depicted in Situation A in Figure 12-1. The circle bordered by the solid line represents the amount of information "of value." The circle bordered by the broken line represents the amount of information used. It is possible, for example, to use information which may be available, but which may not be of value. In the ideal or optimal situation, there is very little information on-hand that is valuable but unused (the leftmost crescent between the solid and dotted circles), or is used but is not valuable (the rightmost crescent between the dotted and the solid circles).

Unfortunately, such a situation is not the only possible case. As Situation B portrays, information used may turn out to be a small percentage of information of value. There may both be (a) a large amount of valuable information which isn't used, and (b) a large amount of information used which isn't of value.

In most situations, more information is collected than is used. In the case shown in Situation C, the information used is a very small percentage of the information of value. Similarly, the organization often collects considerably more information than it uses. The amount of information collected is represented by the dotted circle in Situation C, and the solid circle represents information of value, and the circle composed of dashes represents information used. In Situation C, a small portion of the information collected is used, and only about half of that collected is of value! If the organization were more efficient in using the information it collected, there might be an improvement in effectiveness as well. If the organization strived to insure that the

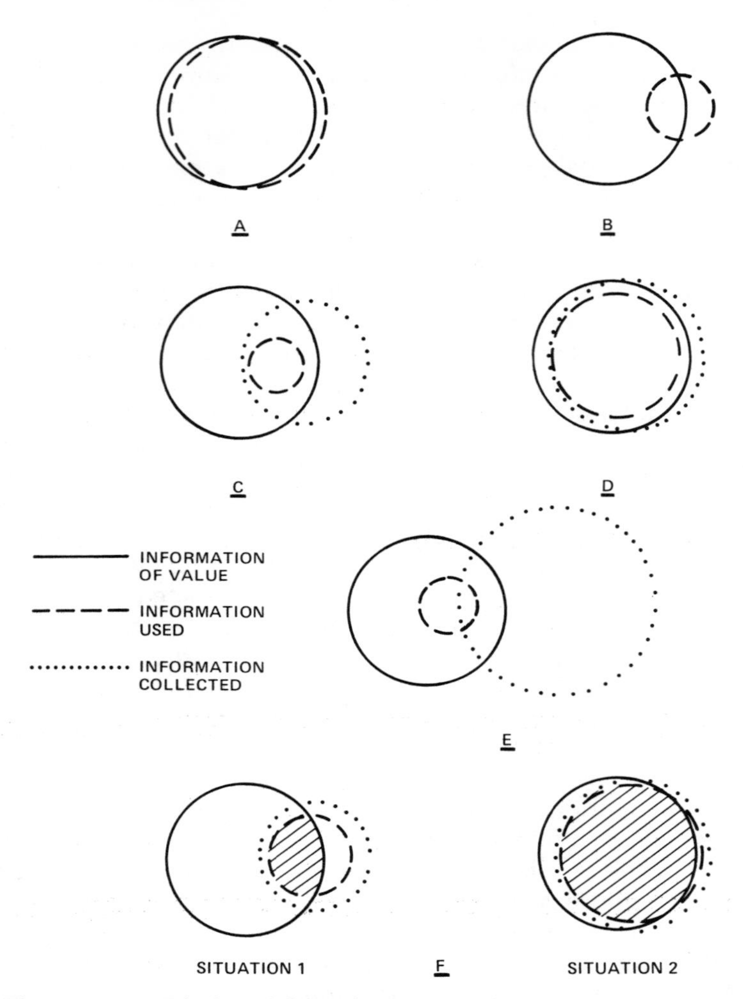

***Figure 12-1.* Distinguishing between information collected, used and valued**

information it collected were used, and the information collected and used were valuable, then the ideal or optimal model portrayed by Situation D might come about. Still another variant of this situation is shown by Situation E. Here, not only is most of the information collected of no value, but most of that which is used falls outside the sphere of value!

When an organization determines what information it needs and if the information contributes towards the achievement of the organization's goals and objectives, that information is *potentially valuable.* If the information is then collected and used, the information becomes *actually valuable.* This is illustrated by Situation F, which has two sub-types. In Sub-type 1, potentially valuable information consists of part of the information currently used, part of the information collected but not used, and information which is *neither collected nor used.* The shaded area, representing the intersection of the three circles, indicates the amount of collected information that has actual value. For an organization to move from Situation 1 to Situation 2 would be an improvement, for the same reasons that Situations A and D above represented improvements over Situations B and C respectively.

Calderone has put forward the hypothesis that the proportion of information which is collected that is used can be taken as a rough measure of *information efficiency*:

$$\text{information efficiency} = \frac{\text{information collected}}{\text{information used}}$$

whereas the proportion of information which is used that is of value can be taken as a rough measure of *information effectiveness*:

$$\text{information effectiveness} = \frac{\text{information used}}{\text{information of value}}$$

This construction does have the virtue of matching the layman's common perception of the distinction between efficiency and effectiveness, as applied to the information resources area. That is, in the first equation, we may use somewhat less information than what has been collected, without bringing in the utility dimension yet. If we "use" only 10% of the information collected, then we are less efficient than if we used 90%. Similarly, moving to the second equation, if it should turn out that 90% of the information used was of value, then presumably we were more effective in achieving our goal, than if only 10% of that which was used turned out to be of value.

USE AS AN INDICATOR OF VALUE

From the above discussion we might be drawn to conclude that use is the paramount, or overriding determinant of value. That simply isn't so; at least, it has not been proven by research. And, indeed, there is some indication that there are many variables involved. Certainly use is an important one, however.

Rich studied the use of information as an indicator of its value.[2] In the context of government programs, one must distinquish, Rich and others found, between primary and secondary values. Primary value in our society must relate to improvements in citizen well-being. These may be such things as quicker service to the needy, a lower accident rate in work places, less taxes required to support programs, better understanding of what government wants and is trying to do, better distribution of values and burdens, and so forth. Secondary values are those which contribute to primary values, such as efficiency improvements.

In this context of government information studies, Rich devised five operational definitions of "value":

- information has value if it contributes to implementing, operating, and monitoring Federal programs;
- information has value if it contributes to the regulatory responsibilities of the Federal Government;
- information has value if it assists the citizenry in understanding and evaluating what the Government is doing and whether it is acting appropriately and within its responsibilities;
- information has value if it assists citizens to obtain Government goods and services to which they are entitled; and
- information has value only if it makes an essential contribution to the operation of a Government program.

Perhaps Rich's most important contribution lies not so much in the above typology, which Rich admits is in no way intended as some immutable scheme, but rather in his frank acknowledgement that conceptualizations of value inherently involve normative judgments. Thus, in the context of the Federal Government, information "of value" involves judgments of specific national priorities. To the extent that such goals are clear, unequivocal, and made explicit, presumably it would be easier for evaluators to determine to what degree information collected and used contributed effectively and efficiently to the achievement (or at least progress toward) those national priorities and goals. Left unclear, muddled and "fudged" by bureaucrats and politicians, the task beomes enormously difficult.

Another dimension to the use/value problem is the philosophical question of whether information collected "according to plan," but used for some other purposes should be considered "of value" in a narrower, resource utilization sense. On this point, for example, Rich says "if intended uses are directly tied to policies which are considered to be of value and information is requested to tie directly into these policies, then comparisons between intended and actual use may be quite important in determining positive and negative value." But, intuitively, one might feel that if useful information becomes available, we would, to use the adage, "cut off our nose to spite our face" if we didn't use it, just because our use was "unintended" rather than "intended." However, we cannot escape the discipline of needing to differentiate between targets of opportunity versus planned targets, in the use of evaluation approaches and techniques.

Donald W. King, in another study endeavoring to develop estimates of the value of scientific and technical information, put forward the theory that a partial estimate, at least, of the value information might be the total social benefits (or "value") provided by scientific and technical journals as the sum of the value of the journal issues actually purchased.[2] The value realized from furnishing a subscriber with a journal can be measured by the maximum price the subscriber is willing to pay for it and can be measured by the demand curve of economic theory. Following this approach, King estimated that the average value of individual articles varies substantially among different fields. For example, he calculated that the value of computer sciences articles could be estimated at over $7,000, and psychological articles about $750. The difficulty with this approach is, of course, that it might be applied at higher, aggregate levels of information outputs but cannot be easily applied at the "micro" levels, an individual report, computer run, survey, or whatever. Of course there are techniques available at that level, such as those suggested by Strassman and others, using chargeback techniques.[3]

EVALUATION AIMED AT DISPOSITION

Going beyond use, there remains the task of dealing with information resources management, in our evaluatory framework, at the last stage of the life cycle—the disposition (or disposal) of information. Traditionally this area has been dealt with by records management programs. That is, when everybody "up the line" agreed they had no further use for the information, it was boxed up and sent to some distant records depository where it gathered dust until it was ultimately destroyed. But too often records disposition schedules and guidelines do not take into account the *re-use* of the information on records (or in computer data banks for that matter); that is, too often the re-use potential of new data is not systematically considered when it is first entered into "the system." As a consequence, when the immediate uses for the data are satisfied, it is too quickly and automatically disposed of.

To the contrary, evaluation analysis should look to whether or not the organization has a program to *recycle* information. Again, analogies with other resources are useful. In the materials, equipment and supplies area, for example, when an item of supply or piece of equipment has outlived its immediate usefulness to the organization, it is placed on a circularization list and its availability thus made known, systematically, to other potential users, both within the immediate department or division and elsewhere. In Government, such an approach is absolutely vital. Horror stories are too well known to repeat them; while agency X was buying sixteen boxcars loaded with paper towels, agency Y was declaring sixteen boxcars excess to its needs and selling them off to the highest bidder at some surplus supplies auction, etc. Why is it that we are far less circumspect about making known the availability of information that may have served our purpose but which could very well meet the needs of someone else? The absence of a vital tool for this purpose, a central Federal Information Resources Locator, for example, has been discussed elsewhere. But even without such a tool, organizational units could establish policies and procedures that would accomplish this simple task of circularization, without elaborate directories or systems.

STUDIES AND SURVEYS

We need to turn our attention now from the evaluation *process* to an examination of evaluation *instruments* conventionally used. The "study" or "survey" are two of the commonest methods by which evaluation is carried out. It is instructive, however, to broaden even further a discussion of survey and study instruments because their use is directly relevant to our purposes. Let us review some of the common "information-related" problems to surveys and studies.

First, collecting relevant and pertinent information. We won't belabor the point made elsewhere, that there is a tendency on the part of most analysts, researchers, and evaluators (by which term I would include auditors, inspectors, compliance officials and others) to collect all possible information "just in case" it might be needed. To be sure, it can be argued that virtually every tidbit of information may have relevance in some context, but that begs the question: which context? While relevancy cannot yet (or may never) be reduced to some mathematical treatment, there are some guidelines available to help us here.

For example, what kind of answer are we looking for? We must have some idea of the range of "tolerable" responses. What kinds of computations are going to be made with the collected data? What kinds of tables, graphs, and charts are going to be prepared? What degree of accuracy and precision are we willing to settle for? And so on.

Next, the credibility and reliability of the information should be tested. Too often analysts and researchers are willing to rush to conclusions based on calculations using the newly collected data without first making some rough approximation of whether or not the data is reliable; that is, what is often referred to as the "ball park estimate." If the dimensions of the data cannot be reconciled in a general way with data previously collected, then the newly collected data should be considered suspect. Too often users are too willing to accept new data without question. This is very often the case when it is determined that the newly collected data comes from secondary sources, whereas existing data is from primary sources. Oftentimes processes of "refinement," "extraction," "extrapolation," "interpolation," and "summarization" leave out vital data dimensions and lead to erroneous conclusions. Again, our six data attributes serve us in good stead. For example, data collected from different sources is often contradictory, inconsistent, and "incompatible." Data with different units of measure suffers from the same kind of problem, and the same can be said for differences in scope, time, and of course quality/precision. At bottom is the question: Are the two sets of data—the newly collected and the existing—describing exactly the same circumstance being measured and observed? Conflicts very often boil down to differences in collection methodology, problem definition, and data definition.

Moving next to structural and management considerations, oftentimes organizations in both government and private industry are ill-equipped to undertake extensive surveys and studies. This is one of those areas where many feel they can perform perfectly well as their own mechanic or physician. As a result, the important processes of survey planning, design, and implementation monitoring are too often slipshod, amateurish efforts, and result in wasteful expenditure of time and resources. Yet professional expertise does abound in many different forms and places. Too often, though, organizations do not maintain a list of contractors, consultants, professional societies, trade organizations, government agencies, universities, and the "think tanks" which do have substantial expertise in this area.

DISTINCTIVE ADVANTAGES

The survey and the study are not the only, nor necessarily the best evaluation instruments available for examining information resources utilization effectiveness and efficiency, but they do have several important virtues not generally possessed by other instruments and methodologies. One of these has to do with the quality of "representativeness" and the other "measurability." The quality of representativeness refers to assurances that an entire population is considered by the survey/study instrument. Other approaches often run the danger of inadvertently overlooking important sub-groups or sub-sets of the population. This is not just a question of the "scientific method" applied to social science techniques. The other quality, measurability, has to do with the degree to which variation in desired results from expected results can be objectively and explicitly considered and appropriately taken into account. To the extent that the value of information lies to a large extent in its ability to reduce uncertainty, this quality of the survey instrument is certainly relevant to that end purpose.

Still another advantage is the discipline involved in documenting findings, conclusions, and recommendations to produce a written record and "memory" which others who may follow can utilize. This, of course, is a central objective of information resources management in the broadest sense. We are not talking about simply "an audit trail." Here "documentation" really gets translated as recording the basic rationales used by an evaluation team such as key assumptions made and why; the reasoning behind decisions to employ direct and indirect methods of data collection; alternatives considered, including a discussion of the pros and cons of each; the preferred alternative and why it was selected over the others; and so on. The survey instrument permits the reconstruction of the entire scenario from initial survey planning to final assimilation of results.

MONITORING THE SURVEY INSTRUMENT

Batts and Powers point out that the daily monitoring of survey activities becomes cumbersome because of the cross-referencing required between the various accounting and management control documents typically involved in large survey projects. They have developed an Automated Survey Control System "to bring together the integral parts of survey support under one basic, efficient, and accurate control mechanism—the computer."[4] Figure 12-2 graphically

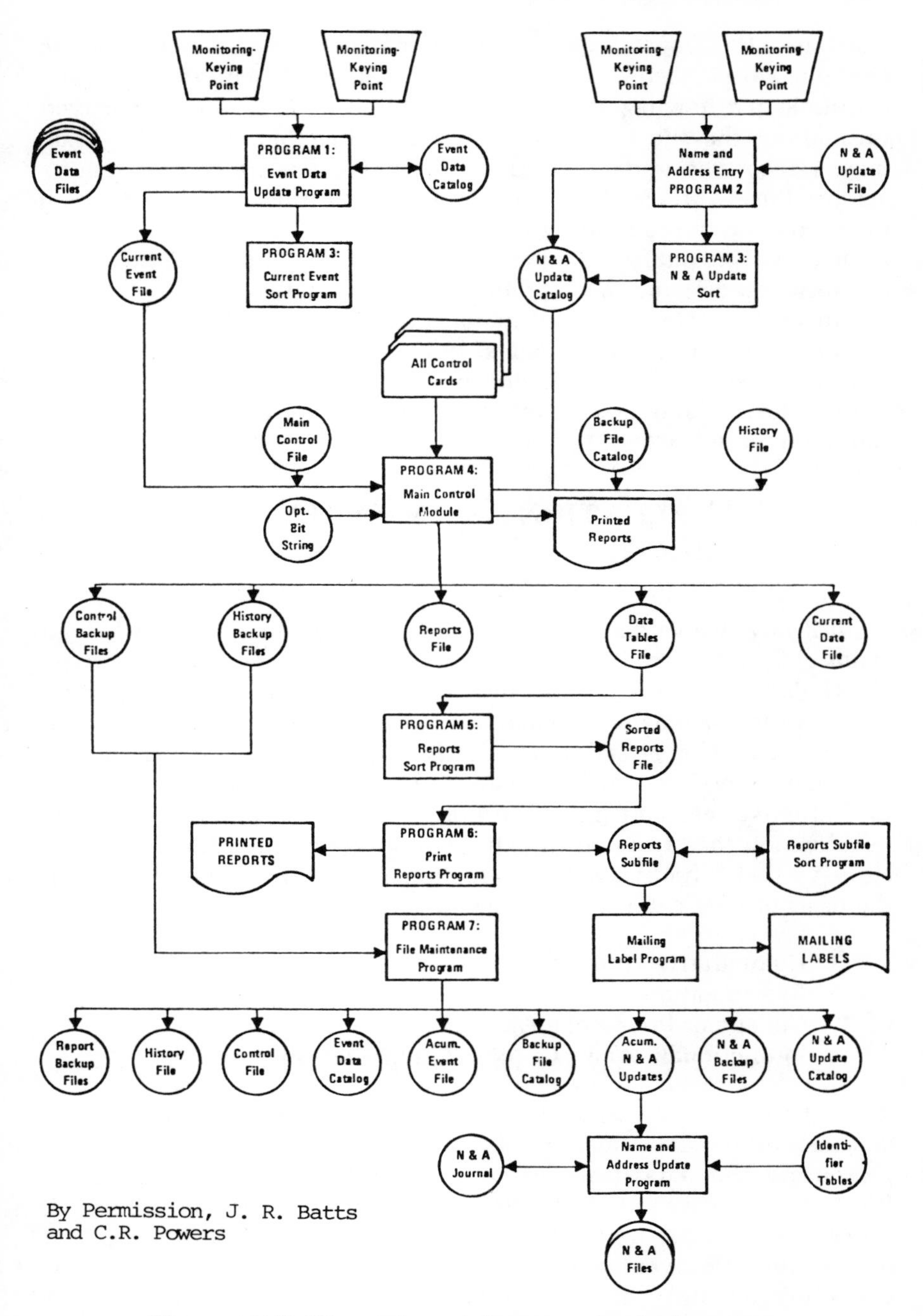

By Permission, J. R. Batts and C.R. Powers

Figure 12-2. **The automated survey control system**

illustrates the flow of data through their system. The control file contains a basic record for each targeted survey element (for example, a sample participant) and, as information is continuously received throughout the life of the survey concerning that target, the basic master record is updated, and various management control reports are produced. Much of the virtue of their approach lies in placing the burden on the computer for extensive survey housekeeping chores, such as mailing out follow-up questionnaires, keeping up with address changes, keeping up with other target unit status changes, and so on. In short, there is a continuous tracking and monitoring system set up, with appropriate "ticklers" such as due dates, suspense dates, follow-up dates, and so on. Additionally, extensive cross-referencing, cross-indexing, and cross-tabulation can be performed on the population total, or sub-sets of the population.

EVALUATION AS AN ANALYTICAL PROCESS

Until now we've dealt with the process of evaluation, and looked at one of the most important instruments involved—the study or survey. Now let's move to the substance of evaluation and relate it to information resources management. Linehan discusses evaluation and analysis in the context of what he calls the "information gap" in statewide planning for library development.[5] Linehan points out that a serious shortage in evaluative mechanisms concerning broad program areas of library development has resulted in a limited ability to plan for the future. He says that, "traditionally, evaluation is usually accomplished on the basis of data collected for four types of analysis:

1. Comparative Analysis
2. Extrapolation
3. Consumer Preference Analysis
4. "Functional" Analysis (correlation analysis, etc.)"

Comparative analysis, as the term implies, makes comparisons and contrasts: Raw data; methodologies for collecting, organizing and presenting the data; findings; conclusions; and recommendations. While comparative analyses have their advantages, such as quick rank order comparisons, highlighting differences, and so forth, they also have serious disadvantages. For one, causes of conditions and phenomena observed and "measured" may remain hidden, disguised, or submerged in aggregates and summarizations. From an "information needs" standpoint, data needed for comparative analysis often comes from secondary sources, and therefore the pitfalls we pointed out earlier, of contradictions and inconsistencies, are very important here.

In contrast, the extrapolation method of analysis requires a different kind of data. Here the focus is on inference. Webster defines extrapolation as the inference "of value of a variable in an unobserved interval from values within an already observed interval." Consequently, the evaluator/analyst must fall back on mathematical and statistical methodology to make the extrapolations. Such knowledge is "data" within our context here, and the analyst must also comply with the laws of statistics and probability in his dealings with populations, samples, projection, estimates of error tolerance, and so forth.

The third method, consumer preference analysis, is in the realm of opinion, attitudes, and behavior patterns and therefore introduces the dimension of subjectivity measurement and the problems of dealing with subjectivity. New knowledge is again needed here, both methodological "technical" knowledge, as well as different substantive analytical data. Whole disciplines have sprung up around psychometric measurement and the field of biometrics. Both the physical and biological sciences have something to offer the social sciences here.

Finally, functional analysis zeroes in on purposes and relationships. Whereas the other three analytical methodologies tend to have a static view of the world, functional analysis looks at people, events, and situations in a dynamic, inter-related context. The functional approach deliberately looks for hidden correlations and relationships which the other methods may overlook.

Linehan asserts that comparative analysis has been the primary mode utilized in state planning efforts for the last decade or so. But he believes "as accountability to legislatures becomes ever more a pressing issue, the need to show how program allocations affect use and users will increase" and consequently there should be a shift to the functional analysis mode which is better equipped to answer these kinds of concerns.

GOVERNMENT EVALUATION STUDIES

A number of evaluation studies have been undertaken by various governmental agencies which touch directly or indirectly on information resources management and are therefore relevant to our interests. Here are some of them.[6]

1. *Appraisal of Government-wide and Internal ADP-Related Activi-*

ties. The General Services Administration has broad Government-wide authority to establish policies and procedures in the ADP area and to establish supportive central services which would most economically meet the needs of agencies. This study report contains a large number of recommendations for both procedural and organizational changes to improve performance in Government's utilization of computers and computer-related information handling resources. The study was undertaken by Fry Consultants, Inc., and is dated March 13, 1972; copies may be obtained by writing the General Services Administration.

2. *General Systems Study Report: Control and Description of Records in the National Archives.* This study report describes the current system for the control and description of records in the National Archives of the United States and outlines a proposed system with costs and benefits. While limited to the National Archives, the approach taken is instructive and the scope of the subject matter so vast as to present a good cross-section of the kinds of records management problems that confront both private industry as well as government.

3. *Computer-Aided Instruction (CAI) Network Evaluation Criteria and Methodology.* This landmark evaluation study was sponsored by the National Library of Medicine as an evaluation of biomedical communications research. The Lister Hill National Center for Biomedical Communications CAI (Computer Aided Instruction) network is reviewed in reference to 50 user's reports, 10 site visits, and a steering committee report. Options are discussed including withdrawal, continuation, expanding, reducing operations, and a shift in emphasis. Ten specific evaluation criteria drawn from the most viable features of the presented options are recommended to improve the effectiveness of the network.

4. *A Systematic Approach to the Evaluation of Drug Programs at the National Institute of Mental Health.* This is another landmark study that is very instructive with regard to the kinds of information needed to evaluate effectiveness and efficiency. This study was undertaken at the request of the National Institute of Mental Health by the Urban Institute, Washington, D.C. The report is dated November 30, 1972. The Institute spent several months reviewing Mental Health program management and administration and systematically interviewed key users of evaluation data. The authors located several gaps in planning and design and suggested changes to make the evaluation programs more responsive to decision-making. The suggested system eventually developed centered around the development of quantitative models which describe the interactions among program interventions, underlying assumptions, environmental factors, and the decision-making process itself.

5. *Organizational Evaluation and Information Needs Study.* This third landmark study in the health area was initiated at the request of the National Institute for Occupational Safety and Health and was undertaken by Decision Sciences Corporation, Jenkintown, Pa. The report is dated January, 1974. Detailed analysis is provided to support findings and conclusions in organizational structure, operations, and information flow processes.

6. *An Employee Evaluation of the HEW Departmental Library.* This report is based on a survey of the job-related library services needs of professional employees in one organizational area of the Department of Health, Education, and Welfare Headquarters in Washington, D.C. The survey found a wide range of needs: 9% never use the department library; 26% use it 21 or more times a year. Substantial dissatisfaction was voiced with the physical appearance, services, and quality of the collection. Alternatives such as interlibrary loans were not found desirable. Recommendations were made to expand both staff and collection, particularly for current, policy-related materials.

In summary, the state of the art of evaluating information management processes is indeed at a primitive stage, and the state of the art of assessing the values of information to users is perhaps at an even more primitive point. Both these areas should receive substantial attention by both Government and private industry, as well as the universities and foundations. In the meantime, studies such as the ones cited above are helpful and should be consulted before evaluation studies are undertaken.

One important point should have emerged from our discussions and examples, and that is that Evaluation and Planning are but two sides of the same coin. As Figure 12-3 shows, one process moves clockwise, the other counterclockwise. Beyond recognition of the fact that the management process is a cyclical one, there are two kinds of evaluation with which we must be constantly concerned. First, substantive program information, the data that is needed to operate programs. The other, the *information process* itself: How effectively and efficiently the organization's information system serves its purpose of communicating data to all of those units and individuals who need it.

Following on our schematic diagrams, if actual information use has been less than 100 percent of planned use, the manager can "correct" by making a course adjustment to the management process at various stages:

1. Redefining program goals and objectives to the extent such

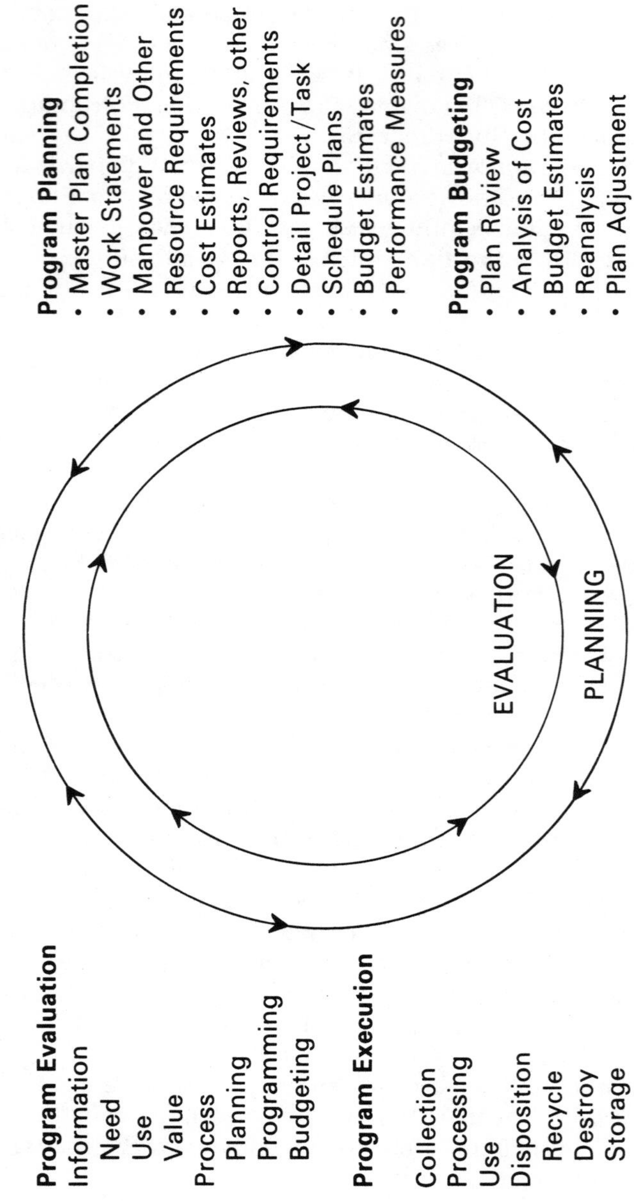

***Figure 12-3.* Program planning and evaluation processes**

latitude is permitted under strategy, policy, financial and other constraints;
2. Redefining needs for information, again within programmatic constraints; and
3. Reexamining the information life cycle to find weak links in the information-communication chain.

A CASE EXAMPLE

It may be useful in concluding this chapter to offer an example of why a systematic approach to evaluating information uses is so important. The example offered has to do with certain kinds of statistical information which is regularly published in professional and scientific journals.

There seems to be little interest shown in attempting to manage much statistical information published in these journals. Abstracts of articles may indicate that charts or graphs are included. But indices of statistical and experimental findings often do not exist.

This problem is illustrative of the broader and more far reaching problem of information reliability. Figure 12-4 is an extraordinary example of "mistakes" which can be made when information use is not evaluated effectively. This table "Thermal Conductivity of Aluminum" presents the findings of 71 papers from professional journals which reported experimental results of research into aluminum conductivity. Each numbered line represents the reported statistical conductivity from the journal article.

As can be readily seen, the distribution of these laboratory findings is very wide indeed. Thus, if a researcher were to read *a* journal article, or even *several* journal articles, he would be unable to accurately cite *the* thermal conductivity of aluminum.

But managing information must be far more than abstracting and indexing. And it is more than keeping track of data files and computer tapes. Managing information is assessing, understanding, and informing researchers that there is no single measure of conductivity of aluminum which adequately explains the phenomenon.

Of course it might be argued that only an "intruder" into the aluminum thermal conductivity field would encounter such a problem; every researcher working in the field already knows the obvious fact that no single figure exists. Perhaps. But I believe it can be argued with equal vigor that as science and technology become ever more specialized and compartmentalized, as well as interdependent (the findings in one field may be directly or indirectly applied to uses

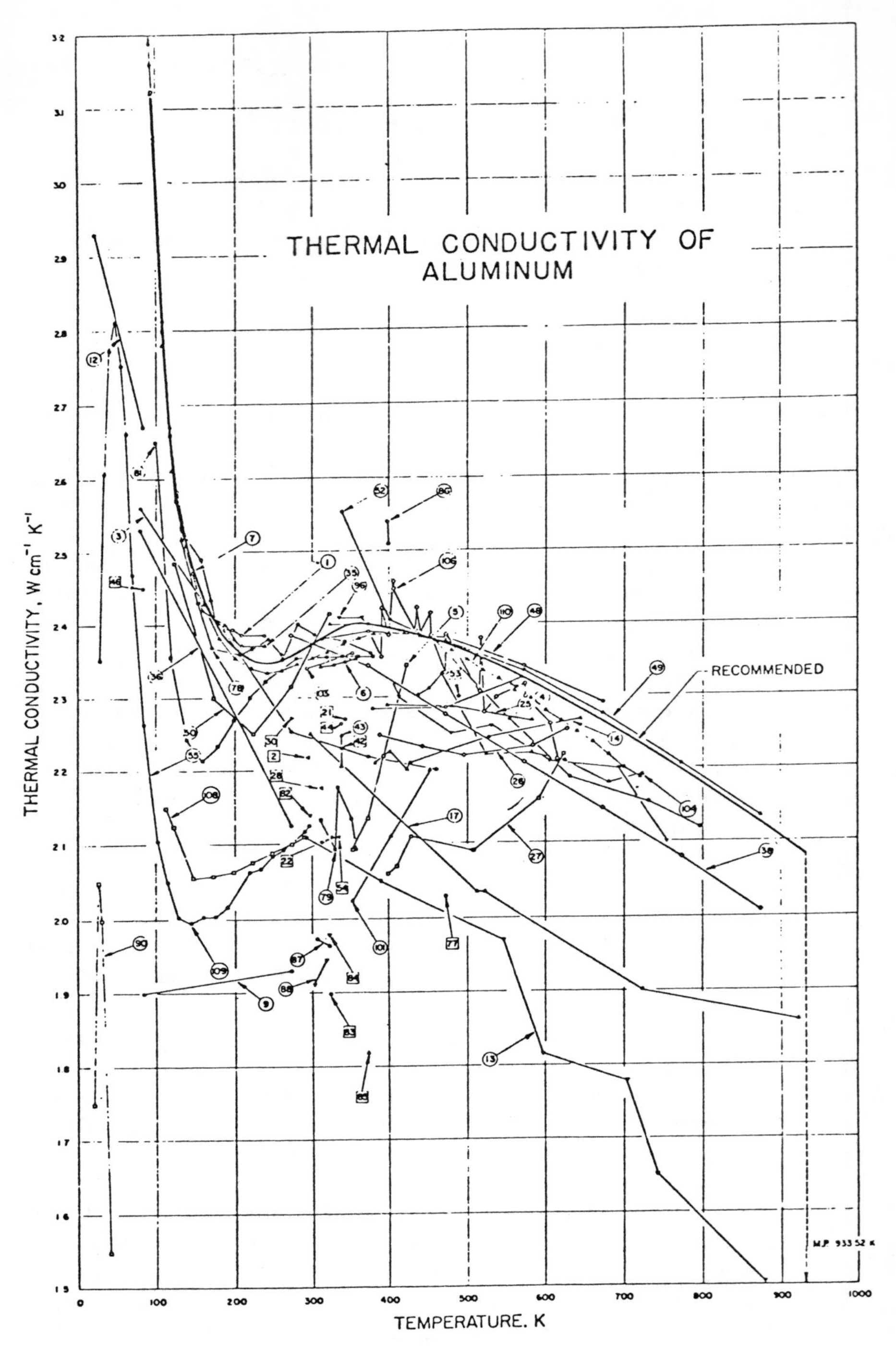
THERMAL CONDUCTIVITY OF ALUMINUM
THERMAL CONDUCTIVITY, W cm⁻¹ K⁻¹
TEMPERATURE, K
RECOMMENDED
M.P. 933.52 K
0
100
200
300
400
500
600
700
800
900
1000
1.5
1.6
1.7
1.8
1.9
2.0
2.1
2.2
2.3
2.4
2.5
2.6
2.7
2.8
2.9
3.0
3.1
3.2

Figure 12-4.

in a related field) the effectiveness of the "invisible college" as the primary means of interchanging information among that select group of researchers operating in any given narrow field, becomes less and less viable. Additional information management alternatives, or perhaps adjuncts, need to be brought into play; the invisible college alone will not do the job.

Thermal conductivity of aluminum as information to be managed illustrates the essentiality of management. No researcher could ever get the right answer from the unmanaged, separate journal articles. By undertaking the task of indexing and comparing the results of research, the information managers were able to construct the chart *and then assess* the information. The assessment results in a "recommended" thermal conductivity of aluminum based on a variety of factors of the studies.

Managing information can result in substantive progress being made in research efforts. The recommended conductivity range can form the basis for uniformity among research. It also offers potent research incentives to discover what factors caused such significant variance and how certain items (number 27, for instance) resulted in distributions which went counter to the trend of other research. Managing information, therefore, can result in meaningful contributions to future research.

Managing information does, however, cost. The table in Figure 12-4 cost $22,000 to compile and analyze. This included the cost of finding, collecting, and abstracting the 71 journal articles, as well as the cost of compiling the table and making the recommendation. The question of prime interest is: Who will pay to manage information?

The $22,000 must be viewed in the context of the original research in order to understand its significance. Each of the numbers on the table represents a single journal article. Each article was the result of considerable laboratory research, financed by research grants, researcher salaries, and other capital and operating costs. Each research report certainly equalled the $22,000 investment in information management. Thus, information management, in this case, is a question of 1 to 2 percent of the research costs. And what do we have to show for that investment? I would suggest that, at a minimum, one study (costing at least $22,000) will be redirected by the findings of research information management. The results could be even more significant.

A final point might be raised about the management of information about conductivity of aluminum. It is Science. Hard science. Replicable in a laboratory setting. And the results of research must be managed to be "right." What, then, about the social sciences? The science of social programs where streets form imperfect laboratories and replication leads to widely different findings. Information management is inherently more difficult, but should be more rewarding. A study intended to form the basis for planning a social program which turns out like item 27, that is, runs counter to all other research, threatens not only the millions of dollars invested in the program, but the lives of tens of thousands of people as well. Information management becomes even more important in such a case, viewed from such a perspective.

QUESTIONS FOR DISCUSSION

1. As has been pointed out in several other chapters in different contexts, we can apply the principles discussed here (i.e. evaluation) to information in two different contexts: the *information process* and *information resources.* Again we might ask here, should the two evaluation processes go along hand in hand, or in tandem, or some other way. In short, what is the relationship between the evaluation of information processes (or simply, *the* process) and information resources?

2. The text makes much of the point that not all information which is collected is used; and not all information which is "used" is of value in terms of helping the organization achieve its stated goals and objectives. Prepare a simple list of factors which you believe would account for the disparity involved here. That is, what factors might account for much unused information; and for much irrelevant information?

3. One school of thought believes that the value of information is almost entirely *in the eyes of the beholder* and is entirely subjective. This group contends that it is virtually impossible to establish *any* kinds of objective yardsticks that might be used to measure and weigh the value of information in any quantitative or financial sense. Debate the pros and cons of this position.

FOOTNOTES

[1]See Final Report of the Information Management Study, Commission on Federal Paperwork, June, 1977

[2]Rich, Robert F., "*The Use of Information as an Indicator of Value,*" (Working paper prepared for the Commission on Federal Paperwork, 1976)

[3]King, Donald W., "*An Estimate of the Value of Scientific and Technical Information Derived from Federal Funds,*" (Working paper prepared for the Commission on Federal Paperwork, 1977)

[4]Batts, J. R., and Powers, C. F., "*An Information Delivery System for Survey Research: The Automated Survey Control System (ASCS),*" Paper presented at the 6th Mid-Year Meeting, American Society for Information Science, Syracuse University, Syracuse, New York, May 19–21, 1977

[5]Linehan, Ronald, "*Statewide Planning for Library Development—the Information Gap,*" Paper presented at the 6th Mid-Year Meeting, American Society for Information Science, Syracuse University, Syracuse, New York, May 19–21, 1977

[6]See "*Federal Program Evaluations, A Directory For the Congress,*" 1976 Congressional Sourcebook Series, Compiled and Published by the Office of Program Analysis, U.S. General Accounting Office, Washington, D.C., PAD 77-5, for sale by the Superintendent of Documents, U.S. Government Printing Office, Washington, D.C. 20402

POSTSCRIPT

This manuscript was completed not too long after one of America's great sons, Hubert Humphrey, died of cancer after a courageous battle which he fought with characteristic tenacity and single-minded purpose that won the hearts and minds of all Americans.

The former Vice President remarked more than once that one of his great fears was that the cure for cancer was sitting in a laboratory file cabinet somewhere, the result of poor information management.

Perhaps. Perhaps not. Nothing is ideal or absolutely certain in the real world in which we live. Thus, study of the real world is prone to a distribution of findings. Only the managing of information which constitutes these findings, I would submit, will produce even approximately "right" answers. The cost of these "right" answers must be borne more fully by researchers and society in order that the resources of research information not be wasted.

That is what Information Resources Management, or "IRM" as it is coming to be called, is all about.

CASES

The five short cases included here may serve several purposes. First, they may reinforce some of the ideas, principles and approaches we've talked about in the more formal chapter presentations, set in hypothetical organizational environments, by using first person, "here and now" style, language and syntax. Second, they offer instructors the opportunity to use the case method as a pedagogical technique in the classroom; alternatively, students of information science may find them useful apart from formal classroom activity. Third, information practicioners may be able to relate to the scenarios in a way that would permit greater internalization of the concepts presented that is otherwise the case, using straightforward text/lecture material alone.

In any event, the cases are not intended as full blown, exhaustively researched and documented histories of actual situations. Rather, they are intended to be rough approximations of generalized scenarios that typify a few of the commoner kinds of problems relevant to our purposes.

THE DEAL FOUNDATION

The Library of the Deal Foundation is considered by the library fraternity in Washington, D.C. to be one of the finest in the city, or anywhere else for that matter. The Deal Foundation enjoys a well-earned reputation for being one of few truly "bipartisan" and professional "think tanks" available to the Congress of the United States. Congressional committees, individual Congressmen and women, and the various staff organizations of the Congress, such as the General Accounting Office, the Office of Technology Assessment, and the Congressional Budget Office, have for years relied on Deal to conduct in-depth, supporting research on a wide variety of high priority, sensitive public policy issues, including energy, environmental protection, consumer protection, and others.

The Head Librarian of Deal long ago decided to use the Dewey Decimal System for classifying, organizing and managing the extensive document and literature holdings of the library. Printed, computerized and audiovisual holdings are very large, and the Foundation consistently supports the Library's budget requests for new accessions and new resources. The Librarian's innovative ideas for extending the outreach of the library to better serve not only the Foundation's own staff, but Congress as well, have impressed key Foundation and Congressional Officials.

In the last two years, the problems of classification and organization of the library's holdings have created operational difficulties for the library staff, the library's users, and the library's suppliers. While the problems are several in number and complex, the central difficulty is inflexibility of the Dewey Decimal System in keeping abreast of changing technologies, new knowledge areas, new disciplines, and changing browsing patterns of library users.

The Library has just signed a consulting contract with the School of Library Service of Columbia University to recommend possible changes in the Library's classification, organization and management schemes and systems, in order to cope with those difficulties and changing patterns. At about the same time, the Library is considering embarking on an extensive microfilm program, involving the use of computers and "COM" (Computer-Output Microfilm). The Foundation has already agreed in principle to such a program and has decided to couple the consulting contract and the microfilming program together.

While the library is primarily a user-oriented, "check-out" library, the Librarian feels extensive browsing is still an important function that needs to be served. The Foundation therefore wants to insure that, whatever new organization and classification schemes proposed provide for a responsive browsing capability. But there are arguments among library staff. Whether the browsing mode should be of the traditional bookshelf type, catalog browsing, on-line terminal browsing, or some other mode is an option left at this time.

Finally, the Librarian is convinced that tracking uses of the library's holdings holds an important key to enhancing the library's overall effectiveness. But at the present time, checkout cards to determine frequency of holding turnover are analyzed only by author and title. No analysis beyond a simple, bibliographic check is made to ascertain patterns of holding use, such as by subject, by family of subjects, by user identity, by accession frequency, or by end-purpose (i.e., for what purpose is material checked out).

You are the Deal Foundation Library, preparing to meet with representatives from Columbia University to make a preliminary review of the various specifications for the proposed consulting contract. The meeting is to take place in two weeks. Answer the following questions:

1. Is there any harm in moving ahead with the consulting contract

and the microfilming contract simultaneously? Discuss the pros and cons. Prepare a two page statement to support your position, pro or con, for use in discussions with Foundation officials prior to the meeting with the University group.

2. What about the browsing policy problem? What kind of policy would you recommend? How do you feel about the argument among the Library staff; what are the implications of this debate insofar as the proposed consulting contract is concerned? How would you handle this matter?
3. How will the question of a "tracking" system for holding uses and users relate to the proposed contract? Should a tracking system be built into the contract as a specific product requirement, or would you handle the matter some other way? If so, how?
4. Assume that the Foundation has directed that you move ahead with the meeting with the University, despite possible misgivings and "unknowns" at this stage. If you were writing the contract, what kinds of products would you call for, and in what sequence? List the products which the contract should deliver, and give an indication of their sequential interrelationships where appropriate. For example, would you start with a "feasibility study" of some kind, or move directly to a specific, identifiable task?

OCOFEC

For some six months now, the Long Range Planning Department of the Organization for Coffee Exporting Countries (OCOFEC) has been struggling with the problem of how to accurately forecast world coffee production and consumption patterns, including the whole array of economic and marketing problems of the availability of coffee substitutes, demand elasticities, income elasticities, and so on. A great deal of trade and tariff information had been collected by member countries before they banded together to form OCOFEC three years ago. But much of this information cannot be used because key terms in the coffee business such as "bag," "barrel," "yield," "commercial grade," "aromatic beans," and so forth, are not standard world-wide, nor are the abbreviations and symbolic code representations consistent. There are many other problems of information incompatibility and inconsistency that relate to both the data itself as well as to the description of the information systems and processes involved such as collecting, recording, formatting, storing, processing, tabulating, and so on.

The squabbles among the multi-national, multi-ethnic economists, statisticians, computer analysts, classification specialists and other personnel assigned to the OCOFEC Long Range Planning Department have reached the attention of the OCOFEC governing secretariat. A summit meeting is planned in the Spring of next year, some nine months away. Many ministers are concerned that OCOFEC will not be in a position to make the necessary strategic planning decisions on whether to increase prices and production, or both, and take other actions, because of the lack of necessary decisionmaking data—aggregated for all countries and cross-tabulated by production, consumption, and so on.

Minister Gonzales, Secretary of the Planning and Economics Committee of the Secretariat, and Dr. Rafael Constanza, head of the OCOFEC Long Range Planning Department, plan to meet in a few days to discuss the situation. Dr. Constanza has been given the task of preparing an agenda for the meeting. Both he and Minister Gonzales consider the meeting crucial to the success of the forthcoming summit meeting because it will be the last chance for setting into motion the necessary machinery to effect changes in the necessary detailed information planning, management, and control. Minister Gonzales has asked Dr. Constanza to make the agenda broad-ranging, and address both short-term remedies that could be implemented immediately, as well as longer-term reforms which may require several years to fully implement, but which, nevertheless, should be identified now and made an explicit part of the OCOFEC planning process.

You are Dr. Constanza. In preliminary discussions you've had thus far with Minister Gonzales and members of your respective staffs, the problems involved seem to break themselves into at least four major groups.

First, there is the policy question of whether or not OCOFEC will adopt existing differing nomenclature and code conventions in use by member countries and, somehow, "live with the situation," or, alternatively, whether OCOFEC will move, and forward to its member countries for a vote, develop a single, standard OCOFEC set of coffee trade and tariff information standards for key names, terms, abbreviations and symbols used in the coffee business.

Second, there is the translation and transliteration problem of developing a dictionary of names, terms, abbreviations and symbols, for use in OCOFEC, whether or not a standard OCOFEC-wide system is approved and developed or not. Inevitably, the problems of reconciling differences in individual country definitions will pose itself, and they already have, for that matter.

Third, there is the problem of what posture OCOFEC should take vis-a-vis the rest of the world with respect to imposing its coffee trade and tariff information definitions and standards on non-OCOFEC countries. For example, at one end of a spectrum of opinion it is contended that since OCOFEC is a monopoly, it should impose its standard definitions (or at least officially promulgated definitions, whether "standard" or not) on non-OCOFEC buyers and sellers, on the ground that other countries are "captives" of OCOFEC. Or, at the other end of the opinion spectrum, some say that OCOFEC should develop a "crosswalk" dictionary that would enable it to translate and transliterate quickly and efficiently back and forth between its own information standard definitions, codes and conventions, and those used by the rest of the world. Under this approach, no attempt would be made to pressure other countries into adopting OCOFEC information conventions.

Finally, there is the technical problem of how to proceed with the changes necessitated by modifying existing OCOFEC member country computerized coffee information systems, all of which currently employ quite different computer, communications and even microform hardware and software. Several member countries, having made enormous investments in such computerized systems, have indicated that they would be very reluctant to make extensive changes to their information system infrastructures, should the cost be high.

Under each of the above four headings:

1. Sharpen the issue posed, if need be. If, for example, there are several subsidiary issues involved, identify them. In short, where necessary break the overall problem involved into smaller sub-problems.
2. List the alternatives open to OCOFEC under each heading. And under each alternative, identify pros and cons. Where assumptions are made, be as explicit, and specific, as possible.
3. Pick a preferred alternative, which you as Dr. Contanza, will recommend to Minister Gonzales. Justify your position fully.
4. Finally, address yourself to an operational course of action, or "scenario," which you will recommend, taking into account the exigencies of the situation: the need for OCOFEC to act quickly; a history of relatively poor collaboration between member countries on questions of this kind; and the need to divide recommendations into both a short term and long term timeframe.

CROWN COLONIES

Crown Colonies has, since the end of the Civil War, been one of the country's leading philanthropic institutions, "seeding" seminal and innovative experiments that might broadly be classified in the Public Policy research area. For example, among the more successful programs it has endorsed with substantial funds in the last 25 years have been these three:

- experimentation with the citizen town hall meeting concept, used in the eighteenth and nineteenth centuries in New England, but in modern inner urban settings in six major metropolitan areas;
- an in-depth, comparative study of changes in western democratic governmental forms in the post-Vietnam era; and
- grants to several citizen action groups, one in the environmental protection area and the other in the consumer protection area, to explore ways to involve a broader cross-section of individuals in government decision-making and problem-solving forums.

Among its fellow philanthropic peers, Crown Colonies enjoys a reputation built on careful, prudent and circumspect grant planning and management. For every grant awarded, nearly five hundred applications are received and considered. A staff of nearly one hundred and ten analysts, representing virtually all of the physical, biological and social sciences, as well as other disciplines and professions, scrutinizes each application to insure compliance with stringent eligibility standards.

The screening committee is now meeting to consider a project proposal from a consortium of six university professors and a prestigious social science research company. Their proposal puts forward three alternatives for collecting empirical evidence to test new geopolitical regional coordinating machinery. One proposal involves melding elements of Federal, regional, state, sub-state, local, and sub-municipal governmental units together, in a series of ad hoc bloc grant planning and mangement bodies.

The three alternatives fit a rather classic pattern of projects of this kind.

Alternative one is a capital-intensive approach. Simplified, would involve Crown Colonies funneling monies through the consortium directly to a variety of selected "actors" in each of the governmental units involved. Those recipients would have wide discretion to use the monies in whatever manner they believed best, subject only to quarterly "management reviews" by the consortium and Crown Colonies.

Alternative two is a labor-intensive approach. Again, simplified, this approach would involve the recruitment of key project personnel all along the chain of evidence-gathering. For example, the consortium would hire a project management staff, the salaries of which would be paid by Crown, but this staff would report to the consortium and carry out a variety of planning, programming, budgeting, data collection, data analysis, report generation, and other jobs. Additionally, specialist personnel would be hired and assigned to field units within the State and local government units participating in the project. In short, extensive "arms and legs" staff would be utilized at all stages and for most steps in the project's design implementation and evaluation stages.

Alternative three is an information-intensive approach. Crown Colonies would expend considerable time, resources and energies in the project's early planning stages, to establish extensive data bases and information systems to monitor project progress and problems. A computerized data base would be developed, along with a storage and retrieval system with microform capabilities. Instead of relying on quarterly summary reports as contemplated in the first alternative, or a delegated approach envisioned by the second, here Crown Colonies would track events in considerable detail.

Your task is to complete the accompanying matrix, using the instruction sheet. Be as complete, specific and explicit as you are able. You may use explanatory footnotes liberally. It may be useful, initially, to prepare a worksheet and structure your preliminary thoughts. You may also identify alternatives where appropriate. Use as much space as need be. If you need additional sheets—or even a full sheet for each of the three alternatives—add them.

		Alternative 1 Capital-Int.		Alternative 2 Labor-Int.		Alternative 3 Information-Int.
FACTOR	SCALE:	5 critical and decisive	4	3 important but not crucial	2	1 secondary factor
1. Program management capability of lower governmental levels.						
2. Resource management capability of lower governmental levels.						

		Alternative 1 Capital-Int.		Alternative 2 Labor-Int.		Alternative 3 Information-Int.
FACTOR	SCALE:	5 critical and decisive	4	3 important but not crucial	2	1 secondary factor
3. Fiduciary/audit and funds control capability of lower governmental levels.						
4. Progress/problem reporting as program proceeds.						
5. Scope and quantity of legal authority delegated.						
6. Scope and quantity of management authority delegated.						
7. Scope and quantity of fiscal administration authority delegated.						
8. Delivery of services and benefits must be quick.						
9. Delivery of services and benefits must be efficient.						
10. Delivery of services and benefits must be accurate and of high quality.						
11. Government-to-people contact necessity (face-to-face).						
12. Legal interdependence of governmental jurisdictions.						
13. Fiscal interdependence of governmental jurisdictions.						

PICK A SINGLE NUMBER FOR EACH OF THE THIRTEEN FACTORS, UNDER EACH HEADING

MAGNETO MANUFACTURING COMPANY

The Magneto Manufacturing Corporation has, recently, been plagued by a series of unauthorized disclosures of closely held confidential data relating to various personnel files of its employees, such as medical and investigative files, and of critical trade secrets relating to the design, operation, and evaluation of several of its key competitive products. Magneto produces a line of large industrial magnets which are used by scrap and salvage companies, auto wreckers, the steel and iron industry, and other major heavy industries.

Daniel Balbour, head of Magneto security, has been in charge of the company-wide investigation trying to uncover the source of the disclosures. He has, so far, looked at four major facets of the company's data security program:

- physical building and equipment facilities protection;
- computer operating program software, including "access keys and codeword systems";
- hardware controls over both the computer and filing and recordkeeping storage equipments, which include safes, cabinetry with locking bars, and vaults to store sensitive information; and
- personnel security measures, including background investigations and investigatory scope and techniques, standards and criteria used, testing policies and procedures, and other measures related to the screening, selection, requirement, promotion, training, assignment, and performance review of key custodial and operating personnel.

Balbour reads widely and knows that crime by computer is a popular subject nowadays. It has been discussed in academic, government, business, and the news media intensively in the last decade. The use of automation techniques, especially computer and telecommunications equipment, has brought a great many benefits and values to processing information. These include the simplification, mechanization, and streamlining of recordkeeping, reporting, and administrative activities in which any organization must engage.

But the advent of the computer and communications technology has also introduced very real concern for the protection of confidential, personal and business data. Considerable study has focused in recent years on developing more effective means of providing security safeguards for computerized files and processes.

Security can be viewed from several different perspectives:

- protection of automated systems from unauthorized access (physical computer room security, and terminal access);
- safeguarding the actual data in automated systems by keeping it from falling into the wrong hands, those for whom it is not intended (unauthorized disclosure); and
- protection of data on individuals and organizations from being misused and abused; protecting the rights of those individuals and organizations which may be jeopardized by inappropriate and illegal use of such data for one purpose when it was collected for another.

Security must be addressed as a problem when the lack of confidence in adequate security measures, whether through knowledge of security violation or not:

- suppliers of data refuse to provide needed data for fear of unauthorized disclosure;
- exchange of needed information between authorized users (for example, two departments within a company) is impeded because of differences in protection standards; and
- protection standards are not made an explicit part of overall organizational policy and procedural guarantees, and such knowledge officially promulgated to all interested and affected parties, including suppliers of data, guardians and custodians of data, and users of data.

Unfortunately, none of the surveys Balbour has undertaken has come up with any promising leads. In each instance, after careful inspection and study of physical, technical, and administrative practices, and procedures, Balbour has been forced to give a "satisfactory rating." And yet leaks are continuing. Indeed, there is some indication they are becoming more serious.

Comment on Balbour's approach. What areas might have been overlooked? What changes might you make in his investigation approach? Where do you suspect weaknesses in Magneto's data security program?

THE PROPERTY MANAGEMENT SERVICE

The Property Management Service is a bureau level unit within the Federal Government's Department of Management Services. The Department of Management Services is the Federal Department charged with responsibility for overseeing the management of real and personal property within the Federal Government. PMS, as it is known in the acronym jargon of Washington, D.C., has in recent years been plagued with ever-increasing overhead costs. While the definition of "overhead" is not prescribed in the internal directives system of the Department of Management Services with precision, nonetheless it can be said that this category of expense generally relates to those items of expenditure which cannot be directly related to the operating programs of the various services. For example, it includes the rents of buildings which house the offices of PMS and the other Services of the Department, expenses related to heating, air conditioning and lighting of these facilities. And a wide variety of it also includes administrative expenses such as printing, computer services, the central library, and many other service-type functions which generally support the operating programs of PMS.

For the last three years PMS budget meetings have been filled with acrimony. Indeed, as budget time now approaches, officials dread the confrontations which they fear will again take place. Perhaps the single greatest friction is between Mr. Barker, the Chief Administrative Officer of PMS, and Mr. Williamson, the Secretary of the Department of Management Services. Last year, for example, the budget meeting in which these two officials met degenerated at one point into a shouting match. This is the dialogue some recalled:

Barker: "I'm sorry sir, I just can't explain why our overhead costs seem to be getting out of hand."

Williamson: "As Chief Budget Officer for the service, you know as well as I that if you were given such an excuse by one of our division heads, you would be up in arms. How then, do you expect me to accept your excuses?"

Barker: "I really can't explain it. My analysts have shown me their charts indicating the demand for certain key general administrative services, such as printing, reproduction, computer services, microfilming equipment and supplies, and the purchase of various expendable supplies such as computer printout paper, microfilm reels and related office equipment, are all going up at an ever increasing rate."

Williamson: "Well surely you have some kind of an analysis; what do they show?"

Barker: "The Division heads are giving me all kinds of excuses. For one, they claim that in recent years, with the budget ceilings that we've had to impose, they are unable to increase their direct hire staffing and therefore have to rely to an increasing extent on machines. For another, they claim that the public whom we serve and the Government clientele we support are both increasing in number, along with the general population. But again they claim they are not allowed corresponding budget increases. For a third, my own analysts tend to verify that to a certain extent productivity increases, that is the work output per manhour of input, is at least keeping abreast with the increases in workload. So I don't think we can say that individuals are falling down on the job. Nor are the divisions becoming less efficient in the methods and systems they employ to keep up with the work."

Williamson: "Seems to me everyone of the areas you just mentioned have something to do with paperwork, information and communications. The computer center, the library, and the printing and reproduction operations all have to do with the processing, storage and communication of our various publications, technical reports and other information products. But I don't recall that the Congress has specifically authorized us to increase our information outputs. Why then, should we be receiving this dramatically increased demand from our own division heads?"

Barker: "Well I really don't know. But I do know that if we don't do something quickly it won't be long before the situation gets completely out of hand. I suggest we put some ceilings on these various paperwork, information and communication categories of expenses. Or at least establish some kind of quotas."

What do you think is happening in the Property Management Service? Why might the demand for the kinds of services involved be increasing? What measures do you think Mr. Barker might institute to find out what is going on?

APPENDIX A

USEFUL DEFINITIONS RELATED TO INFORMATION RESOURCES MANAGEMENT

1. *Data.* A representation of "raw" facts, concepts, or instructions in a formalized manner, suitable for communication, interpretation, or processing by humans or by automatic means, but not usually in context.
2. *Information.* The meaning that a human assigns to data by means of the known conventions used in their representation.
3. *Information Life Cycle.* The five stages through which data passes in order to transform it into information, use it effectively, and dispose of it when it no longer serves a useful purpose. The stages are requirements determination, collection, processing, use, and disposition.
4. *Information Resources.* All of the data and information facilities, sources, services, products, and systems needed by the agency manager to support and fulfill his information requirements.
5. *Information System.* A combination of human, material, and equipment services used to collect, process, store and disseminate information to support the management of Federal resources and/or programs. An information system may be computer-based or manual.
6. *Information Requirements Determination.* The first stage of the information life cycle. Information planning. All of the steps necessary to set forth, explain, justify and cost (both expected values and benefits as well as expected burdens and costs) the establishment of new information flows.
7. *Information Collection.* This is the act of bringing information from one or more sources to a central processing point. This is the second stage of the information life cycle.
8. *Information Processing.* To copy, exchange, read, record, store, transmit, transport, or write information from one medium or format into another. This is regarded as the third stage of the information life cycle. *Data Processing* precedes information processing. Data processing programs assemble, process, associate and structure

data into information. Data processing programs accept data input and output information.

9. *Information Reproduction.* This is the active process of copying recorded ideas, facts, and data by any medium.
10. *Information Interchange.* This is the process of sending and receiving data in such a manner that the content or meaning assigned to the data is not altered during transmission.
11. *Information Storage.* The action of placing information into a storage device and retaining it for subsequent use.
12. *Information Retrieval.* The action of seeking out and recovering specific information needed from stored data.
13. *Information Dissemination.* The active process of communicating recorded ideas, facts, and data by any medium. Sometimes the term 'information transfer' is used.
14. *Information Disposition.* The steps taken to determine whether data should be destroyed or maintained for residual value.

APPENDIX B

THE INFORMATION FLOW PROCESS IN GOVERNMENT

The accompanying narrative is designed to be used in conjunction with Figure 6-3. The numerical coding scheme (e.g. 1.2, 1.3, etc.) used in Figure 6-3 is synchronized to the narrative in the following descriptive material.

The information flow process in government depicts step-by-step tasks that are performed to plan, define, collect, process, and use information in support of program objectives. The tasks shown demonstrate the complexities and impact of information requirements inherent in any program. These tasks show also how peripheral paperwork cycles can be generated to support the main line information process.

Detailing of the process clearly illustrates the impact and burden on both the collecting agency and on the respondents who must provide the data.

Clearly even the following detailed process still understates the full magnitude and complexity of the information process. Indeed, some critics may allege that the process herein "barely scratches the surface." But we must begin somewhere.

1. LEGISLATIVE AUTHORIZATION

Legislative Authorization is that part of the information process which starts when Congress considers a multitude of public interests and demands for a public good or service. This phase concludes when Congress legislates a program. Inherent in each program is some need for information.

The following steps are a part of the Legislative Authorization Phase and represent one of the sources of information demands.

1.1 PRESENT INTERESTS

A variety of groups present (or demand) their interests to Congress for assistance or regulatory programs. Interests may be presented directly by the public or by special interest groups. Or they may be represented to the Congress by Executive agencies or the President. Events such as the 1973–74 oil crisis also stimulate the need for Congressional action.

1.2 CONSIDER INTERESTS

Individual Congressmen or Committees and other groups within the Congress consider the various interests presented. If significant, additional information may be developed by the committee, executive staffs, agencies, or public interest groups.

1.3 SPONSOR BILL

If considered to be in the interest of the public, a bill will be drafted and sponsored by one or more members of Congress.

1.4 DEBATE

Interest issues, and an accompanying proposed program strategy are debated by Congress. The debate may require development of additional information, and hearings on the subject are typically held.

1.5 LEGISLATE PROGRAM

Following debate, the bill may be amended prior to vote. If and when a bill is passed as public law, some program information requirements may be explicitly stated, while others may be implied.

2. PROGRAM PLANNING

This phase in the information process deals with planning and preparing for implementation of legislated programs. It also encompasses the determination of information needs by agencies. These needs are added to those statutory requirements for information expressed in legislation.

2.1 PLAN PROGRAM IMPLEMENTATION

The agency assigned responsibility for the program defines existing organizational resources, establishes goals and objectives, estimates resources and establishes a time table for the program. Requirements for coordination are also identified.

2.2 DEFINE PROGRAM FUNCTIONS

Specific functions which must be performed to operate the program are defined. The program operational and administrative organization may also be structured.

2.3 ESTABLISH THE INITIAL PLANNING STAFF

Candidates for managing the planning effort, as well as the subsequent operations of the program, are selected and the planning organization is formed.

2.4 DETERMINE INFORMATION NEEDS

An important part of the program planning process is identification of information that will be needed to support the program. The first requirement that must be met is information expressly identified in the legislation, along with additional information required to operate the program. This type of information requirement may be reviewed by higher levels of management in the agency. At the program level, the program manager and the planning staff may determine the types of information that may be useful for management of the program, as well as for use by higher agency management. At the same time, needs for Congressional oversight may be defined. The essential question in this definition is, "Can everything that might be asked about the program be anticipated?" There is an overriding concern of "not knowing" and thus looking bad in front of the Congress, superiors, peers and subordinates. Information to support budget appropriation needs is also defined. In addition, there is a likelihood that the program may subsequently be expanded in scope and/or intensity. Therefore, information outside existing program scope may even be defined as needed.

2.5 COORDINATE INFORMATION NEEDS

After information needs for the programs have been defined, these needs are coordinated within the program planning staff and with other organizations that may be associated with the program, its management and evaluation. In situations where a program may not have a precedent (i.e. a new, unique program), some agencies may use a research staff to collect and analyze data. Research needs may thus be included in overall program information needs. In some instances, where other agencies are operating in the same broad functional area, information needs may be coordinated with these agencies. The coordination process generates a peripheral paperwork flow to support the basic information process.

2.6 PRESENT TO MANAGEMENT FOR APPROVAL

Defined information needs are presented to management for

review to determine whether or not essential items, especially for higher management and Congress, have been inadvertently omitted.

2.7 DESIGN COLLECTION INSTRUMENTS

After information needs have been defined, coordinated, approved, collection instruments and their accompanying instructions are designed. Assistance may be obtained from various paperwork specialist groups such as records management, and data processing organizations. The design effort may therefore involve several other staff organizations.

2.8 OBTAIN CLEARANCES

The designed collection instruments will be reviewed by agency management organizations and subsequently, in some cases, by OMB or GAO for clearances. This very coordination process generates a paperflow between the interested parties, as well as an information collection and maintenance process within the clearance agencies themselves.

2.9 DETERMINE SYSTEM SUPPORT REQUIREMENTS

During or following the clearance cycle, the planning group will focus on how the collected information will be maintained and what types of reports should be produced. Depending on the quantity of data to be collected, and the frequency and variety of permutations and combinations of the data, this information may be processed by manual or by an automated system. If computer support is already available in the agency, the decision may tend toward an automated system. In short, the quantity of collected data, as a decision factor, may become secondary to the flexibility and variety of output products that can be obtained. For a manual system, some type of office equipment may be purchased and a series of detailed procedures and instructions prepared. For an automated system, the system must be designed, applications programs written, and hardware support obtained.

2.10 DESIGN SYSTEM

The system design task involves conceptually structuring a series of programs to screen collected data for validity, maintain a file of collected data, and produce output reports. The design identifies each program needed, functions that must be performed, the exact sequence of the events, and how the incoming data, files, and products will be portrayed and presented. The design task alone may be performed by special agency staff, or it may be accomplished by a contractor. In any event, a large paperwork cycle is generated by this task. A feasibility study may first have to be conducted. The feasibility study is followed by a justification document and an estimate of costs. If this or subsequent tasks are contracted, an additional justification may have to be developed. Funds must be obligated and an RFP prepared. The RFP may require additional coordination between contracts, data processing, and agency management organizations before issuance. Maximum point values will be assigned to factors outlined in the RFP and a weighting scheme devised. An evaluation team will analyze proposal responses, score, and select a successful bidder. The selection must be documented and justified. Contract terms are developed and the contract is then negotiated. A cyclic progress reporting schedule will be implemented for contract monitoring. The system design task, with peripheral activities in obtaining design assistance, either internally or by contract, are paperwork-intensive. The sole product of the design task is documentation (paperwork).

2.11 DETERMINE HARDWARE SUPPORT REQUIREMENTS

After the system has been designed and processing quantities estimated, the hardware required to support the system is defined. Again, this task may be performed by an inhouse staff or a contractor. The product is a hardware functional specification document.

2.12 OBTAIN HARDWARE SUPPORT

Based on the estimated capacity and performance requirements, hardware will be obtained to support the system. Hardware within the agency may be adequate to provide the support. However, if current capacities may be exceeded by the new system requirement, the existing system will have to be upgraded. If new hardware or upgrading is necessary, an RFP will be developed for a procurement. This procurement must first pass through a justification and approval of specifications. The paperwork cycle generated by this task is similar to that outlined for Task 2.10 "Systems Design." However, the hardware procurement cycle is usually more intensive in paperwork demands for coordination, evaluation, and award.

2.13 IMPLEMENT SYSTEMS DEVELOPMENT

After required hardware support has been obtained, implementation of the system is initiated. Again this task may be performed by an in-house staff or contractor. If sources outside the agency are obtained, an RFP-Proposal-Evaluation cycle will be repeated. This task involves preparation of system specifications, design of test procedures, and programming of system modules.

2.14 PLAN COLLECTION AND PROCESSING METHODOLOGY

After systems development has been initiated and systems specifications have been prepared, the program planning staff will develop methodologies for collecting and processing information. Functions will be defined for determining respondents, assuring that all are polled during collection, and that responses are accounted for, reviewed, and processed into the system. Estimates will be made of response volumes, and consequently, the size of processing staff.

2.15 STRUCTURE PROCESSING ORGANIZATION

Based on the tasks defined for collecting and processing information, the information processing organization will be structured. Specific functions will be assigned to each unit and staffing levels will be determined.

2.16 PREPARE PROCEDURES

Based on functions that must be performed to collect and process information, and on organizational relationships, procedures will be prepared. These procedures are usually coordinated with key participants or proposed chiefs for each processing unit.

2.17 HIRE PROCESSING STAFF

Based on the organizational structure, staffing levels, and functions to be performed, job descriptions will be written and skill requirements determined. Staffing, grades, and budgets may have to be justified. This task, like others in the process, generates a flow of paperwork such as advertising position openings, and review of resumes from applicants for a competitive selection process.

2.18 TEST SYSTEM

After programs have been written and individually tested, the entire system will be tested with specially prepared data, and then samples of live data. In some cases the data and procedures used for testing are documented. The processing organization, program management, and users may participate in the testing and review of results to determine system acceptance.

2.19 PREPARE SYSTEM DOCUMENTATION

Concurrent with or following system testing, the system will be documented. This documentation may include an overall systems description; a description of each component program; description of source documents, input media, files, and report outputs, and a data base dictionary; a system overview for management; instruction manuals for processing personnel; and a quality assurance procedures manual for subsequent system maintenance. The product of this task is paper.

2.20 TRAIN PROCESSING STAFF

Using instruction manuals and procedures prepared for the system, training aids will be developed, and the staff will be trained in the collection and processing of information along with how to use the system.

3. PROGRAM IMPLEMENTATION

The Program Planning Phase provides the base line or framework for Program Implementation. During the preceeding phase, information needs were defined, collection instruments designed, and a mechanism and organization for processing information were established. This phase, "Implementation," launches the program and its associated information collection and thus has a direct impact on respondents. It is this phase that levies the information demand on a respondent, either external or internal to the government. Although the term "implementation" is used in the context of a new government program, this phase can be considered to be a repeating phase where information collection is initiated on a cyclical or recurring basis.

3.1 RESEARCH AND IDENTIFY RESPONDENTS

This task is performed principally to support regulatory, enforcement, compliance, and revenue collection functions. It insures that the subject population is brought under "coverage" of the program through an information or related collection process.

For example, each industry or business discharging waste into streams, rivers, lakes, or estuaries must apply for a waste water discharge permit. To insure that all industries comply with an application, industrial inventories are developed within each Federal region. Permit applications are checked against these inventories to insure that all have responded, and are complying.

This task may generate a paperwork cycle by requesting local governments or associations to furnish a list of all organizations in their area that are subject to the program. A respondent research group may also extract or obtain information from other sources such as Dun and Bradstreet directories.

3.2 COMPILE RESPONDENT CONTROL LIST

Information developed during the research and identification of respondents is compiled into a control list or inventory. For programs whose objectives are to "provide and assist," a control list may be developed from the responses received. For example, application forms may be distributed to convenient locations so that applicants may apply for benefits or assistance under a particular program. From those applicants who are determined to be eligible, a control list may be compiled. The list may include all applicants, identifying both those who are eligible and ineligible. This type of list may be inherent in collateral sources. For example, to be eligible, a person must also presently be a participant in another program. A collateral list of these program participants may thus be used to screen applicants for the new program.

The compilation of control lists or inventories of a program population is usually a recurring task that results in a "mini information system" for maintenance and revision of respondent identification records.

3.3 INSTALL SYSTEM AS OPERATIONAL

The information system, tested in Task 2.18, is installed as operational to support either implementation or operation of the program. During the implementation phase, the system may be used to produce mailing labels from respondent control lists.

3.4 ESTABLISH RESPONSE CONTROL

Based on respondent lists and inventories, specific procedures may be established for controlling and insuring that the subject program population complies with responses. This type of control may be integrated into the automated system, or it may use system products (listings) to assist a manual control operation.

3.5 INITIATE COLLECTION OF INFORMATION

The program implementation phase is concluded by initiating the collection of information. Collection forms and instructions are either mailed directly to subject respondents, or the requirement for submitting information may be publicized. In the latter case, respondents must obtain required forms from public or designated sources. The task of initiating information collection is principally a paper distribution task.

4. RESPONDENT COMPLIANCE

The initiation of information collection is followed by the Respondent Compliance Phase. During this phase, a respondent either complies with requirements of regulation, enforcement, and revenue collection programs, or applies for benefits under benefit, assistance, or service programs.

This phase represents a direct burden on the respondent. However, all the preceding planning and initiation tasks, and subsequent operation tasks also represent a burden. Their costs, in the form of taxes or portions of the price for goods and services must be borne by both respondents and non-respondents. These costs, are "indirect" in that they are not discretely identifiable to the reporting requirement. Since the public must comply with revenue collection programs to support these costs, costs would be more apparent if labels with the following information were attached to each collection form and sent to respondents as well as non-respondents:

> The costs of planning, producing, and issuing or distributing this form have been: $ ________
> (This includes all costs for Phase 2 and 3 allocated directly for information.)
>
> Your pro-rata share of these costs is: $ ________
>
> The annual costs to process and use this information will be: $ ________
>
> Your pro-rata share of these annual recurring costs is: $ ________
>
> Your costs for collecting, maintaining, and furnishing the requested information, if you are a respondent, are: $ ________

Add pro-rata costs for planning and subsequent processing to your costs for furnishing information. This is the total cost to you as a respondent or non-respondent to this report: $ ________

This illustration focuses only on the cost burden and does not consider other burdens such as psychological or loss of production by the diversion of effort to assemble, compile, and furnish information.

4.1 RECEIVE AND CONTROL INFORMATION REQUESTS

The respondent, if a large organization, may follow some receipt and control procedures for complying with mandatory information requests. Requests may be assigned and routed for response to one or more units within an organization. The control task is also used to follow-up and insure that the response is made on time. The magnitude of this task can vary from a simple mental note made by an individual respondent to a large and complex inventory system for a giant corporation. For example, Exxon maintains a computerized, comprehensive inventory of all forms that must be submitted to Federal, State, and local governments, and associations. This inventory lists over 425 Federal forms and reports that result in more than 2,600 submissions a year. Thus, for some respondents the quantity of requests may give rise to a peripheral information support system with additional paperwork.

4.2 DETERMINE IF INFORMATION IS CURRENTLY AVAILABLE

After the information request has been assigned to a unit for response, the unit must examine existing records to determine if the requested information is available. Several situations may exist. The information may not currently be collected and maintained, or only a portion of the information may currently be collected. There may be similar information, but for a different time period. Only gross information without supporting detail may be maintained, or the detail required may be imbedded in other combinations of detail information. In any event, requested information may not be readily available from existing records.

4.3 IDENTIFY SOURCES FOR INFORMATION NOT MAINTAINED

If information requested is not currently maintained, sources for this information must be identified. These sources may consist of records maintained at a lower organizational level, or sources may be a point within an organization where information can be counted, compiled, and collected.

4.4 ESTABLISH COLLECTION MECHANISM

After sources or potential sources of requested information have been identified, a series of channels and procedures for the collection must be defined and established. This may require written notifications or a set of instructions to sub-level respondents. Respondents may have to implement an automated collection and maintenance mechanism, depending on the quantity of information requested, the level of detail required, and availability. For example, one Washington, D.C. firm, employing several thousand professional and support personnel, had to design and install a special, single-purpose system just to gather data to satisfy EEO reporting requirements. Respondents may also have to make minor adjustments in organization or methods of business in order to segment, identify, and count items that must be reported.

The collection process may require detraction of effort from normal administrative or production operations, or it may even require the hiring of additional personnel to handle reporting workloads.

4.5 DESIGN COLLECTION INSTRUMENT

Depending on the number of sources and types of information required, one or more collection forms may be designed and reproduced. These forms may also be accompanied by instructions.

4.6 INITIATE COLLECTION OF INFORMATION

Collection forms are distributed to the sources of information identified in Task 4.3. This task in essence repeats, at a sub-level, the collection initiated by the requesting agency.

4.7 RECORD INFORMATION

Respondent units that are sources for data will extract from local records or initiate collection procedures to capture required information. Collection may involve the establishment of counting or recording stations, or it may consist of polling employees for information. The collected information is recorded on internal feeder forms.

4.8 CHECK AND VERIFY ENTRIES

To insure that recorded information is accurate, entries may be checked against original tallies, or entries may be totaled and balanced. Recorded information is then forwarded to the central response organization.

4.9 RECEIVE AND CHECK INFORMATION

The central response organization may screen feeder reports to insure that information is reasonable and complete, and that all units have reported.

4.10 ORGANIZE AND MAINTAIN INFORMATION

Feeder reports collected by the central organization may be arranged and maintained in working files until the close of the reporting period specified for response. Depending on the volume of information collected, information maintenance and subsequent compilation tasks may be supported by an automated system.

4.11 COMPILE NEW INFORMATION

At the cut-off date for response, new information furnished in feeder reports will be compiled for final submission.

4.12 COMPILE INFORMATION FROM EXISTING SOURCES

Where the central responding office already maintains a portion of the requested information, this is also compiled. This type of information may require extracting and re-summarizing to meet the agency request.

4.13 BALANCE AND CHECK COMPOSITE INFORMATION

Information from existing and new sources will be merged to provide a composite of the information requested. Usually this composite is balanced and checked against other records or reports for reasonableness.

4.14 TRANSCRIBE INFORMATION TO REQUEST FORM

The last step in the Respondent Compliance Phase is transcription of the collected and compiled information to request forms. This is probably the least burdensome task to the respondent. However, an extreme transcription case is represented by a single report form from one regulatory agency. This form contains 178 pages. Of more significance is that there are over 17,000 discrete items of data which the collecting agency plans to enter into an automated system. Since keying this data from respondents will present a critical, peak burden on the collecting agency, the agency is considering whether or not to require respondents to furnish this information on magnetic tape. The estimated cost for a service bureau to transcribe information from the report form to magnetic tape (an additional step to original transcription of information to the form itself) is at least $2,000 per respondent. This cost plus the original transcription cost, may be relatively minimal compared to respondent costs incurred for collecting, recording, organizing, compiling, and summarizing 17,000 items of information prior to transcription.

Following the transcription task, information is checked to determine if all items have been completed and if entries are accurate. This verification step may include addition and cross-balancing to verify transcription of entries. Completed forms are sent to the requesting or collecting agency. A respondent control point may be notified of this transmission to indicate and record that the request has been satisfied.

5. PROGRAM OPERATION

The Program Operation Phase encompasses the receipt, handling, control, maintenance, and processing of information collected from respondents. This phase terminates with the production of report information for use in the Program Administration Phase.

The tasks in this phase may be manual, automated, or a mix of both techniques. Even if the task is automated, there is usually significant manual or clerical processing prior to entry of information into a computer system. This pre-processing may be reduced where information from respondents is furnished in digital form (see Task 4.14).

Whether this phase is performed manually or with automated support, the steps or tasks are almost identical. The significant differences are the quantities of information collected and handled, the number and variety of processing steps relating to data manipulation, the quantity and frequency of report information produced, and the time span within which processing is accomplished.

5.1 RECEIVE AND LOG-IN RESPONSES

Usually all information responses are processed to control receipt. This is true of mandatory responses for regulation and enforcement as well as applications for assistance or benefits. The control may consist of a log, or it may also include assignment of a serial control number for tracking the report through subsequent tasks in the process. Statistics for incoming response loads may also be produced on a weekly or other periodic basis for management review.

5.2 IDENTIFY NON-RESPONDING

Using the respondent control list compiled in Task 3.2, and notations of received responses, a periodic report of non-responding entities may be prepared. This step is more likely in an enforcement, regulation, or revenue collection programs.

5.3 INITIATE FOLLOW-UP

Using the report of non-responding entities, correspondence may be drafted or a form letter used to follow-up the original information request. This may require establishment of a suspense file for use in subsequent follow-up at the end of a specified time limit.

5.4 REVIEW RESPONSES FOR COMPLIANCE AND COMPLETENESS

In many information processes, responses will be screened or reviewed for completeness and general validity. This may be performed through sampling, or it may consist of a 100 percent inspection.

5.5 INITIATE FOLLOW-UP

Incomplete forms or forms containing information of questionable validity may be returned to the respondent. This step requires a special letter or pre-printed form. Like Task 5.3, a suspense file may be used for subsequent follow-up.

5.6 LOG-OUT TO INPUT KEYING

All responses passing initial screening are usually logged-out and sent to an input keying function. Log-in and log-out steps are typical in an information process. They serve as a control each time paper changes hands. The losing organization usually logs-out information to verify that it has left its sphere of responsibility. The gaining organization usually logs-in information to prove that they have not received items for which they might be erroneously charged. Each logging operation is usually accompanied by periodic compilation of statistics. Logging may consist of controlling groups or batches of responses by count, or it may involve recording each response by a unique control number. Individual logging facilitates subsequent tracking of responses. The larger the information collection effort, the more chance for loss or misplacement or reports or applications during the processing cycle. This problem generates an intensive record-keeping operation.

5.7 KEY RESPONSES FOR INPUT TO SYSTEM

Responses passing the pre-screening steps are keyed for input to the system. This is usually the last of a series of duplicative transcription steps in the information process. Information in whole may also have been transcribed several times by the respondent prior to transcription or entry of information on request forms submitted to the agency.

In manual operations, a step similar to input keying may be performed. Information from responses may be typed (transcribed) to 3 × 5 cards or other types of manual reference records. This transcription provides a cross-index to locate different types of information contained in responses. Another example that demonstrates the multiple transcription or cross use is a system operated by a large information intensive agency. Incoming reports are reviewed to identify and mark key place names, proper names, and words identifying important subjects. These documents are microfilmed. Documents are then reproduced from film to a 5 × 8 paper size. Based on the number of names or terms marked in a document, that number of copies is reproduced. Each of these copies is then filed under the selected names or subject terms in a master reference file. This technique provides direct access to all relevant reports, without having to consult a crossreference index and then find the document (single copy) in a serial file.

These are a few examples of the same types of facilities provided by an automated system. The exception is that a computer can make multiple uses of data without multiple manual transcription. To provide these facilities, a computer also actually copies or transcribes information electronically.

5.8 KEY VERIFY INPUT

All information previously keyed for input is usually key verified through a second keying process. Although information is not in actuality transcribed again, key verifying is a form of dual transcription. In this process, information from responses is re-keystroked. The keystroked characters are compated to those characters already keyed. Differences indicate errors either in the original keyed information or in the verification keystroking.

5.9 CORRECT KEYING ERRORS

Transcription errors detected in the verification step are corrected. This type of correction addresses only keying transcription errors and does not deal with validity of the information substance.

5.10 PROCESS AND EDIT INPUT

Reports, transcribed to a machine readable language, are processed by specialized software designed for the collected information. This software was defined in Task 2.10, implemented in 2.13, tested in 2.18, and made operational in 3.3. The incoming response information is compared to a range of criteria that has been determined to represent acceptable data. For example, dates earlier than a specified reporting date may be rejected as unacceptable. Simple tests such as months greater than 12, or day dates greater than 31, may also be performed to screen out errors in responses. Some items of information may be compared to identical items in an existing file to insure that incoming information matches a prescribed condition. For example, updates of corporate information may be processed to compare a portion of the company name and identification number to comparable information in an existing master file of corporate information. This insures that incoming data are applied to appropriate records. If both the name and identification number do not correspond to one in an existing file, the response information will be rejected.

The editing process cannot validate or verify the substance of most information. For example, income information on a welfare application may have to be sent to both an employer and a bank for verification. Or financial information from a corporation may be verified through an audit of corporate records. These types of verifications create another peripheral information cycle and constitute a degree of burden on respondents other than those who were original subjects of the program.

Information screened by the edit process is listed and those errors that can be detected are noted.

5.11 CORRECT DETECTED ERRORS

Detectable and identified errors are researched against responses and possibly against collateral files and documents to determine correct information. This task may require a follow-up with the respondent to determine what information is correct or appropriate. This may cause a paperwork cycle of correspondence and suspense files similar to those in Tasks 5.3 and 5.5.

5.12 ORGANIZE AND MAINTAIN INFORMATION

After new or incoming responses have been corrected, this information is organized and applied to a main or master file containing all response information. Maintenance of this file includes addition of new records of information, insertion of new data in existing information records, changing or revising information in records, or deleting parts of, or entire, records.

In automated systems, surrogates of this main file may be generated and organized in a sequence representing an inversion of the original file. This proliferation of information is used as a cross-reference to the main file, or it provides direct access to the body of information through another usable sequence. In manual systems, this is accomplished by reproducing or typing several copies of information extracted from the response. These copies are then organized into multiple files maintained in various sequences to facilitate cross-referencing and location of information.

5.13 PRODUCE REPORTS

Information from the main file, and possibly ancillary files, is reprocessed "cosmetically" to arrange and format this information and produce a variety of information products. Information Reports may be produced in multiple copies, or they may be reproduced in large quantities on high speed copying machines. Generally, three types of reports may be produced. These are:

- Individual profiles of collected data
- Composite details from respondent submissions
- Composite summaries of respondent data

Each of these types of reports may involve total, selected, or exception information. The individual profile represents a report which contains all, or a selected part, of the information for a single person or respondent organization. Computerized history financial statement for a corporation represents this type of report product. A composite detail report contains detailed information for classes of people, organizations, or events. Personnel listings showing names of employees, job titles, grades, dates of birth, etc., are representative of these types of reports. Composite summary reports contain a compression of details and represent profiles of a class or group. Statistical reports, and employee strength tabulations fall within this category of reports.

These types of reports may be generated on a fixed periodic reporting cycle. However, many automated systems offer the capability to produce ad-hoc reports on a demand basis. Where time shared, remote access to a system is available, authorized users may access an information file and produce any number of ad hoc reports desired. Some systems also offer direct access to discrete information. This can eliminate some of the paper output reporting requirements.

6. PROGRAM ADMINISTRATION

The preceding phase was concluded with the production of report information compiled from responses. The Program Administration Phase encompasses the use of this information for one or more of the following:

- Statutory Requirements
  (Explicitly mandated or implied)
- Program Management and Administration
  (Allocation of resources, budgeting, expending, scheduling, work load problem solving and performance measurements.)
- Program Operation
  (Regulating, enforcing, providing, assisting, defending, protecting, and collecting revenue.)
- Program Research
  (Planning, evaluating effectiveness of program impact, improving program in scope or intensity.)

The Program Administration phase may involve additional transcription of information into reports, memos, or briefing charts. However, this transcription usually applies only to condensed information and not to the entire response detail. This phase may conclude with the determination that additional information is required or that some information can be eliminated.

6.1 REVIEW AND ANALYZE INFORMATION

One of the most important functions in program administration is to obtain a view of the program, its operation, its impact, and associated problems. This view is obtained through information furnished by respondents (Phase 4) and the processing of this information into reports (Phase 5). The quantities of this information that must be examined reach their largest proportion during this task. In respondent compliance, the magnitude is viewed as the number of discrete questions that must be answered. However, in this phase, where collected information is examined for program use, the magnitude is expressed by a different measure annual data volume. Although proliferation, multiplicity, and other terms may be used to describe this magnitude, they do not adequately impart a feeling for the actual size. Data volume is expressed by the product of three specific counts for information collected. First is the number of questions or data elements on a report which must be answered by a respondent. Second is the number of times per year that a respondent must submit a report, i.e., 12 for monthly submission. Third is the number of respondents submitting reports. The product of these three counts indicates the potential magnitude of information items that are collected and maintained for a single report. However, other multipliers must be applied to this product to represent the various sequences and permutations of this data that can be compiled and displayed as processed information products. The frequency with which these products are generated also becomes a multiplier. In essence, the greatest magnitude of information occurs at the use point which represents the large end of a funnel. Quantities of collected information are figuratively exploded into much larger information product quantities.

During this task, the information is reviewed and analyzed to determine:

- How the program is progressing
- Where there may be problems in program progress or implementation
- Where there may be individual case problems
- Performance of program personnel
- What types of information should be brought to management's attention
- Current status of costs
- Areas for expanding program activities and impacts

6.2 INITIATE OPERATIONAL ACTION WHERE NECESSARY

Based on significant facts determined through examination of information, action impacting operation of the program may be initiated. Prior to taking action, coordination of intended action and exchange of information may take place.

6.3 EXTRACT AND RECOMPILE INFORMATION

Generally before coordination, exchange of information, or briefings to management take place, sets of information pertinent to a subject must be extracted from the totality of information collected and processed. More often than not, this information must be recompiled or organized in yet another format or sequence to satisfy a specific use. This represents the beginning of a series of information transcriptions, to support a variety of needs. These transcriptions, however, usually involve only a portion of the total information collection.

6.4 PREPARE TABLES AND GRAPHS

Trends or comparative relationships are sometimes better depicted in tables and graphs rather than as absolute values. Thus to satisfy coordination and management reporting needs, tables and graphs may be prepared. This represents an additional transcription or re-configuration of information.

6.5 PREPARE NARRATIVE REPORTS

Information, even though it has been extracted, re-compiled, and re-configured usually cannot stand on its own. Narrative explanations or interpretations are then prepared to accompany tables, graphs, or portions of collected respondent information. These narratives may add a new dimension or value to the original information and constitute another information product. Narratives may be combined with other information materials and reproduced and transmitted as reports. This is another form of the information proliferation, a synthesis of the original information.

6.6 PREPARE BRIEFINGS

If the information reported is considered to be of high significance to program operations or objectives, this information may be transcribed again and re-configured to briefing charts for a different audience.

Original reports may also be re-written for oral presentation. In some instances, condensations of reports may be prepared and reproduced as handout material. This is also a part of the series of information proliferations. The total number of iterations cannot be estimated. However, each transcription involves processing costs, and the number of copies distributed involve a cost of reviewing and studying by each recipient.

6.7 REVIEW PROGRAM PROGRESS

Proliferated information produced in the preceding steps may be reviewed by a number of people horizontally within an organization, as well as, vertically at different organization levels. Usually program progress is frequently the topic of the first review. This review may concentrate on whether or not the program is progressing according to schedules, if there is a backlog of cases in benefit applications, enforcement actions, etc., status of the budget compared to program accomplishments, and what management actions may be required.

6.8 EVALUATE PROGRAM EFFECTIVENESS

Following a review of program progress there is typically an evaluation of program effectiveness. Information is analyzed to determine how well the subject of the program is being impacted, the objective achieved, or if there are areas outside the program that should be included. In some cases, information originally collected from respondents may not be adequate for this assessment. A special survey may have to be initiated or an inspection team may be ordered to conduct an audit.

6.9 INITIATE PROGRAM ACTION

Based on a review of program progress and an evaluation of program effectiveness, corrective or stimulating action may be initiated by any level of management. This requires an action plan as well as a statement and assessment of the problem. Thus another report, re-configuring some previously used information, may have to be prepared. Additional coordination may also be required. The levels of review for program progress, evaluation of effectiveness, and program action may include Congress, in addition to internal agency management. How much of the original collected information is used in various presentations, and how much of this information is useful in indicating whether or not some action must be taken, is usually not known. Also, there is additional information that must be collected to provide answers to questions posed by agency management or Congress.

6.10 ESTABLISH NEW PROGRAM GOALS

Based on the review of program progress, program effectiveness, actions taken, and consequences of these actions, program managers or agency management may establish new goals for the program. These new goals may represent an intensification of the program within its present scope, or it may represent broadening of program scope. Changes in program goals will require justification. Even without a change in goals, the very status of the program may also require justification. If a change in scope or intensity is considered, this may require information outside the present respondent population or subject area covered by the program.

6.11 DEVELOP AND SUBMIT BUDGETS

The annual budget cycle requires the development of financial information profiling operation of the program. This information is usually maintained in both the accounting and budget organizations of an agency. Due to the dissimilarities in definition and record keeping between these two organizations, this information must be reconciled during preparation of budgets. A third source may be the program information base, particularly if the program is involved in dispensing financial benefits, collecting enforcement fines, or collecting revenues. A fourth source for budget information are the agency personnel or payroll files. These files will provide program staffing information to support the budget.

The budget preparation process is thus characterized by handling, rehandling, compilation, and recompilation of information from several sources.

6.12 PRESENT PROGRAM PROGRESS

Just as important as financial information is a profile of program progress and effectiveness. Although previously compiled information may be used to justify budget requests, depicting program progress may require recompilation and reconfiguring of information for agency budget briefings and Congressional hearings on the budget.

6.13 JUSTIFY BUDGET REQUESTS

Financial information, along with information on the program, its progress and impacts, is used to justify the budget request. If there is a proposal to increase intensity or scope of the program, additional information will be used to profile potential benefits or show what problems might arise if program goals are not expanded. In some cases, additional information may be required to demonstrate why a program has not progressed as originally anticipated. Even though a wide variety of information may be assembled, all questions asked in an appropriation or oversight hearing cannot be fully anticipated. An additional information collection and compilation cycle may be initiated as a result of these hearings.

6.14 REASSESS PRESENT INFORMATION

The inability to answer some questions in a hearing or the difficulty encountered in isolating a program problem usually results in a reassessment of the information that has been collected. This reassessment may involve only the examination of data validity. But more importantly, it may focus on identifying additional information that is not presently available.

6.15 DETERMINE NEW INFORMATION NEEDS

The reassessment step usually leads to the conclusion that new information must be collected to support existing or new program goals. This new information may consist of a finer detailing of existing information or it may consist of a totally new set of data not previously collected. In some cases currently collected information may be inaccurate and the accuracy cannot be improved. Or an item of information, after examination, may be of less significance than originally anticipated. Along with the determination of new information needs, some types of information may be omitted from future collection.

This determination step usually results in a re-entry to the information process at Task 2.4. This may cause modifications to collection instruments and to the processing system. Or it may cause a complete overhaul or "upgrade" of processing capabilities. This impact is not uncommon since it is difficult, at the outset, to anticipate and forecast all information needs. Experience in the use of information results in refinements and changes until the optimum information support is achieved. Also impacting information needs are current events and changes in direction dictated by these events. The information system and the process must constantly adapt to these changes to support program needs.

Phase 2, the planning phase, may be repeated periodically. This represents the beginning of a new information system life cycle and the end of the previous system's life cycle. The costs associated with these changes represent additional "One-time" costs that are a part of the total information process.

Phases 4, 5, and 6, which involve respondent compliance, processing information responses, and using information products, are cyclic and may be repeated on monthly, quarterly, or annual cycles for the life of the program. These phases represent recurring costs of the information process.

INDEX